D1632150

Danny La Rue

FROM DRAGS TO RICHES

My Autobiography

WITH HOWARD ELSON

FOREWORD BY
DONALD SINDEN

VIKING

VIKING

Penguin Books Ltd, 27 Wrights Lane, London W8 5TZ (Publishing and Editorial)
and Harmondsworth, Middlesex, England (Distribution and Warehouse)
Viking Penguin Inc., 40 West 23rd Street, New York, New York 10010, USA
Penguin Books Australia Ltd, Ringwood, Victoria, Australia
Penguin Books Canada Ltd, 2801 John Street, Markham, Ontario, Canada L3R 1B4
Penguin Books (NZ) Ltd, 182–190 Wairau Road, Auckland 10, New Zealand

First published 1987

Text and illustrations copyright © Dan-De-Lion Investments (Pty) Ltd, 1987
Foreword copyright © Donald Sinden, 1987

All rights reserved.
Without limiting the rights under copyright
reserved above, no part of this publication may be
reproduced, stored in or introduced into a retrieval system,
or transmitted, in any form or by any means (electronic, mechanical,
photocopying, recording or otherwise), without the prior
written permission of both the copyright owner and
the above publisher of this book

Made and printed in Great Britain by
Richard Clay Ltd, Bungay, Suffolk
Filmset in Monophoto Baskerville

British Library Cataloguing in Publication Data

La Rue, Danny
From drags to riches: my autobiography.
1. La Rue, Danny 2. Impersonators, Female
– Great Britain – Biography
I. Title II. Elson, Howard
792.7   PN2598.L24

ISBN 0–670–81557–8

Dedicated to the memory of
a wonderful human being: Jack Hanson

Contents

Acknowledgements

I would like to thank the following people for their great assistance and endeavours in helping me with this book, and for jogging my memory:

My sister Nancy and brother Dick

Barry Cryer, David Ellen, Clifford Elson, Ted Gatty, Hughie Green, Peter Hepple, Davy Kaye, Wayne King, Toni Palmer, Noel Talbot, Barbara Windsor, Peter Woodthorpe, and the Grand Order of Water Rats

Michael Burge, Tony Claydon, Erica Elson, Robert Finikiotis, Anne Galbraith, Carolyn Whitaker, and Ann Zahl

Special thanks to Donald Sinden for his kind words.

Danny La Rue
August 1987

Foreword *by Donald Sinden*

In the so-called legitimate theatre great plays require great actors. Sometimes the play is written first and the author then has to find the actor to fill out the role. At other times the author writes with a specific actor in mind – as Shakespeare did for Richard Burbage. But the world of entertainment covers a wide spectrum from which, very occasionally, a true original evolves. The Niagara Falls, for instance, awaited the day when Blondin could traverse them on a tight-rope. Perhaps only convicts had foreseen the day when there would emerge an Houdini to give escapology a good name. The time, the place, the era, the climate must all be in tune.

The Americans have always been prepared to nurture and exploit these rare talents. We must not imagine that in Hollywood there were numerous scripts lying around waiting for a talented child actress, but suddenly there was a Shirley Temple and the scripts hastily followed. The rare bloom was packaged and the world's cinema-goers became aware of what had been missing from their lives. The same could have been said of Sonja Henie and Esther Williams: there was a skater and there was a swimmer, both apparently created to fill a void that no one had previously thought existed. Mankind had danced for centuries before a genius was discovered in the shape and style of Fred Astaire, and people were suddenly prepared to sit back and watch him dazzle them. God created the supply, the moguls marketed it and the demand followed.

During the war of 1939–45 thousands of men were thrown together, often in battle situations but sometimes in long periods of boredom with no entertainment save for an occasional visit by an E N S A troupe. They therefore created their own. A large number of today's finest comedians were to start in this way, but who was to provide the glamour of the opposite sex? Many a seviceman found himself donning a home-made wig and a skirt, but few people, if any, could have foreseen that a remarkable talent was to emerge, a true original, in the expressive form and admirable movement of a young Irish boy named Danny Carroll. As Vesta Tilley had held up a mirror to the follies and foibles of the male sex, so Danny mirrored the image of the eternal woman and brought back feminine glamour to an austere world. His success has been phenomenal, and for thirty years he has reigned supreme.

My family and I have known him as a loyal and great-hearted friend for some twenty-five years, and we all find an aura of 'goodness' about him. I know he would not wish me to recall his acts of kindness to colleagues and strangers, but they are many. I admire his unique talent, envy him his energy and am honoured to be asked to write this foreword to his book. As Danny himself puts it so succinctly: 'There will never be another Danny La Rue. There are very few one-offs in show business; I am unique because I am the only man in a glamorous frock who has become a major star, not only in Britain, but also in Canada, Australia and New Zealand . . . There has never been anyone like me before . . . I have retained my position all the way because I am a product of the people and desperately try to live up to them. The audiences dictate what every performer does in his career. They make demands and we follow.'

Introduction:
'You can't take that, darlin', 'is trousers'll fall down'

I looked at my watch for what seemed like the fiftieth time. It was only four thirty. Still nothing had happened. I suddenly felt that slow, cold sensation of panic starting to grip my body from the inside. My heart fluttered; my stomach rolled and knotted in anticipation. All kinds of thoughts raced through my mind. What if they can't get it in time? What if I have to cancel the tour? What if . . .?

I took another look towards my upturned wrist. Four thirty.

'Come on. Come on. *Please.*'

My first day on American soil was turning into a nightmare. I was nervously pacing the floor of the waiting room in the British Consulate in New York, trying to be patient, trying to be calm, as I waited for news. Any news. Good or bad, it didn't matter. I just needed something.

Only a handful of hours earlier, I had stepped ashore, wide-eyed and open-mouthed and gazed at the sight before me. The city of New York is a breathtaking place with its skyscrapers and vast fingers of concrete and glass. Awe-inspiring. I was speechless at its sheer magnificence. It had a strange beauty. Sinatra was right. I was excited at the prospect of exploring this new Aladdin's cave, though my only regret was that there wouldn't be enough time to take in everything I wanted to see, and do it justice. New York was to be the briefest port of call en route for my first overseas season in Toronto, Canada. I didn't want to miss a moment.

My company and I had travelled over luxuriously on board the *Queen Elizabeth II*, and had landed in the midst of the noisy chaos of the crowded dockside. A strike had meant that Captain Arnott, the pilot and crew had carried out an incredibly complex docking operation unaided by tugs. But as people on shore rushed here, there and everywhere, busying themselves and oblivious to our presence, the new arrival pulled alongside. Immigration formalities had been completed on board by the US officials. The obligatory 'Have a nice day,' had followed a piercing scrutiny and down had come a firm hand bearing a

13

rubber stamp, killing off any ideas of the stay on Ellis Island that had filled my movie-conditioned mind. We were passed through quickly, delighted to step ashore in a city whose fabulous silhouette we had watched come alive at sunrise as the great lady of a liner manoeuvred into her berth. Then on to the noisy, bustling hubbub of the customs hall, where my party were swiftly waved through . . . all except me. I was eyed with suspicion by one particular customs official. Apparently, I was wearing a snakeskin belt to which he took great objection.

'Can't import no animal skins into the US of A,' he said, his mouth chewing all the time. 'No, sir. Can't do it.'

Polite and anxious not to cause offence in my first few moments in a new country, I was prepared to give way. 'But surely,' I said almost apologetically, 'that rule doesn't apply to personal wear.'

Just then, my long-time and ever-resourceful leading lady, Toni Palmer, bellowed from an adjoining counter, in a fearful Cockney brogue that seemed to hang precariously on the air and echo around the official building, taking the uniformed American off guard: 'You can't take that, darlin', 'is trousers'll fall down.'

The ice was broken. All dissension disappeared in a burst of laughter. Out came the chalk and I was through. But it was that moment of distraction which brought disaster. In the briefest of encounters, an unknown hand reached inside my coat pocket and very niftily relieved me of my passport. With typical British politeness, I had actually apologized to the racy-looking character who had bumped into me, and who had then rushed off into the maelstrom of people surrounding us. It wasn't until we'd arrived at the Plaza Hotel that I discovered my loss. I started to panic. I tried desperately to hide that awful sinking feeling, and the air of desperation that followed, from the rest of the party. But it was difficult, I could feel myself shaking, literally, with nerves, or fear, or sheer frustration.

What a mess! Because of my heavy workload, my trip to North America had taken six years of negotiations and re-scheduling to fix up. Here I was, just one hour into it, and my passport – my lifeline – with my US visa inside had vanished into the thin New York air. In ninety-six hours, we were due to open a much-heralded and publicized season in Toronto.

The feeling of alarm spread.

'Don't worry,' I told everyone grandly. 'I'll phone the British Embassy. I'm sure they'll do something. It must happen every day.

They're used to this kind of situation. No problem.' My bravado concealed my fears.

I subdued my panic and dialled the number. A friendly voice calmed me down. 'Come over as soon as you can and we'll see what we can do.'

The welcoming smiles of the consular officials changed only slightly after I arrived and told them I needed to travel to Toronto on Saturday.

'Jeez,' said one. 'It's the weekend you know. But don't worry, you can fly through to Toronto on Tuesday.'

'I don't fly,' I told them. 'That's the whole reason for coming by sea. The rest of my company has gone on ahead. With just a small party, I have appeared in cabaret on board the *Queen Elizabeth II*, as part of the trip, working my passage.' I laughed nervously. 'But I won't fly. I just won't.'

They looked puzzled. It was already after normal working hours back home in England. The next day was Saturday and the British Consulate needed to establish and verify a vast amount of information from the London files before they could even think of issuing a new passport. Time was desperately short.

'We've got to make inquiries,' said a top official. 'It's pointless you waiting here, Mr La Rue. Why don't you go back to your hotel and wait, or, better still, get out and about and see something of the city? Enjoy yourself for a while. Relax. We'll sort you out. Come back here by about four o'clock and we'll see what we can do.' His smile was reassuring. 'Oh, and keep your fingers crossed,' he added in afterthought, and smiled again.

I had now been waiting for an anxious half-hour since my return, getting the occasional encouraging, though non-committal, smile from various members of the consular staff as they hurried about their diplomatic duties.

The tiny smile on the approaching face of the very English official, however, brought hope. As she reached me the smile beamed into a grin. A brief hesitation and then her hand was raised, clutching the deep blue and shining gold of a British passport. I sighed in anticipation.

'Mr Carroll, we made it.'

I gave another, audible sigh of relief, followed by an even bigger thank you to each of the four officials who had come through for a chat now that the formalities were completed successfully.

'I'm very grateful,' I enthused. 'But, for a while, I thought you weren't going to get the information you needed, particularly with the weekend coming up. How did you make it so quickly?' The question came more in relief than anything.

'We nearly didn't,' replied the lady. 'The problem at such short notice is identification. Of course, in these circumstances, people have *lost* their main source of identification.'

She smiled again. 'In your case, we were able to assure London that you really are who you say you are. They accepted that yours is one of the faces that is its own passport. Now, please, would you mind if we asked for a few autographs – in your professional name, of course? We've included that you see . . .'

She handed me the passport, open at the title page. Name of bearer: Daniel Patrick Carroll – *Professionally known as Danny La Rue.*

As I signed each of the sheets of paper before me, I turned the phrase over and over again in my mind. *Professionally known as Danny La Rue.*

My first day on a new continent, in a new world. Me, the kid from a worker's tiny home in Horgan's Buildings in Cork, Ireland. Son of handsome Tom, a father I scarcely remembered, and Mary Ann, a gentle, but strong mother who had done so much for me and her other four children in the hard times that followed her husband's death at a tragically young age . . . and who afterwards devoted her life to her growing family. I was proud to bear their name, but proud, too, of the name I had made known for myself to the point where it was now my mark in the world. Proud and moved by the phrase that ran through my head.

Professionally known – that was the important thing. From my earliest days in the chorus, I had always tried to be professional, to respect my profession and receive respect myself in return.

Danny Carroll, the tiny lad from St Patrick's School in Soho to where Mary Ann had taken us in search of a better life . . .

The altar boy, who served mass in the church where his mother and sisters scrubbed the flagstone floors, which was the most service Mother Church would accept from her daughters at the time, unless they chose to become nuns . . .

The teenager, who had run pell-mell through the London Blitz, lungs bursting through a screaming chest as he dodged the rain of falling shrapnel, in a race to get home safely, because he knew if they were all going to die that night, the family just had to be together . . .

The bombed-out refugee, who came out of the air-raid shelter to find his home a smouldering ruin and his sobbing mother wondering why she had brought her family out of Ireland for this . . .

The evacuee, who found a new and satisfying life in Devon, and who later took his mother on a weary pilgrimage back to Ireland and war-torn Belfast where his shipwrecked brother was thought to be dying from the effect of long and terrible hours in the murderous Arctic sea . . .

The young man, who lied about his age to join the Navy and who, in the dying embers of the Far Eastern war, took a sheet from the officers' quarters and pinned it round himself to play the part of a dusky, South Sea beauty, Tondelayo, in the ship's production of *White Cargo*, a torrid drama of sex and passion in the steamy jungles of Borneo . . .

Daniel Patrick Carroll – *Professionally known as Danny La Rue*.

1
'You'll none of you ever be as good-looking as your father'

For a man who has made a vast amount of money from a lifetime in show business and who has lost an equally huge amount in a much shorter space of time, the greatest gift I own, indeed my most treasured possession, is my name. *Dan*. It is such a simple name. So ordinary.

It gives me no end of pleasure to walk down the road and hear people calling to me from across the street: 'Hello, Dan, how are you?' Or London taxi drivers shouting above the roar of rush-hour traffic – 'Wotcha, Dan, good on yer.' In Australia, it's 'G'day, Dan, mate.' I like that; I feel I belong. I feel part of the public.

It is a smashing name and I thank my mother for her splendid choice.

I loved my mother very deeply. She was a marvellous lady and very special. I never called her mother. To me, and the family, she was Mary Ann – it was such a lovely name and sounded so nice – because she was like a best friend. She was always there to comfort and to help me, always there to encourage. She shared my joys and triumphs, my sorrows and often my innermost secrets. She was someone to confide in.

Mary Ann was a very pretty woman, very striking with flaming red hair and a smile that could light up a dark sky on a dreary day.

She taught me so much. She had style and taste and looked smart at all times, even when there was no money to buy clothes. She had a dry sense of humour and a sharp wit, which I believe I have inherited. She also had almost undying self-discipline. 'You have no right to discipline others if you can't discipline yourself,' she would often say. She had great dignity.

Above all things, my mother instilled into me a sense of good manners and politeness. Manners were everything. We always said please and thank you and if a woman came into a room I would stand up immediately without being asked. It was a sign of respect. Mary Ann taught all her children the right way to behave and it has proved a great asset all through our lives. One thing I hate when I travel is to

18

see rude children. I can't bear it. I find some of today's children little monsters with no manners at all. That's sad. Parents are even worse for allowing them to get away with it. They have a lot to do with how their children behave.

My mother had a hard life, but a happy one. She worked solidly for her family, yet never complained. Sometimes she would have a little moan, but it was short-lived. That's why I spoiled her when I was able, and I was delighted to make a tremendous fuss of her. She deserved it, and had waited a long time to be spoiled. I gave her minks and diamonds, but she had too much style to be flamboyant and vulgar like some show-business mothers.

Mary Ann could hold her own in any company. She sat next to Prince Philip at one special Variety Club luncheon and was perfectly at ease with him. The Prince was enchanted by her and afterwards took me to one side. 'It's easy to see where you get your charm, wit and good taste from,' he said. 'Your mother. She is a very gracious lady.' Perhaps it was the Irish in her that gave her such flair. She was pure Irish.

The Dennehy's were country people from County Cork, good Irish farming stock, although my mother's father was a local headmaster. The family was comfortable rather than well off, and devout Catholics.

Mary Ann Dennehy was born in the village of Ahavrin on 22 May 1897. She had a very strict upbringing with her sisters, Annie and Hannah and brothers Dan – after whom I am named – and Jack. Many years later, Jack's son, John Dennehy, was elected Lord Mayor of Cork, and in 1984 he led an official civic reception of welcome for me when I played my first theatre engagement in my home city.

Religion, and the Catholic attitude, were very powerful in Ireland at that time. To quieten a child, parents would never say, 'the bogey-man will come and get you'. They would simply threaten to send for the local priest, which put instant fear and trepidation into any youngster's mind. It had a very profound influence on me as a young boy. I was frightened of all clergy until I reached an age when I realized that priests were only human beings and quite as vulnerable as the rest of us, if not more so. But I hated that attitude. Religion should never be used as a weapon of fear.

My mother married very young. It was a common fact in Ireland that the daughters of large, happy Catholic families seemed to marry young, many of them still in their teens. Two of my sisters married early in their lives. I think it's marvellous because it allows a mother to grow with her children and that can only make for a much closer relationship and a stronger family bond.

It would be romantic of me to say that my mother ran away from home to marry my father, and they eloped together. She didn't, although she did marry without her parents' consent, which was almost as bad in such a close-knit Irish community where everyone knew each other's business. However, I doubt very much if the family would have allowed her to wed my father even if she had sought permission. I am sure they believed she could do better with her life. But Mary Ann's mind was made up. She loved her handsome Tom, and became a devoted and caring wife.

One of the great regrets in my life is that I never knew my father. I long to have known him better. In parts of Ireland, they still talk about him today. He was well respected.

Tom Carroll came from the tiny village of Coachford, fifteen and a half miles west of Cork. Even in the mid-sixties, the population was only just over 130 people. He was born in 1895 – a great romantic at heart, who revelled in his Irish heritage. Everyone agrees that he was a distinguished, good-looking man. 'You'll none of you ever be as good-looking as your father,' my mother would tell any of us who might get carried away with our own self-esteem. Tom was a big man, six feet two inches tall, and the shortest in his family. Those who knew him well say he had a fabulous singing voice.

He was a cabinet-maker by trade, a fine precision craftsman and very artistic. My brother, Dick, who is an interior decorator, has inherited his talents and skills.

Tom Carroll met my mother at a local village platform dance, which were very popular in the countryside throughout Ireland. People came along and simply put a wooden platform down in a field or by the side of the road; a fiddler or accordionist – sometimes both – would strike up; and very soon people flocked from all over the neighbourhood to take part and let their hair down. It was spontaneous and infectious entertainment, similar, I would imagine, to a hoedown in America.

They were married in 1914 at the village church in Ahavrin. My mother was seventeen; my father nineteen.

The evening before the ceremony, on my father's stag night, he and his best man, a flamboyant Italian called Lou Cessi, who later became one of my godparents although I only ever met him once, spent much of the night escorting each other to their respective homes. After a heavy drinking session together, Lou Cessi decided the time had come to leave for home and insisted that it was the best man's solemn duty to ensure the bridegroom got home safely. So they set off. When they arrived at my father's house, he in turn insisted that he should escort the best man back to his house in case he came to any harm. It must have been some drinking session, for when they staggered across to Lou Cessi's house, he then decided that he wouldn't be doing his job correctly unless he could see my father safely back to his home. It went on all through the night, backwards and forwards they trudged to each other's houses, almost right up until the wedding ceremony itself, before the effects of the imbibing finally wore off.

After their wedding, my mother and father set up home together in a terraced worker's cottage at 10 Horgan's Buildings in the city of Cork, where they raised their family.

When I was a child, the house at Horgan's Buildings seemed as big as a mansion, and it held such wonderful memories for me. Yet, in 1984, when I returned to Cork to appear at the city's Opera House, I went back to see the home I had left behind, imagining it to be as large and spacious as I remembered it. My illusion was shattered when I arrived and saw it. It was tiny. A young couple who had bought the house invited me in for tea. It was a poignant and very moving moment for me coming home after all these years. All I wanted to do afterwards was to pick up this tiny doll's house and take it back to London with me.

My eldest sister, Molly, was the first child to arrive, two years after Mary Ann and Tom's marriage. She was born in 1916 and grew into a raving beauty. My niece, Mary, who is one of the most attractive women in my life, resembles Molly greatly. She is a stunning girl to look at and so, too, was my sister. We have all inherited our looks from both parents. We are fortunate enough to be an extremely attractive family.

Molly had such a tragically short life I hardly knew her. She was married at seventeen in 1933 to a boy named Michael Cotter, and left Horgan's Buildings to live in Cork city centre. In 1947, at the untimely age of thirty-one, she died of pneumonia, leaving behind a young widower with two children to raise on his own. It was a great shame, and such a waste of a young life.

My sister Joan was born on 21 September 1918, followed three years later on 21 October 1921 by Nancy. Three years after that, on 4 October 1924, my brother, Richard, arrived. I think my parents had a special arrangement, some grand three-year plan, because another three years went by before I made my début on Tuesday, 26 July 1927. I was the youngest member of the family, and was actually born in a hospital in Cork, although the vast majority of children born in those days were delivered at home. I was christened Daniel Patrick Carroll.

The rhyme says that 'Tuesday's child is full of grace', and I like to think that I am, if grace is measured in behaviour and good manners. In both my personal and professional life, I have never knowingly offended anyone. I would be most upset to do so.

The great depression that hit the world during the late twenties and thirties did not spare Ireland. It embraced the country in a vice-like grip and virtually sucked its lifeblood away. Ireland, like so many countries, suffered badly. Food was scarce and work was in very short supply. My father was an ambitious man. When he found great difficulty in obtaining work at home, he decided he must search much further afield to support his wife and growing family, and in 1924 he chose America where he was contracted to work on the interior designs for the great Macey's store in New York. A lot of his contemporaries went over to England to find work at about the same time, but I don't think anything in the world would have persuaded Tom Carroll to go there. So he left for America two months before Richard was born and didn't see his new son for over two years, until he returned to Cork in 1926.

America was a new challenge, a new world, and a new start in life. He liked the country enormously and had every intention of taking his family back to New York with him to live permanently just as so many of his countrymen had done. He saw it, like thousands of immigrants before and since, as a land of opportunity for those with the right credentials and abilities. As a very talented craftsman, his exceptional skills were in great demand across the Atlantic. Sadly, Ireland could no longer offer him even hope.

He returned home determined to save enough money to take the family to America as soon as he was able. Yet his great American dream for us all faded away on 19 February 1929.

Some months earlier, he had contracted tuberculosis and, despite constant nursing from Mary Ann, he died. He was thirty-four. I had barely reached eighteen months. So the joy of sharing my life with a father was snatched away from me in an instant. I think I would have enjoyed the experience. At least it would have been nice to try. Had he lived, everything would have been totally different. My life, I am sure, would have changed dramatically. As it was it would be another forty-seven years before I followed in his trail to New York.

After my father died, my mother devoted herself completely and utterly to her children. I didn't realize until I was a teenager exactly what she had given up for us. Although she had a widow's pension from the Irish government, money was still in short supply and I'm sure that her own family were very supportive towards her and helped her out from time to time. It was never mentioned. Mary Ann also supplemented her income by making shirts, for sixpence each. One of her customers was Jack Doyle, the famous boxer.

Throughout the so-called hard times, however, I never really felt poverty. I would love to say romantically that we starved and lived like paupers, but we never did. It didn't seem to be a struggle at the time. We always ate – I can never remember going hungry. I think this is one of the reasons now that I hate fancy food. I find it boring. We were brought up on very ordinary food, good and wholesome, and we loved it. To this day my favourite dish is a simple casserole.

During my early childhood, however, I never had anything I could call my own. I was so small in stature that I existed on hand-me-downs from my brother, Dick, and from relatives. I was six when at last I had my very first pair of new shoes – not just second-hand and new to me, but spanking new, straight from the shop. It was wonderful and I was so proud that I wanted to share my good fortune with our neighbours and show off my shoes to them.

Though it had been raining outside and the pavement was quite muddy, I was still determined to show off my shoes. So I went round the house collecting up old newspapers and laid them down outside our house like a trail of paper stepping-stones to our neighbours to ensure I could walk safely between the two houses without spoiling the shoes.

I have always been very good at looking after my clothes, and it was instilled into me right from an early age. It was respect really. As kids, we had to make do with what clothes we were given, so it was essential we cared for them and didn't abuse them. Clothes have been important to me all my life and I have been careful with them at all times. Even in times of adversity, I have protected my clothes first and myself later.

I was coming up to five years old when I went to school for the first time, to St Mary's of the Isle primary school in Cork, run by nuns. On my very first day, disaster struck even before I reached the playground. I caught my hand in the school gate. One of my fingers was completely flattened and burst on impact, spurting blood all over my clothes. I've still got the scar. Although I was in agony, I was far more terrified that I would be told off for spoiling my clothes. I thought I had done something wrong, and it was all my fault. I ran home in tears.

I never actively disliked school despite such an inauspicious start. However, I can't say that I enjoyed myself there. It never did much for me, either. I was good at mathematics, a legacy from my mother's side of the family, but I was never meant to be an academic. I was lucky, life was my tutor. I am always proud when people talk about the importance of carrying on with an education through to university to tell them that I haven't done badly without a single qualification, and I keep a large number of people in continual employment, working for me. I didn't need university, some people do – but I firmly believe common sense is the greatest form of education in this world.

Yet school did give me a taste for drama, which I adored. I was a great extrovert from an early age and loved to perform in front of an audience. I had a way with me that endeared me to almost everyone I came into contact with, so consequently I was spoilt and pampered.

I loved to fantasize about everything in my life. If I didn't like something I drew a veil across my mind and blanked it out altogether, hoping it would go away. I play-acted a lot, and I enjoyed appearing in the little playlets we presented at school. Looking back, they were probably dire, but I loved the chance of being the centre of attraction. Whenever I had to read out loud to the class, I was aware that I sounded better than anyone else in the class. I was different from the other children, I realize that now, and I think I probably realized it then too.

My mother greatly encouraged my developing taste for theatre and entertainment. My first experience of the theatre came at Christmas 1932 when I was taken to the Cork Opera House to see Jimmy O'Dea in the pantomine *Mother Goose*. I was in awe of this great Irish comedian playing dame, and I scarcely took my eyes off him throughout the performance. It was so exciting. He mesmerized me.

Jimmy O'Dea was probably Ireland's foremost comedian of his day and without my knowing obviously influenced me tremendously.

Eamonn Andrews used to work with him as a feed, and his leading lady was Maureen Potter, who is probably the finest comedienne in Ireland today.

Jimmy was a diminutive man, but with a big talent. He created a marvellous character called Mrs Mulligan – 'the Pride of the Coombe'. When he died, his widow sent me one of his famous snuff boxes, still containing a little snuff, as a gift. She wrote to me saying she knew how much I admired and respected her husband and she wanted me to have something that belonged to him. It was a very touching gesture, and I was deeply moved by the sentiment. The snuff box had been given to Jimmy in 1940 by Evelyn Laye (Boo), who became a dear friend of mine, when they appeared together in pantomime in Dublin, with O'Dea playing Buttons to Boo's Cinderella. It was inscribed on the back: 'With Love from Boo'. It is a treasured memento.

On display in the Cork Opera House today, my photograph hangs alongside a picture of Jimmy. I regard it as a tremendous compliment to be in the presence of such a great star.

We made our own entertainment at home as well. All Irish families loved to sing and perform. Many of them gathered around the piano. But none of us could play an instrument, we couldn't afford one anyway, so we just sang. Like my father, my mother's singing voice was a wonder to hear. We also listened to the wireless a lot and, whenever there was any money available, we went to the local cinema. I can remember the first picture I ever saw was a religious film.

Religion has always played a vital role in my life and as a youngster I spent most of my time in church. We went to several in Cork. There is a certain glamour in Catholicism and I have found a great sense of romance surrounds the Church. In those days they were packed to suffocation point because that aura kept families together. But, today, the influence of the Church has faded tragically and, with it, the congregations. Churches are almost empty, even in Ireland, where there are more churches than public houses.

My religion is with me all the time. I can be totally alone, and yet I am never alone. Faith has been my strength. Catholicism suits me fine and works with me; it has helped me greatly. It goes back to my roots and it would now be difficult to shake off. I believe completely, utterly and without question. All life is ordained, so I accept everything that happens and nothing ever disappoints me. Everything is intended.

In Ireland in the early thirties religion was totally dominant. People lived their lives by their religion and the Church's power was wide and embracing. We suffered a bereavement once when some distant aunt or granny passed away, and my sister Joan discovered that, if there was a death in the family, everyone connected with that family had to wear black. It was a mortal sin if they didn't comply with the doctrine. So, she went out and bought a dye and then set to work dying black every piece of clothing she could find. Even our white shirts and socks suffered the treatment. She thought it was the correct thing to do, like they did in Italy. My mother went mad. Yet, it was a very important custom in Ireland to wear black in mourning and a widow had to wear it for a whole year or she was labelled a hussy.

We had tremendous respect for Mary Ann. She was the head of the family. Even when my sister got married and moved away, her respect for mother was unwavering. When I was a boy at school, all my classmates had a mother and father. We just had Mary Ann who became both mother and father to us all, and it brought the family much closer together. We adored her. She was the governor. She was tough and she was strict and she would often threaten to hit us. 'If you do that again, I'll kill you,' was a stock phrase when we got up to our childish pranks, but, of course, she never touched us.

Dick and I were good friends, although like all brothers we got up to all manner of mischief, and could often be found punching the living daylights out of each other. Love has a strange way of manifesting itself in brothers. We hated each other one minute, while the next, we were the best of friends.

Once, after a brief scuffle, Dick threatened to punch me. So, not wanting to be on the wrong end of a hiding, I ran away and hid behind a closed door. I waited until I could hear him approaching the door, and then opened it quickly, smashing it into his face. It knocked him out. I didn't wait around to see what damage I had inflicted, but I sensed I was in trouble. So I ran away and hid in another room. I got all the coats and various pieces of clothing I could find, threw them on the floor in a heap, and then hid myself under the great mound, like an ostrich burying its head in the sand. I thought no one would ever find me. I figured that if I couldn't see anyone, I couldn't possibly be seen myself. It didn't work!

Several years later, when I first started out in show business, and was in the chorus, struggling to find my way, my brother was the first to give me the odd pound note to help me along. He never expected anything in return. We were brothers.

Dick and I have always been close. He is a very gentle and kind man with great modesty. In all the years since I established my name, he has only ever asked me once to use my position and standing in show business to help him out. In a pub near to where he lived, I was asked to knock over a pile of coins for charity. Dick had been using that particular public house for five years, yet no one knew I was his brother. He hates showing off.

In 1937, unaware of the imminence of war in Europe, friends of the family in England arranged for my sisters Joan and Nancy to travel to London to work. Jobs had been fixed up for them in the Downham Tavern, a small private hotel in Bromley. Everything was paid for, food, board and lodging, and they also received a small salary in return for their hard work. It was only a small business and they were expected to help out with most things.

So they left their home and their family to make the great trek over the water and start a new life on a foreign shore. Yet, it was only the overture for us all to join them as soon as we were able. Since my father's death, I believe the seed of travel had been implanted in my mother's mind and she seemed restless and unsettled in Ireland. Perhaps the country held too many painful memories for her.

Together with friends, my sisters managed to organize accommodation for us all in central London, in a flat above a dress-hire shop in Earnshaw Street, between New Oxford Street and Shaftesbury Avenue and on the verge of Soho, where there was a large Irish community. The necessary arrangements were made to bring us over from Ireland.

A few weeks later in the spring, my mother, my brother Dick and I gathered together our possessions and set off on what seemed to a young boy of nine years old like a great adventure. We turned our backs on our homeland in Ireland in return for a new life in England.

We travelled by ferry from Cork to Fishguard on board the *Inishfallen* – I'll never forget its name – and then on to London by train, not really knowing what destiny had in store for us, but looking forward to meeting it head on.

Nearly fifty years later, in 1984, when I returned home to appear at the Cork Opera House, I told the audience on opening night: 'See what they did to me in England. I left here in short pants, and I have come back . . . in a frock.'

2
'They used to call me a little angel – little devil, more like'

London was alive. It appeared like the centre of the world. A vast city pulsating with energy and life, with a new adventure lying in wait around every corner for a young, inquisitive and unsuspecting boy not yet ten years old.

It was a very different world to the one I had left behind in Ireland. Cork appeared quaintly rural by comparison; a beautiful city, it's true, dominated by its sprawling terraced hills and its white limestone buildings, its elegant Georgian houses and stately bridges. Yet, although it was Ireland's second city and a thriving seaport, sitting astride the River Lee on its journey into St George's Channel and then on into the Atlantic Ocean, it lacked the drive and determination, and the sheer ambition that drew people to London from all over the world. Cork was a city content to doze; London was wide awake and raring to go. It never slept. I loved it. True to my beliefs it had been ordained that I should come to London. I felt at home almost immediately, and revelled in its rarefied atmosphere.

In the spring of 1937, London was a great hive of activity as it prepared to celebrate, with typical British pomp and circumstance, the coronation of George VI, following the abdication of his brother the previous year. I'd seen nothing like it back home in Ireland. We had romance, fantasy and poetry, but nothing so grand and so splendid as a real-life coronation.

There was a marvellous feeling of togetherness in the capital: a great feeling of unity, as a country and its people paid homage to its new king. Flags and bunting of all colours hung from every building and every lamppost on the London streets, while pictures of the king and his queen were on display in almost every shop window along Oxford Street, Shaftesbury Avenue and Charing Cross Road. And everyone on the streets seemed to be smiling. It was infectious. Daily news of the preparations for the great day were broadcast on the radio. The whole country was engulfed in the excitement, including three new arrivals from Ireland. It was completely theatrical.

We moved into a flat in a large house in Earnshaw Street, in sight of St Giles-in-the-Fields, unfortunately not a Roman Catholic church. The flat had several biggish rooms, or so they appeared at the time. They were probably tiny, but so was I. My mother had a room, I shared a bedroom with my brother, Dick, and the two girls had a room to themselves whenever they came up from Bromley to spend odd weekends with us. But it felt as if they were always at home.

With the few possessions we had brought from Ireland and some other bits and pieces Nancy and Joan found for us, it didn't take us long to settle down and turn a tired old apartment into a cosy and loving home.

Although we had left so much behind us in search of a new beginning, we were still faced with a mountain of problems, none more so than money. My mother's pension was barely adequate to keep herself and her rapidly growing two sons. My sisters helped out with regular contributions and I determined to do my bit for the family funds. It was the natural thing to do. We needed money, so we worked. One of the greatest strengths we possess in our family is that we are all workers. It has never been a chore to any of us, least of all Mary Ann, to work hard, very hard. With a combination of cheek, luck and Irish charm, I managed to get a job delivering newspapers for a man who owned a shop on the corner of Charing Cross Road and Newport Court, and virtually on the doorstep of Leicester Square Underground station. I was up at five each morning and finished my round by seven. I was paid a few shillings a week, which I gave immediately to my mother. In return she gave me a handful of coppers.

When I started to make a name for myself in show business in late-night cabaret in London's West End many years later, I used to buy my copies of the *Stage* newspaper from the same shop. One afternoon the owner stopped me as I was leaving the premises with my usual paper.

'Your face is very familiar,' said the old man. 'I keep telling my wife I'm sure we've met before. I know you.'

'Yes, you do,' I replied, knowing full well he couldn't possibly have seen me appearing in cabaret. 'I used to be your paper boy.' He was flabbergasted, but he remembered with a little prompting.

St Patrick's Church, standing on the corner of Sutton Row and looking out over Soho Square, is a large red-bricked building that has been a beacon to Catholics in London for nearly a hundred years. The imposing Gothic-styled building looks older, but it was opened on St Patrick's Day as recently as 1893. The church itself stands on the site where, in 1778, a Chinese pavilion at the back of Carlisle House was converted into a Roman Catholic chapel to become the first Catholic chapel in England to be dedicated to Ireland's own patron saint.

We became part of St Patrick's congregation as soon as we arrived in London. It was the first church I ever went to in England; it is my parish church today, and remains my favourite. I still attend Mass there regularly.

The church provided for all our needs, spiritually and physically. Dick and I were enrolled at St Patrick's school, housed in a narrow road just off Oxford Street and tucked away behind Dean Street. My mother was given the job of looking after the schoolchildren, cooking for us and generally acting in a matron-like capacity. She was ideally qualified.

St Patrick's was a small school and boasted very few scholars. We were a mixed bunch of nationalities: Spanish, English, Italians, Irish, all joined together by the common thread of Catholicism. And there was a sense of empathy between us all.

I still wasn't very academic, but I had carried my love of theatricals with me from Ireland and my greatest delight came from appearing in the school plays. Anything to do with drama and performing to an audience had me spellbound. I was always the first to volunteer for the end of term play, or the Nativity productions, in which I seemed always to end up playing one of the Wise Men. I felt as if I was rehearsing all the time.

We had a club room at the church, in the basement, which is still there, where we presented our pantomimes and plays to an enthusiastic audience of parents. I always imagined it was like the London Palladium, but really there were only a handful of seats for the audience to sit on.

Despite coming from Ireland, I didn't actually possess a broad Irish accent. It was more like a gentle lilt. In fact I thought I sounded very English until I set my heart on being the very best in the class in the subject of English. At the end of term, the top pupils in various subjects were given books as prizes and I desperately wanted to win one. When I didn't get a prize, I was most disappointed, but my mother was as philosophical as ever. 'Don't worry,' she said, 'you'll win it next time,' and she made me read more. She was rarely wrong.

Over the years, I have discovered that the Celts – the Irish, Scots and Welsh – actually speak English better than most English people. Since it's their national language, the English tend to be very lazy and careless with it. From an early age, I determined to be as articulate as possible. Strangers have great difficulty telling where I come from because I have no obvious dialect, except when I get very excited. Then, certain of my pronunciations are *broad* Irish, but it is the only time.

Next to her family, my mother was devoted to her church. She served both with love and distinction. It was part of her Irish background. She attended Mass nearly every day and what spare time she had left after seeing to the wiles and demands of her two uncompromising boys was spent in the tranquil surroundings of St Patrick's, cleaning, arranging flowers, washing the lace or scrubbing the white flagstones. They were always immaculate.

St Patrick's became a vital force in our lives. We had a wonderful priest called Father Wood who made Catholicism come alive for me. He was great fun and I can remember thinking that priests in England were much lighter in attitude than their counterparts in Ireland. They were warmer hearted, somehow friendlier and more human. It was just a thought but the feeling brought me closer to the Church. Tragically, Father Wood died very young. I don't think he was forty. But he played a large part in my life.

We were practising Catholics, but my mother never made us go to confession. It was left to our own conscience. You can take holy communion without taking confession, for part of the theology is that an individual is a sort of self-confessor. By recognizing any sins and understanding them, you can rectify the situation yourself. I have always gone along with that line of thinking. Too many people who go into the confessional make it all up, and don't really say what they should. You can say what you like to a priest. You can confess lies if by taking penance it makes you feel better. But to me there is only one form of confession, between yourself and God. I don't think a third party can help very much.

I became an altar boy and soon had an obsession for the Church. I truly believed my vocation in life was to become a priest when I was old enough. I was in St Patrick's as much as I was at home, and if I went missing, people always knew where to find me. 'Look in the church.' I attended church like other boys played football, almost

31

every day, and it was nothing for me to be involved with three or four services a day, particularly on Sundays. My mother soon put a block on any ambition I might have nurtured to become a cleric. But when I was a child, I believed all priests were saints and wanted to emulate them. All through my life I have met some highly dedicated priests who do a magnificent job.

As an altar boy, it was my duty to fill the incense burners and to wait on the priests taking each service. I took my responsibilities very seriously. I loved wearing a cassock, and I adored holding the altar candles and incense because it was a theatrical gesture: I was on display and playing to the gallery. Even as I headed towards my teenage years, I was still a very tiny boy and in my long, flowing ankle-length ecclesiastical robes, which I am sure were taken up and shortened otherwise they would have swamped me, I looked and acted the picture of innocence. I had large brown eyes that dominated my tiny face, and jet-black hair cut in a fringe, which sat easily on my forehead, just above my eyebrows.

'What a little angel,' I would often hear members of the congregation whisper to each other during a service as they saw me going about my business, and it made me feel very special. I suppose I did have a grand air about me, and a presence associated with angels. I loved the pomp. My mother said I could charm the birds out of the trees. But really I was more like a little devil and was always up to mischief with the other boys.

One of our regular tricks after attending to our duties was for us all to congregate out of sight of authority and take large illicit swigs of communion wine. One day, one of the boys drank far more than was good for him, and reported for altar duty blind drunk. He had to be taken home in disgrace, though at that precise moment, I don't really think he cared too much. Another time, my brother and I found a discarded packet of cigarettes and, ever inquisitive, smoked them all between us, avidly trying to figure out exactly what all the fuss was about. I couldn't understand why people liked smoking: the cigarettes tasted awful and made us cough violently. The episode didn't do Dick any good because he actually fainted at holy communion shortly after-wards from the effects of inhaling too much smoke. That taught us both a lesson, and we have never smoked since. I hate cigarettes, I don't like the smell of them, I hate having them near me or in a room. I find the habit loathsome and it all stemmed from that single incident.

St Patrick's Church was packed to the rafters three times a day on Sundays, serving the very cosmopolitan Roman Catholic community of Soho. Sunday was a special day, too, for the Carroll family. It was the one day on which my mother could afford to treat the kids to cakes. It was our one little luxury in a life of necessities. After Mass I could contain my excitement no longer and literally flew out of church, down Greek Street, over Old Compton Street and into the Bertaux pâtisserie next door to the Coach and Horses public house. The shop was owned by two partners, lovely men both, Messieurs Bertaux, from whom it took its name, and Vignaud, and we became very good friends. They watched me grow from a boy. Monsieur Vignaud later bought his partner out and took over the pâtisserie, which is now run by his dear wife. She never acknowledges me as Danny La Rue, to her I am simply Dan. When I starred in my own show at the Palace Theatre at Cambridge Circus, for over two years I was a regular visitor to the shop, treating myself to their lovely cakes and pastries. Madame Vignaud also made me the most beautiful birthday cakes.

I adored Soho and everything it conjured up. It was the Bohemian centre of London and as such it appealed to my romantic nature. It was a fantasy world and my formative years spent there were very happy and contented.

Soho was a village within a city, like Montmartre in Paris, and like a village, everyone in the community knew each other. It was a close-knit society based on friendship, like a large family. If anyone was in trouble, a neighbour would rally round; if help was ever needed for any reason, there would be someone to lend a hand. There was an unspoken code of conduct.

The area was filled with many marvellous characters, some totally eccentric, and a strange mixture of artisans, shops and street traders. The shopkeepers prided themselves on knowing the name of every one of their customers and went out of their way to be of service. Nothing was too much trouble. Standards were high, and anything could be made or purchased for a price.

There were picturesque restaurants, which served a range of exotic foods and delicacies from Spain and Greece, Italy and France, to the locals, many of whom had travelled no further south than Victoria station, or Margate if they were lucky. Quaint old-fashioned tea shops and cafés were available for the more conservative, delicatessen for the more adventurous, and the homely, but inviting, public houses for the more down to earth. The smells and the sights and sounds of Soho were stimulating, the atmosphere compelling. An air of camaraderie permeated the whole place which meant you were never alone. Everyone worked for each other and together they built a fine community with strength and respect running right through it. They had all the right kind of values, too.

On Sunday mornings, people thought nothing of going out to collect their milk or newspapers in their dressing gowns and slippers. Then, oblivious to the rest of the world, they would spend the next half an hour or so talking on street corners to neighbours and friends. It wasn't out of place at all, just expected and very much part of the local colour. Soho was never dull.

I still can't understand why it has all been allowed to disappear under a hail of sex shops, pornographic clubs and rip-off joints. It saddens and amazes me that we could let it all go so easily . . . and makes me very angry.

When I reached puberty, I started to understand just how much my mother had given up for her family. I suddenly realized that we had a beautiful lady in our midst who had had no man in her life for many years. Other ladies I knew had boyfriends, and several of my mates had 'uncles' who dropped in and stayed from time to time, but we had nothing like that. The joke was that when I became important in show business I became my mother's boyfriend. However, we did make a lot of friends amongst the neighbouring families. It was hard not to in Soho, but strangely enough, most of our friends were Italians. I can't remember us ever having any close Irish acquaintances.

One particular Italian family, the Anselmis became our great friends and neighbours. They were lovely, genuine people, as much aliens in a foreign country as we were. The father and head of the household worked as the maître d'hôtel at the famous Mirabelle restaurant in Curzon Street, and several years later he kindly organized a job for me there as a commis waiter. I had left London during the war and been evacuated to Devon, but I was back in the capital for a brief stay with my sister Joan and needed something to tide me over. I lasted a week. The Mirabelle was the most chic restaurant in London, with style in abundance. It was my job to assist a more senior waiter and set tables. However, it wasn't for me. I hated it, particularly serving at table. Still, the tips were impressive. Each one of the waiters pooled his gratuities into a large box called a tronk. At the end of the evening session, the money was shared out equally. When I told my superior I wanted to leave, he was reluctant to let me go and even offered me a larger share of the tronk because he thought I was good at the job and had great flair. I was on display again, playing to the gallery.

Mr Anselmi was most disappointed that I didn't stick with the job longer. I felt slightly saddened because I had let him down, but it would have driven me mad if I'd stuck it out. In 1976, when I was lucky enough to be given a tribute luncheon at the Savoy Hotel by the Variety Club of Great Britain to celebrate my twenty-five years in show business, it was arranged and organized by Anselmi's son who worked at the hotel in charge of banqueting. It's certainly a small world.

I made Dame Anna Neagle roar with laughter once when I told her the story of my days as a commis waiter. I explained to her that we had first met at the Mirabelle. She arrived one evening at the restaurant for dinner with friends and I had the great pleasure of holding the chair for her at the table, while she sat down. I was sixteen, and it made a great impression on me. She didn't remember me at all, of course.

Anna and I became great friends. We would often meet at show-business functions, and she and her husband, Herbert Wilcox, were patrons of my nightclub in Hanover Square. In 1965, I knew Anna was facing a major decision in her long and eventful career. She had been offered the leading role in a new musical, *Charlie Girl*, which was to open in the West End. I knew she was a little apprehensive about accepting the contract. I found out she had a liking for yellow roses, and sent her a large bouquet hoping it might help her to make up her mind to agree to play the role. She did, and she was marvellous in it, just like I told her she would be. Anna related that story when she was a special guest on my *This Is Your Life* programme in 1984. She was an elegant lady, a great star and a splendid actress. Her death in 1986 was a sad loss.

After a full day at school and church, our evenings were spent at home. Mother had little spare money to take us out, so most of the time we went to bed relatively early. I had to be up at the crack of dawn for my paper round. Steam radio provided much of our entertainment and both Dick and I were avid listeners. We liked all the music programmes, but especially enjoyed the comedy shows that featured all the great comedians of the day: Flanagan and Allen, Max Miller, Will Hay, Robb Wilton, Jack Warner, Elsie and Doris Waters, and Charlie Chester; Arthur Askey and Richard Murdoch in *Bandwagon* were also very popular. But the show we never missed when it started broadcasting in the summer of 1939 was Tommy Handley's *ITMA*. It was absolutely hilarious. We soon slipped into a regular routine of listening.

Most Saturday afternoons, Dick and I would travel north by Underground or bus to stand on the terraces at Highbury and watch the famous Gunners along with 50,000 other cheering, well-behaved supporters. We were season-ticket holders and great Arsenal fans. They were the all-conquering team of the thirties and we saw some truly magnificent players – Crayston, Bowden, Drake, James and Bastin.

I have always been stage-struck, right from an early age. I still am. I loved the glamour and excitement of show business and I was always keen on collecting autographs. Living so close to London's theatreland, I would often visit the theatres in Shaftesbury Avenue or Charing Cross Road and just stand outside gazing at the billboards and front-of-house photographs. However, I remember seeing Frances Day at the Phoenix Theatre and being totally enchanted. The Palace was another favourite haunt where I would wait for what seemed like hours at the stage door hoping for a glimpse of a star name or famous face. The stagehands and usherettes soon got to know my face and on many occasions they would secrete me in through a side door to watch the show for free. Thirty years later it would be the scene of one of my own theatrical triumphs.

Gracie Fields had always been one of my favourite stars for as long as I could remember and I regarded her as the greatest of all the variety artistes. She had magic. In 1938, she appeared in a special concert at the Phoenix Theatre in Charing Cross Road for some kind of benefit or charity. Armed with a pencil and a piece of paper, I waited patiently outside the theatre's stage door for the great lady to emerge after the show. When she did, she opened the door with such force that it smashed into my face and almost knocked me unconscious. I had a beautiful black eye for several days afterwards. It was a total accident, but Gracie was so upset and apologetic at what she had done to me. She picked me up and gave me a huge hug and a kiss and kept asking if I was all right. I nodded, feeling slightly stunned, but only my pride had been really hurt. I certainly didn't mind the pain or the black eye, at least I had managed to meet, and talk to, one of the greatest stars of the British theatre. I was thrilled.

I told that story to Gracie thirty-six years later, in 1974, in my dressing room at the Prince of Wales theatre where I was appearing in my own show. We had been friends for some time by then. Norman Newell had brought her along to see my show to celebrate her seventy-sixth birthday on one of her rare visits to London from her home in Capri. When I knew she was coming to see the show, I arranged for the orchestra to busk 'Sally' and I warned the sound engineer to stand by with a tape recorder in case anything happened. Halfway through the show, I started singing 'Sally' and introduced Gracie Fields to the audience. Immediately, she rose out of her seat and sang the song with me and then walked up on to the stage. The audience went wild. The applause was rapturous, she was held in such high esteem by everyone. We chatted briefly on stage and then she sang a marvellous parody of the Dean Martin song, 'Volare', making up the words as she went along, and changing the lyric to 'My Danny'. It was very touching, but afterwards I very nearly killed the theatre's sound engineer. He was so excited and so entranced by such a gracious lady that he forgot to switch on the tape recorder . . . and I lost a priceless memento. But I have retained it in my heart.

Gracie was a remarkable woman. She could have been your favourite auntie, up from the country, she was so ordinary. But she had so much magic when she entertained. So much charm and charisma. We appeared together again in 1978 at the London Palladium in the Royal Variety Performance. It was her last performance. She died a year later.

Not long after her death, when I was in Capri, her brother, Tommy, took me to her home and showed me around. It was a very beautiful house. He took me into the drawing room and there on the grand piano was a photograph of Gracie and me together, taken at that Royal show. Tommy told me his sister loved the picture and kept it permanently on display. He added that she regarded me as she would her own son.

As I was leaving the house, Tommy gave me a tiny straw fan that had belonged to Gracie Fields and with which she would often fan herself when she was living on the island. It is one of my most prized and cherished possessions and goes everywhere with me. I touch it and I get a strange feeling: Gracie is here with me *still*.

It cost ninepence to sit in the gods in most of London's theatres in those days and that wasn't cheap. When she could afford it, my mother would take us to the Princes Theatre (now the Shaftesbury), which was literally down the road from our flat. On other occasions, in more affluent days, we would travel to the Metropolitan at Edgware Road, where they presented music hall and variety. We saw most of the great stars of the day, including Randolph Sutton, whose signature tune was 'On Mother Kelly's Doorstep', Jimmy O'Dea, Leslie Henson and Arthur Lucan as Old Mother Riley, who became an enormous star by dressing up in women's clothes. There is a strange and almost chilling parallel between my act and that of Arthur Lucan. I project the glamorous showbiz image, while he portrayed this old lady, Mother Riley. But under the skin they were sisters. I depend upon the use of masquerade and we both achieved fame from an image that was not our own.

In the summer of 1986, while I was appearing in my own show at the Spa Theatre in Bridlington, I was given the great honour of unveiling a bronze memorial bust to Arthur Lucan in a converted bakery in Paragon Street, Hull. It stands on the very spot where the creator of Old Mother Riley collapsed and died in the wings of the old Tivoli Theatre on 17 May 1954.

Apart from the theatre, we were also taken to the cinema, but I wasn't impressed. Movies did nothing for me, they lacked the intimacy of live theatre; there was no rapport between the audience and the performers. How could there be? I can honestly say that I have not liked many films. Of course, there were exceptions. Walt Disney's *Snow White and the Seven Dwarfs*, the first full-length colour cartoon feature film, made a great impression on me. So, too, did *The Wizard of Oz*, and I fell instantly head over heels in love with its star, Judy Garland. Little did I know that, within a handful of years, I would be slapping the great star's backside because she got too drunk, or that I would be entertaining another screen legend, Betty Grable, to dinner where she poured out her heart to me and asked for my advice, or that I would be singing to the piano accompaniment of Noël Coward and Liberace. Such is the frightening power of show business.

The threat of war was apparent from the moment we arrived in England. We knew that it was on the horizon, but few people spoke about it, hoping it might go away. The wireless was our only source of information and Alvar Lidell became a national figure as he read out the daily bulletins, telling us about the ambitions of Herr Hitler and the Third Reich in Germany and their imperialistic plan for Europe. The bitter reality of conflict had been drummed into us through the

Spanish Civil War with its grim stories of terrible suffering, death and destruction. We hoped it wouldn't be allowed to happen here.

The menace from the continent only served to bring the people of Britain closer together. A tremendous sense of solidarity descended on the nation, kindling a great spirit of unity. People changed, they behaved differently. Barriers between rich and poor were broken down, discrimination between the classes disappeared. Everyone mucked in together for the common cause. We were all brothers and sisters under the same flag. If we were threatened, then we would fight shoulder to shoulder together. Patriotism was high. We put our trust in our political leaders. They wouldn't let us down. But when Hitler annexed Austria, doubts began to show.

I can remember vividly listening to Neville Chamberlain's voice when he returned from Munich in September 1938 waving his piece of white paper in the air. I was eleven. After he promised us all 'peace in our time', my mother grew apprehensive and restless once again. She was worried about what might happen. She feared the worst. Why had she brought her family over the water for this? Maybe the best solution would be to go back to Ireland and safety? She almost convinced herself that would be best but my sisters managed to talk her out of such notions. 'We're all happy here,' they told her. 'All our friends are here. London is our home. We'd all like to stay.' We were united in defiance.

So we stayed put in Earnshaw Street and got on with the daily business of living, while we prayed in St Patrick's for peace and salvation.

With an unwavering sense of the inevitable, London – and the rest of the country – prepared for war as 1938 slipped quietly away and into 1939. While Hitler was preparing to invade Czechoslovakia in March, we travelled to Gray's Inn Road to pick up our government-issue gas masks, to be carried with us at all times. The posters on the street told us to: 'Hitler will send no warning. So always carry your gas mask.' I had a horrible black one which I carried in a cardboard box around my neck on a piece of string. It was awful.

The government went to great pains to tell people about the dangers of poison gas after the appalling casualties it had inflicted in the trenches during the First World War, and they assured us it would be a major weapon in any future conflict. Leaflets and handbooks were distributed. While posters were pasted up throughout the capital, council workmen went all over London painting the tops of GPO pillar boxes with a bright yellow gas-detecting liquid which supposedly changed colour in the event of poison being in the air. Well, that was what we were told anyway!

There was an invasion of a different kind, too, as sandbags and barbed wire were brought into the city, and men and women arrived in uniforms of all kinds. Shopkeepers made ready to board up their windows if hostilities broke out, and buildings with large basements and underground cellars were prepared and converted into air-raid shelters. Recent history suggested Hitler would attack us from the air. A large shelter was opened up underneath Soho Square to be used by local residents, which became a life-saver when bombs destroyed St Anne's Church near by, and Carlisle House at the other end of the Square.

Soho was changing before our eyes. It became painfully noticeable when the iron railings that had enveloped the Square for over 200 years were taken down unceremoniously, carted away and salvaged for the war effort. Iron was a useful commodity for munitions, every ounce was precious.

Sunday, 3 September 1939 was in many ways just like any other Sunday in Soho. St Patrick's was packed for Mass and the Square itself, and side streets, were awash with people from the break of dawn. Soho woke up very early. It was not unusual.

Back at home, every household that could, tuned into the wireless set to listen to the Prime Minister. At eleven fifteen on that tense morning Neville Chamberlain's voice crackled into life through the static:

'I am speaking to you from the cabinet room of 10 Downing Street,' it began, and within the briefest moment, the short statement concluded . . . 'consequently this country is at war with Germany.'

The bad dream we most feared had become reality.

But then . . . the strange thing was that *nothing* happened except for a brief and terrifying false alarm in London just seven minutes after Chamberlain had finished speaking. An unidentified plane had been spotted nearing the capital. Sirens screamed into action, people panicked . . . and the plane turned out to be one of ours. German aircraft had been predicted over London and we expected to be bombed at any moment. But the skies remained clear.

On the home front, Britain went about its daily routine as usual with a renewed sense of urgency as what was called the 'phoney' war gripped the country, and autumn turned to winter. Life went on much as normal, albeit for a few minor irritations like ration books, identity cards, coupons and blackout curtains.

However, London was preparing for the worst to happen. Vast barrage balloons were launched into the city skies, anti-aircraft gun emplacements were sited in the most unlikely places, and the city was ringed by a network of giant searchlights.

To a young impressionable twelve-year-old caught up in the feverish activity, there was a marvellous sense of drama and excitement. Far from being scared at what could become a tragic outcome, I looked upon it all as just another big adventure and took all the upheaval in my stride.

Shortly after the declaration of war, most of London's schools closed for the duration and for many parents it meant separation from their children, who were evacuated to the safer reaches of the country or seaside, away from any bombs or devastation.

What bombs? We stayed in town.

The wireless kept us in touch with the outside world and what was going on. We heard of people being killed in Europe, which was a terrible shock. We were told of the fall of Norway, Denmark and Belgium, and cheered when Winston Churchill became Prime Minister in May 1940. We cried when we heard of the retreat at Dunkirk and rooted for the heroic seamen in their daring rescue attempts.

Soho became the scene of some ugly incidents in June when Mussolini threw in his hand with Hitler and Italy declared war on Britain. Retribution against the Italian community in London was swift and terrifying. The windows of many Italian restaurants and shops were stoned and smashed. Slogans were daubed on walls and doors, and friends verbally abused in the streets. Anti-Italian feeling ran very high, indeed. It was a great tragedy, because most of the Italian families in residence in Soho, Covent Garden or Seven Dials had lived in London for generations, many were born there, and the vast majority of them were very pro-British and identified more with this country than their own. They were piggies-in-the-middle of a highly volatile situation. Emotions ran sky high. Soon afterwards, the police started rounding up German and Italian immigrants throughout the country for questioning and ultimately internment at centres on the sea coast or on the Isle of Man. Some were even sent to Canada. Our good friend, Mr Anselmi, was spared the indignity of it all – I think he was too old anyway, but the husband of one Italian family we knew well was picked up and sent away to one of the detention centres. Tragically, he died, and his widow left Britain to make her home in Sydney, Australia. She contacted me there when I was in Australia for one of my tours, and we renewed our friendship.

Amidst all the uncertainty in our lives, we did have one cause for celebration. In the summer of 1940, my sister Nancy married Walter Christopher, a dashing young man from Devon whom she met at the hotel in Bromley. She was eighteen. Normally, I think perhaps they might have waited to get married, but there was a war on and Walter was in the Army and about to leave on active service. It was almost certain he would be posted overseas. Wally was a smashing man, and we welcomed him lovingly into our family. The couple started their married life together in the tiny village of Kennford, three miles south of Exeter in Devon, where Wally had been born and raised.

Meanwhile my other sister, Joan, had taken a job in the catering department of *The Times* newspaper, near to Blackfriars Bridge, and she was now living permanently with us in the flat at Earnshaw Street.

Then it happened. In the late afternoon of Saturday, 7 September 1940 – just over a year since the declaration of war – Hitler took the first step in what he was convinced would ensure victory over Britain and lead to a successful invasion of the island.

At about five o'clock, the blue summer sky over London was filled with the eerie shapes of a thousand German planes, each one carrying a deadly cargo. It was like a huge black raincloud about to unleash an awful downpour. The terrible droning noise of engines was incessant as they set about their mission to wreak death and destruction upon the helpless city below. The sky seemed to throb with the sound. The East End took the full force of a relentless onslaught as the Luftwaffe squadrons sought out London's docklands with the intention of crippling the heart of the city. The raid lasted over an hour, and, by the time the bombers left, the sky had turned crimson red with fire as the capital blazed away beneath.

The bombers returned for a second onslaught within sixty minutes. The nightmare was beginning.

Our routine had been well-rehearsed. As soon as the sirens screeched out their warning, my mother, Joan, Dick and I would each grab a blanket and a bag of food, and hurry across the road to the YWCA

(Young Women's Christian Association) building in Great Russell Street, off Tottenham Court Road, which had been turned into an air-raid shelter. We were told it was one of the deepest shelters in London; we hoped it was also one of the safest. Once there, we queued for a few short moments to register and then, with great speed and clinical efficiency, the wardens regimented us downstairs where, in the converted gymnasium, in the bowels of the building, we were allocated our own section and settled down for the night. It was a well-run system.

I was amazed by the sheer volume of people inside the shelter. Masses of men, women and children were huddled together in sleeping bags, on top of mattresses and bunk beds, and under blankets, in what resembled a huge subterranean barracks room. People from every walk of life were thrown together in times of adversity. They coped extremely well. In a very short space of time, the YWCA became a thriving underground community as friendships were forged and the refugees from the Blitz banded together in camaraderie and brotherhood to share whatever fate had in store for them.

War has this irresistible quality that brings people together as one in comradeship. It may be silly to say it, but I believe it was the best time for England. The same spirit was shown during the Falklands crisis in 1982. It seems that when the very quality of life is threatened, the British rally round to defeat the common enemy, as if people *need* a war to snap them out of an apathetic streak and unite them. Why this attitude of solidarity cannot be retained at all other times is beyond me.

The YWCA in Bloomsbury became our second home for many months, and played several vital roles in my life. I still have a great respect for it. Nostalgia, I suppose. After the war I joined an amateur dramatic society that was based there; and it must surely be a unique situation that an unknown thirteen-year-old boy in short pants should return as a star in adult life and book rooms in the building for his own company and himself to rehearse whenever he had a new show to present in the West End.

Our gymnasium home became a hotbed of activity each evening, often to relieve the sheer tedium of all the waiting and worrying. We sang together, danced together, played charades together and an assortment of games, or simply chatted away the boredom. Card schools were in session well into the small hours and beyond, in various corners

of the room. Someone played a mouth organ, another beavered away
on an accordion, someone else strummed a banjo. The shelter also
boasted a piano and a fair share of willing hands to play it. There was
never any shortage of accompaniment. Occasionally a shout of 'quiet'
or 'shut up' would echo around the building and punctuate the hubbub
as a lonely figure fought to get to sleep, but mostly spirits were high.

One night, I befriended a young girl called Trixie, who worked at
the Maypole Dairy packing butter. We soon became good mates and
spent our time crocheting slippers together which we later sold to
anyone who would buy them. Even at the age of thirteen, I was
business-minded, a budding young entrepreneur in the making.

The intensity of the air raids on the war-torn city had meant that all
of London's theatres had closed down, all that is, except the redoubt-
able Windmill which 'never closed'. Some cinemas stayed open and at
one time the Granada chain offered entertainment, which included four
or five feature movies, newsreels and a community singsong, *and* shelter
through the night in an effort to gain customers.

Several West End nightclubs also kept their doors open to the public,
preferring to take their chances against the might of Germany's air
force in order to take money from grateful punters starved of entertainment. Churchill's, where I was later to start my own nightclub career,
was one of them.

George Shearing, the blind American jazz pianist, was a regular
performer at the Bond Street nightspot during the war. He would often
call into the YWCA shelter on his way to and from engagements and,
quite naturally, he would be gently persuaded to play the piano. I got
a great kick out of singing along with him. I had an audience, albeit a
captive one, but it made no difference. 'On Mother Kelly's Doorstep',
'We're Gonna Hang Out the Washing on the Ziegfried Line' and
'Underneath the Arches' were guaranteed to set the gymnasium ringing
with song.

Trixie, George and I shared a great rapport, and we became almost
inseparable. But love was blossoming in another direction, and it came
as no surprise when Trixie and George married. Shortly afterwards,
George Shearing's career took off in a big way and he became a major
star on both sides of the Atlantic, and well-respected in music circles.

When the war was over, George returned to London for a series of
appearances. We had lost contact by them, but I thought it would be a
marvellous gesture to go and see Trixie and George again after all

these years. So I put on my best suit and went to visit them at their hotel. But they didn't want to know me and wouldn't see me. I was devastated. It was a tremendous shock and upset me greatly. We had been so close at a time when we needed to be close, and I couldn't understand what had happened. What had changed? I felt shattered, badly let down. The incident stayed in my mind and influenced me greatly when I became a star in my own right. I vowed then never to act like that myself towards anyone at all, no matter who. Civility and sincerity cost nothing, yet count for so much.

Throughout our nightly ordeals I was never scared. I have never been frightened of dying. To me death is just an extension of life and not to be feared. Even when I was exposed to the bombing on the streets after being caught outside away from the shelter during an unexpected air attack, I ignored the inferno and the bombs dropping all round me in a great effort to rush back to the YWCA as quickly as I could. My only concern was that if anything *did* happen that night, the family had to be together. If we were going to die, we had to die together. But I was not afraid for my own safety, not even when I was only inches away from oblivion. There was a kind of excitement and stimulation about it all.

On one occasion I can remember sprinting down Tottenham Court Road towards Great Russell Street with the German planes overhead. Instinctively I looked back and saw a bomb drop at the other end of the road virtually in the same place where a few minutes before I had been standing. I ran on unconcerned by the danger.

Apart from the bombs themselves, flying shrapnel was another potential killer, and I must have dodged my fair share. I used to take my life into my own hands regularly because I started collecting shrapnel. I went round the streets picking it up. I thought it had such marvellous shapes, weird, wonderful and strangely beautiful. I took as much home with me as I could carry. I was oblivious to the terrible consequences that might have been.

Many a time I would see motionless bodies on the pavement, or lying in the debris of a bombed-out building, obviously dead. I couldn't relate to death – to me they were sleeping and looked like tailor's dummies. There was no fear.

People say that children have a steel nerve. They are rarely frightened. They can cope very well in crises. I have certainly found it to be true when I have visited children in hospital. They put up with so much pain, suffering and discomfort that their courage puts most adults to shame.

It didn't take me long to discover that many of London's Underground stations were being used as air-raid shelters and that thriving communities just like our own at the YWCA existed on the Bakerloo Line, or the District or the Metropolitan. What was even more thrilling, was that tube trains continued to run right up until ten thirty at night. I spent many an adventurous evening travelling up and down the Northern Line from Tottenham Court Road, jumping out at stations to spend a pleasant few minutes chatting to these underground villagers, until the next train came along and I was off again. It was an amazing sight. Platforms were piled high with a network of iron grid bunk beds, seething with human life. People settled down on the concrete floors, and I learnt that once the current had been extinguished for the night, hammocks were slung across the open tunnel mouths to provide even more sleeping accommodation. Just as in our shelter, there was a terrific camaraderie.

However, it wasn't all good news. Several stations were bombed. There was a major disaster at Balham where dozens of people lost their lives in a direct hit, while Camden Town and Trafalgar Square were other stations to suffer damage. News of this destruction was spread through rumour and gossip, although nothing appeared in the newspapers or on the radio reports. It was bad for morale and spirits *had* to be kept as high as possible.

The Blitz on London continued for several weeks – it seemed unending – throughout September and October into November to Christmas and the New Year. At first the East End bore the brunt of the onslaught, but within days every corner of the capital was pounded from above. No one was left out. Hitler didn't discriminate in this case.

The engines droned on and on overhead, with remorseless regularity. With the same relentlessness, we kept our early evening appointment down below in the shelter. Even when there was a temporary halt in the frenzy and Goering's aircraft turned northwards for fresh pickings in Coventry, Birmingham and the Black Country, we continued with our own night shift at the YWCA and stubbornly refused to be lulled into a false sense of security. Others did, and paid the ultimate price with their lives when the bombers returned unexpectedly. We stuck to our routine and never missed a night – it saved our lives.

One morning, after a particularly bitter night, we emerged from our shelter into the daylight bright and early, and crossed the road for home. Earnshaw Street wasn't there any more. It had gone. Hitler's bombers had scored a direct hit. The entire road had been flattened, totally destroyed. In its place desolation and chaos – a smoking ruin. Firemen and salvage experts scrambled over the rubble searching and listening desperately for any sign of life, tearing at the debris with their bare hands.

My mother and I, Joan and Dick stood dazed amid a small crowd of people rummaging away. The noise of confusion was deafening, yet we were utterly alone. Speechless, not daring to think that we could all have perished under the devastation that now stared back at us, we shared a single, chilling thought.

Amid the shattered buildings, we hadn't actually lost an awful lot. We had few possessions, but in a way we had lost everything. We had lost our home . . . and that was hard to take. My sister cried. Two boys looked bewildered, while my mother sobbed, and I could read the thoughts running through her mind: 'If only we hadn't left Ireland . . . if only we'd gone back . . . if only . . .'

That night, and for the next few days, the family was temporarily split up as officialdom decided what to do with us. Dick and I were billeted in a nearby church hall; mother and Joan went into a hostel.

The authorities in their wisdom recommended that my brother and I be evacuated from the city like thousands of other children had been before us. We hated the idea. It meant we would be separated for an even greater period of time, and Dick and I might be split up and parted. Besides, we had heard several stories from other evacuees who were beaten and treated badly in their new 'country' homes. The thought was abhorrent to us both. If possible, we wanted the whole family to be together and we didn't want to be sent just anywhere, we wanted some kind of say in our destiny.

In the end, my sister, Nancy, came to our rescue, and solved the problem for everyone, officials included. Since her marriage, she had been living in the Devon village of Kennford with her parents-in-law, who were a very prominent family in the area. As soon as she heard of our plight, she started organizing the family once again. With the Christophers' help, she arranged for us to leave London to live in the West Country. Only Joan remained behind, preferring to stay in the capital and continue with her job at *The Times*.

We were on the move again.

3
'I don't like men who dress up as women, but you make me laugh'

I spent some of the happiest days of my life in Devon. After the horrific bludgeoning London had taken in recent months, and was still experiencing, the peace and tranquillity of *real* village life had a profound effect on a thirteen-year-old from the Smoke, who was inclined to be romantic. I'd stepped out of a holocaust and into a fantasy world. It was just like my very own Shangri-la, and I was willingly swallowed up by the whole ideal.

Kennford, and its twin village of Kenn, had a rare beauty, a picture postcard charm, so tiny and quaint that at times you could almost feel the silence. The whole area was heavily wooded and everywhere the earth was a deep, rich red. It could have been in Ireland and I firmly believe that was one of the reasons we loved it so much. I'm sure my mother, more than any of us, sensed the very close resemblance. I had never seen her so relaxed and contented; she sparkled like a precious jewel. After all, she had originally come from a tiny village in County Cork, and Mary Ann adored the country, she wasn't really a city woman.

The whole pace and atmosphere of village life was different, slower by comparison with London. The quality of that life appeared better, too. In a few years, Devon turned a young boy into a man. It was indeed my destiny to be sent to the West Country, to enjoy what I have called my quiet period, because it gave me an inner calm and tolerance, a sense of quality and restraint. It was solid and reliable, and proved to be one of the most vital parts of my life experience. Without Devon, I definitely wouldn't be the person I am today. Yet it wouldn't have happened had there not been a war.

The Christopher family had arranged accommodation for us in the village with a man called Bert Yeo, who lived with his sister in a large house, so there was plenty of room for the extra visitors from London. The Yeos were a lovely family, gentle folk, kind and wonderful. Bert was a market gardener by profession and we had the pick of the fresh fruit and vegetable crop. It was such a dramatic change from London where things were in very short supply and we had to queue for most items with our ration books at the ready.

Almost as soon as I arrived, I decided I had to get a job. I have always been a worker, so I felt it was my duty to help provide for the family. I was lucky enough to find work on a local farm, sweeping up, mucking out and generally tidying the place up, which at that time was totally alien to my nature. I had never done anything like it before. But I think I must have done well because I was regularly given a dozen eggs for my efforts, which at that time was a king's ransom. In the large cities, eggs were a precious commodity and in very short supply.

It didn't take us long to integrate into Kennford village society. We were never made to feel outsiders by our hosts; on the contrary, we were made to feel very much at home by everyone. Their warmth and generosity touched us all. Maybe the strangers from London were viewed as a novelty and our arrival made a welcome change of routine for the friendly community. Perhaps my sister, Nancy, a villager by marriage, had something to do with it. She had such charm. Either way, the villagers took us to their hearts and we were encouraged to join in with all the local activities. There were many. We went to whist drives, I loved playing cards, and to the shilling hops in the village hall, which always seemed to take place on Thursday evenings. Amateur dramatics were also very popular. Everyone mucked in together for their own enjoyment, in a community where everyone was a friend, and in many cases, a relative. It was that kind of village.

I made friends quickly and easily, and I loved talking. Jimmy Ratcliffe was a particular friend, and we did most things together. He taught me how to ride a bicycle, which was a new experience for me. I had never cycled in London. After several painful attempts to get the co-ordination correct, which saw me falling from the saddle sideways invariably into a clump of stinging nettles, I persevered enough and eventually mastered the simple act.

Cycling opened up new horizons for me. A small gang of boys and girls from the village would often ride miles together, all over the district, exploring new and exciting places. There was always something to see and somewhere different to go, even in the rain. It didn't matter. Villages with such romantic names as Clyst St George, Doddiscombeleigh, Powderham and Topsham were in easy reach of our pedals, and I spent some happy moments just getting to know the beautiful county. On many occasions, I left the bike at home and rambled aimlessly over the countryside, just looking, taking it all in and savouring its delicacies. It was idyllic and safe.

I also became a Boy Scout, joining the Kenn St Andrews Scout Group, led by John Waldron. I enjoyed scouting immensely and soon mastered the rudiments of morse code, cooking, first aid, knot tying, and tracking. Swimming in the outdoor pool near by was another energetic pastime. We went camping, too, but I hated it so much that I left the site and went home after just a handful of hours under canvas.

We kept in touch with the latest developments in the war through the newspapers and radio, but its harsh reality hit us hard one evening when we saw the sky glowing bright red in the darkness, as Plymouth, a mere thirty miles away, suffered a terrible basting from the German air force as they attacked the naval dockyards. A sickening stillness hung in the air to the west. Exeter was also on the receiving end of a battering. But the war rarely touched Kennford.

Jimmy Ratcliffe's mother Winnie became like a second mother to me during my time in the village. I used to visit her cottage at weekends to share a supper of homemade pasties and cakes, and then we would spend a pleasant few hours chatting together. She was a delightful lady. Sadly, she died in the same week Liberace passed away and, in the space of a few days at the beginning of 1987, I lost two dear friends.

School, like most of Kennford, was tiny. Mr Rowley was headmaster of a one-roomed, one-class establishment where the boys outnumbered the girls and the curriculum gave everyone the same solid, down-to-earth education and basic grounding. Devon sharpened my confidence as a boy. Even though I was small, I was never shy: I was always well-mannered and sort of proud.

Kennford was three miles away from Exeter and once a week I was allowed to get the bus into the city and go to the pictures. Whenever possible, I tried to see a Betty Grable film – I adored her. On Saturday evenings, the last bus home left Exeter at six thirty and it was usually packed. One night, after seeing Betty Grable in *Moon Over Miami*, I was at the head of the queue and caught the bus as normal. But, before it left the stop on its journey through to the villages, it became so full that the conductor reluctantly turned a pregnant woman away, and refused to let her board. It seemed a great injustice to me, so I got up and gave her my seat and then walked back to Kennford on my own. I thought nothing of it. However, my mother was terribly upset with me for being late, she had expected me home at a certain time and when I didn't arrive, she started to worry. She told me off in no uncertain terms because she hadn't known where I was. I just told her I missed the bus. On Monday, the headmaster heard about the incident and spoke about it at morning assembly in front of the whole school, commending my actions. But it had been an instinctive reaction. I had been brought up to act in that way.

Besides being well-mannered, I also possessed a kind of arrogance which gave me very definite ideas. I stuck firmly to what I believed in. Nothing on earth would shake me from my beliefs. I suppose it was youthful stubborness. It manifested itself early in my life.

One morning in school, a boy sitting next to me in class suddenly flicked an ink pellet at the headmaster's back as he was writing on the blackboard. It hit him on the nape of the neck. Mr Rowley reacted immediately. He turned and stared at the class, his face reddening with anger. A deathly hush fell over the assembled children. It was pretty obvious from which direction the missile had been launched, so the headmaster asked me to stand up. His eyes burned into mine.

'Do you know who threw this pellet?' he asked.

'Yes, sir,' came my confident reply as I knew I'd done nothing wrong.

'Who was it?' he snapped.

'I'm not telling,' I snapped back.

Rowley's brow furrowed and he barked out an order, calling me out to the front of the class where he unceremoniously threatened me with the cane if I didn't reveal the name of the perpetrator of the crime. It had become a battle of wills. He knew I was not guilty, but I was sticking to my principles.

'You're not going to cane me,' I said defiantly. 'I shall leave.' So I did, before he could say anything further. I walked out of the classroom and went home to explain to my mother exactly what had happened. She backed me all the way, and returned to see Mr Rowley herself, and asked him to apologize to me for his actions. Then, and only then, would she allow me to go back.

I don't remember getting an apology, but I certainly went back to school that afternoon, and I definitely *wasn't* caned. After that incident, Mr Rowley and I saw each other in a different light.

We acted Shakespeare at school with the boys playing many of the female parts as the author had intended, not through any great dramatic revelation, but through necessity. We had too few girls in the class. I got the pick of the roles. I was small which was a definite advantage, and the headmaster realized I had some flair. I think even then he recognized the actor in me. Looking back there were qualities in me that were different to the others, but it never occurred to me that I was any different. I had charisma, so I was called upon to play such parts as Rosalind and Portia. My Juliet was also very convincing. It was a great challenge to act, but I had no intention of taking it up as a permanent career when I left school. That was the furthest thought from my mind.

We made our own scenery, and costumes, too, using coloured crêpe paper. Those who saw the plays thought the costumes were magnificent, yet we hardly dared move on stage for fear of ripping the paper. My own stage costumes have come a long way since then!

At that time, I was very worried that I might never grow tall. I was always much shorter than my brother, who at five feet six inches seemed to tower over me, a mere four feet nothing. I was getting tired of looking like a cherub and being called a little angel. I hated it. I wanted to grow, *desperately*.

Then, without warning, I shot up to five feet eleven, leaving Dick in my wake, which pleased me no end. I was tall and loved it.

In the summer of 1942, my elder sister, Joan, persuaded my mother to let me travel to London to stay with her for a few days. She had a small flat, and as the bombings had stopped permanently and the city was considered relatively safe, she was eager to put me up for a brief holiday. Much as I loved Devon, I was anxious to see London again. I hadn't seen my sister for a good eighteen months and I realized that in that time I had grown considerably. Yet I hadn't noticed myself just how much I had changed.

When I arrived at Waterloo station, Joan didn't recognize me. More than that, she ignored me. She had no idea I'd grown so much. She still had a picture of me in her mind as a little boy, the baby of the family, even though I was now fifteen. I stood at the ticket barrier, watching her reaction. She walked up and down the platform looking for me, scrutinizing the faces of all the passengers who had disembarked from the Exeter express. I think she was starting to panic that she couldn't find me. When I eventually revealed my identity she was so shocked she nearly fainted.

That same year, Dick left home for the first time after enlisting in the Royal Navy. He was off to fight the war.

We lived with Bert Yeo and his sister for well over a year, until Bert married and we were forced to move. His sister was terribly upset to lose us and we didn't want to go, we had become dear friends and like one big happy family. But it simply wasn't practical to stay on.

We moved less than a mile down the road to the village of Kenn and into the Lodge house on the Trehill Estate in sight of the country manor. I felt very grand and special living so near to such splendour and imagined it was mine, and that I was lord of the manor.

We lived in what can only be described as converted stables set around a courtyard. The whole building looked to me like a fairytale castle with its solid walls and huge wrought-iron gates standing sentry at the bottom of the driveway to the big house. The Lodge house itself was far too large for Mary Ann and me to live in on our own now that Dick had joined up. So Nancy and her young son, Percy, moved in to share our home. My sister's husband, Walter, was away fighting for king and country. Nancy was always good company.

There were no Catholic churches in the twin villages, so our God was worshipped at home. Once a month, my mother took us on a pilgrimage by taxi to church in Exeter, where we took communion and renewed our faith. We couldn't afford to go more often.

When I was fifteen, I decided it was time I got a permanent job to do my bit and help support my mother. School hadn't really done anything for me, although Mr Rowley wanted me to stay on and continue my education. He pleaded quite vehemently with Mary Ann to use her influence to help me change my mind. But it had been made up for quite some time.

I took a job earning one pound a week in the bakery in Coulson's store in Exeter High Street. I used to be given bread as one of the perks of the job, and tins of fruit which I was convinced had been stolen. But I kept my mouth shut and said nothing – there was a war on. The job didn't last very long, I couldn't stand the intense heat from the ovens. I asked to be transferred and, at no increase in salary, was made lift boy in the same store, which was later taken over by Debenhams.

I hadn't been in my exalted position long when I was befriended by a most elegant lady who used the store restaurant each day for lunch. I later found out her name was Mrs Payne. She was a sophisticated woman and very fashion-conscious, even in such austere times. She was tall with tremendous presence and charm. I estimated she was in her forties. She took quite a shine to me and, after a few weeks of exchanging the customary 'good afternoons' and other normal pleasantries on our brief journeys upwards, she told me she thought I was completely wasting my life as a lift boy. She added I was far too intelligent for such a mundane job. I hardly knew the woman.

'You should be more ambitious,' she said as the lift ascended to the chosen floor. 'Do you like fashion?'

I'd never had much cause to think about it before, but I nodded in agreement. 'Yes,' I replied. I was game for anything, but I couldn't really see the point of the conversation.

'Well, I have a job available for the right person, as a trainee window-dresser at J. V. Huttons across the road, on the corner of Queen Street. I think you'd be ideal . . .'

The lift slowed to a halt.

'After lunch come over and see me,' she enthused as she stepped out of the lift, 'and we'll sort everything out,' and disappeared into the restaurant.

I started work at Huttons each morning at seven thirty after travelling what was now four miles from Kenn to Exeter by bus. I handed over my twenty shillings weekly wage to my mother each Friday, and if I needed any money for myself, I only had to ask. I rarely did.

J. V. Huttons was a general outfitters, selling coats, hats, dresses and all the various accessories. The elegant Mrs Payne managed the shop along with her husband, who was also in charge of window-dressing. Although there was severe rationing, and clothing coupons were like gold dust, business was doing very well, and the company was able to employ ten full-time staff, all women, except for me and Mr Payne.

Each Monday morning, all the display windows were cleared out and re-dressed completely, which was Mr Payne's special responsibility. During the week, we used to titivate. I was told to watch what he did and to listen to what he said, and to learn. Maybe one day I might just get the opportunity of designing and dressing a window myself. I took it all in and absorbed the things Mr Payne told me meticulously. He had taught me all he could in a matter of weeks and it didn't take too long before I was better at the job than he. I had a natural artistic flair, I suppose, and a theatrical disposition, which helped. He was a shrewd man and could see my potential, and after a while he simply handed the job over to me. I had to dress every window in the shop. It was hard work, but a great challenge for me, and my salary rose accordingly to thirty shillings a week. I enjoyed my time at Huttons very much indeed, and was grateful that I had found something for which I had natural talent and feeling.

I got on very well with both the public and the sales assistants. I would think nothing of chatting up new and potential customers to help them make their decisions over which outfit to buy. They always listened to my opinions and advice and respected my judgment. That way I helped to make sales for the girls, but I always told the truth. I never flattered for the sake of it. If I believed a garment didn't suit a customer, I told them so, and then helped them look for one that did.

On occasions when I was dressing windows, I became the centre of attraction for passers-by on the pavement, through my antics. I think people have a fascination for watching window-dressers at work. They laughed when I had to take the clothes off the dummies because they knew the models were naked underneath, so it was always a bit of a giggle. One thing I hadn't bargained for was the terrific heat given off by the huge plate-glass windows. Standing there for several hours at a time was almost unbearable. I thought I had left the heat behind in the bakery.

There were other problems, too. I once knocked over a dummy and sent it sprawling through a window in a shower of broken glass on to the pavement outside, much to everyone's horror inside the store and out. Shortly afterwards, I arrived at Huttons one Monday morning, eager to start work with some new designs to re-dress the windows, only to find them all shattered. Exeter had been bombed the night before and every piece of glass in the shop had smashed.

Once work had finished for the day, I involved myself entirely in amateur dramatics. It gave me a wonderful outlet in which to express myself. We rehearsed for weeks and weeks and then presented our offering in the village hall for a couple of nights. Then we started all over again preparing our next production. Winnie Ratcliffe was one of the leading ladies of our village drama society and we appeared several times together in plays like *The Farmer's Wife*, or evenings of revue with everyone on stage making utter fools of themselves. But that's what village life was all about, good wholesome fun.

There was also a spate of village dances, where I discovered that I was an excellent dancer. I often partnered a lovely girl called Honor Preece, who later married Jimmy Ratcliffe, my best friend. Occasionally, I went into Exeter to visit the theatre. My life was full and active, and I was enjoying every second. I was completely and utterly contented. I often wonder what might have happened if I hadn't followed my brother Dick into the Navy not long afterwards.

My religion has always taught me to accept everything without question, and to take nothing for granted. Everything that happens is intended. I believe God tests us all the time and I don't believe we should ever become complacent or big-headed if things appear to be going well. The situation can change so suddenly and our world can come tumbling down at our feet in seconds.

In 1943, shortly after I had reached sixteen, my mother received a telegram from the War Ministry. It was grave news. The ministry wished to inform her that HMS *Berry*, on which my brother Dick was serving, had been torpedoed by U-boats while in the Arctic Ocean with great loss of life. Thankfully, he was among the survivors and had been picked up from the freezing waters. He had been taken to a military hospital in Belfast where he was in a critical condition. There was little hope he would pull through his ordeal. The effects of the icy Northern waters, exposure and severe shock could prove too much.

Mary Ann and I made the journey to Northern Ireland by train and sea. It was agonizing. We realized the seriousness of Dick's condition when we were given special permission to enter Belfast. Although there was a war on, there was still a great divide between the north and south of Ireland – and we were originally from the south. We were convinced we were going to say our goodbyes to Dick, whom we were told could die at any moment. We prayed and hoped we wouldn't be too late.

Throughout our journey we discussed the future over and over again. A future *without* Dick. Should we bring his body back with us, or should he be buried in Ireland? Fortunately, the questions never had to be answered. When we arrived at the hospital, we found my brother sitting up in bed, laughing. He *was* seriously ill, but making a sterling recovery. He had been in the sea for hours and by rights he should have been dead.

Then two days before D-Day, on 4 June 1944, my sister's husband, Walter Christopher, was killed at Anzio, during the Allies' advance north through Italy. I will always remember his face; he was such a nice man. The tragedy devastated the tiny community and everyone in Kennford and Kenn felt great sadness and grief. He was known and well-liked by all the villagers. They had lost one of their own. Nancy's daughter, Mary, was just a few months old. News of Wally's death came two days after his brother, Don, had been reported killed.

I returned to the twin villages of Kennford and Kenn in the summer of 1982 while starring for the season in Paignton. The local independent television company took me back to my Devonian roots to make a short documentary on my life and times in the area. It was very moving and an emotional homecoming to Trehill. Memories came flooding back as soon as I saw the place: I could hear my sister Nancy crying again after she had heard the news of her young husband's death.

Shortly after Walter died, I volunteered to join the Royal Navy and signed on for three years, much to the annoyance of my mother and sister who both tried to talk me out of going. I was due to be called up for national service anyway within a year of my seventeenth birthday, and I wanted to emulate my brother's lead and follow him into the senior service. If I had waited for my official call-up papers, I might have been drafted anywhere without a say in my own future. I didn't fancy the Army, so this way I was sure of going to sea. Had Dick joined the Army, I would have followed him just the same, although being near to the sea, with Dawlish and the coast only a few miles to the south, affected my decision greatly as well. I love water – a legacy from my childhood in Cork. If I could live by water all the time, I would indeed be a happy man. That is one of the reasons I adore Australia so much. My mind was made up and destiny, with a little prompting in the right direction, had taken a hand.

On my first day in His Majesty's Royal Navy, I left Exeter station and headed north and east to Skegness on the Lincolnshire coast, where Billy Butlin's very first holiday camp had been commandeered by the Admiralty at the outbreak of war and used as a recruitment centre and training establishment. It had been re-named H M S *Royal Arthur*, a concrete ship as they were called. It became infamous a few weeks into the war when Lord Haw-Haw, broadcasting the latest Nazi propaganda from Germany, announced, 'H M S *Royal Arthur* has been sunk with all hands.'

New recruits into the service from all over Britain reported to Skegness immediately they had signed on. Here they spent the next few weeks of their life getting to know the Navy. It was their introduction to national service, and they also had to undertake the various medical examinations and aptitude tests to determine what type of position they would be suited to in uniform, and to which jobs they would be assigned, before being dispatched for basic training. I was classified a Devonport rating: Carroll, D. P. D L X 741517.

The naval authorities tried to match up suitable jobs for all recruits as near as possible to the type of work they had been doing before they joined the service. When they asked me what I had done in civilian life, I told them I had once worked as a waiter at the famous Mirabelle restaurant in London, which was perfectly true. It sounded glamorous and it didn't really matter that my employment there had only lasted a meagre seven days. No one knew, and the assessment board was suitably impressed. So I became a steward: a waiter by any other name.

I was transferred from Skegness after six weeks to HMS *Duke* in Malvern, Wiltshire, for training. It was tough. It was meant to be. Whatever branch of the Navy you went into, you still had to do the requisite square-bashing, pack-drill, physical training, weapon training and rowing. I hated it. I wasn't cut out for it, and yet I loved the Navy itself. I found it interesting and exciting. It was never dull, though I doubt if, by choice, I would have made a career for myself as a sailor. It was something that *had* to be done like a chore.

Once training at Malvern was completed, recruits were sent off to one of three depots, at Chatham, Portsmouth, or Devonport. I arrived in Devonport via Appledore in North Devon. It was an ideal posting for me, so close to my home and my family.

I had been in the Royal Navy for less than six months when I was attached to my first ship, HMS *Alaunia*, a converted Cunard liner, seconded by the service and now classified as a depot and repair ship. The whole of the interior was like a vast factory. When the ship docked, damaged vessels would come alongside for repairs or refurbishments, just like going to a garage for a service. Others would simply come for supplies. The ship was to be my home for the next six months, shared with a crew of over 1,200 men.

HMS *Alaunia* was just part of Lord Louis Mountbatten's invasion task force, destined for the Far East and Australia, to help mop up the Japanese war. The war in Europe was rapidly coming to a close, but Japan was proving to be a stubborn adversary. On board ship, I was assigned as a steward to the officers' mess, which really was quite a cushy number. There were several of us together, so we delegated the duties between us. The officers were very pleasant, although I wasn't overfond of the Commander, whom I thought a pompous idiot.

Many years later, a strange thing happened. In the autumn of 1966, I was invited to a party in honour of Sir Georg Solti, the celebrated conductor. It was given by Dorothy, Lady Hulse, a patron of the arts who was a great fan of mine and who had been to see *Come Spy With Me* at the Whitehall Theatre on a number of occasions. During the course of the party, I was trying to circulate among the guests to talk to as many as possible, when I was suddenly confronted by a man with a look on his face that said we were long-lost friends. He smiled and shook my hand.

'You don't remember me, do you, Carroll,' he said. I was taken aback. Here was I, known to millions of people as Danny La Rue, and here was a man I couldn't place, insisting on calling me by my *real* name, and my surname at that. I thought him extremely rude and arrogant.

'Should I?' I was matter of fact.

'We served together on the *Alaunia* during the war, remember?' he offered by way of explanation. 'I was your commanding officer.' He was triumphant.

'Oh, yes,' I replied, and we tentatively exchanged small talk.

Then he asked me if I had seen the splendid Rolls-Royce parked outside, and did I know who owned it?

'Oh, yes,' I said. '*Me*.' I paused. 'And what are you doing now since the Navy?'

'I'm in insurance.' He was enthusiastic again.

'*Well, don't try to sell me any.*'

In my life, it is the pompous people I have never really liked.

Our voyage to the Far East was an eventful one. I celebrated my eighteenth birthday on board HMS *Alaunia* in July 1945, and we hadn't been long at sea when news reached us that the Allies had dropped the atom bomb on Hiroshima and Nagasaki. Japan had surrendered. The war was over. It was history in the making, but none of us knew then what a terrible inheritance had been unleashed. No one could foretell the nuclear future.

With the war over, new orders were received on board. It had been decided at Admiralty level that instead of completing our voyage to Australia as had been originally intended, HMS *Alaunia* would now remain in Singapore. We were all bitterly disappointed with the news, but I'm certain it was fate lending a hand once again. Maybe if I had gone to Australia at that time in my life, at eighteen, and had loved the country as much as I do today, I might well have stayed there and never returned home. I can't say.

However, there were still plenty of other ports of call on our route east to Malaysia, and we intended to make the best of them. We docked in Gibraltar, which had been hardly touched by the war, and in Malta, which I found intriguing. There was a particular group of us on board ship, all about the same age, who were young and eager and out for a good time, to make up for all those lost opportunities back home in England. So we went out on the town and ended up 'down the gut', Malta's equivalent of Soho, filled with Spanish dancers, sleazy cafés and the island's low life. It was certainly an eye-opener, but I was captivated by everything I saw – it was fabulous. I was surprised not to see any devastation in the aftermath of war.

After a brief stop-over in Aden, we sailed on to the west coast of India, where I was so disappointed with Bombay. I had heard so many exciting stories about the place and I was expecting some kind of oriental masterpiece. It never materialized. My most vivid recollection of the whole Indian sub-continent came when I was travelling by train from the city on an excursion to see the sights. I looked out of my carriage window and saw a sleek, black panther keeping pace with the locomotive, stride for stride, and running almost as fast as the engine itself. It was a magnificent sight. Fascinating.

Although we were at sea for such a long time, we were kept very busy on board attending to the everyday needs of running such a large ship. The work was tedious and hard, but we had plenty of time to ourselves to relax once our duties were finished for the day. There was always plenty to do. Evenings were filled with silly things like bingo, though we called it housey-housey, and film nights. Several of the ship's company were accomplished and talented musicians, so we were never short of musical soirées and recitals. There was a healthy debating society and lectures. We had quizzes and often competed against other sister ships near by in the task force, using the radio link-up. Everything was well-organized, and there were always new lists going up on various noticeboards asking for volunteers for this activity or that.

One of the ship's officers had had theatrical experience and got permission to start a concert party troupe on board. Volunteers were duly called for once again and auditions held. If you could speak well, it virtually guaranteed you a place in the troupe. I was very lucky because I always had a good speaking voice, which was something I had cultivated from an early age. When I told the officer in charge that I had acted in amateur dramatics back home, I was in. I volunteered, in the first place, not through any great desire to perform on stage, but basically because I saw it as a good way of getting off duties. One always finds a reason at the time.

True to the spirit of amateur dramatics, our concert party troupe spent more time rehearsing than actually performing. It was worth it, though – I was put on part duties because of my involvement. We presented to our fellow crew members a wide and varied range of entertainment, two or three times a week, from old-time music hall to revue, and everything else in between. They were a very appreciative audience. Some of the senior people in the company had dabbled a bit in the profession. There were a few old stagers aboard.

My first part was in a send-up of Leon Gordon's *White Cargo*, a play about two tea planters in love with a native girl, set in the jungles of Borneo. I'd seen Hedy Lamarr in the film role in 1942 and was a great fan. I played the native girl, Tondelayo. I looked stunning. I was a very good-looking young man with jet black hair, and the sun had turned my skin dark when we were at sea. I looked like a native. All I wore for the part was a bed sheet, nicked from the officers' quarters, and tied round me like a sarong. Apart from my crêpe paper outfits at school in Devon, it was the cheapest costume I've ever had. It must have proved something. I didn't have a large part, in fact I hardly spoke at all, but I got lots of laughs. The raucous belly laughs and applause from my shipmates were stimulating.

At that time, I wasn't consciously aware of being, or of wanting to be a female impersonator. I had never seen a female impersonator in my life. As far as I was concerned I was just putting on a costume to play a part – I was acting. I had no desire to be a woman, but I was good-looking and I made people laugh as well. I suppose the foundations for my future career were laid in that one small part, because I was good at it, and because the audience liked me, and *that* made all the difference.

Until then, female impersonators fell into two distinct categories: the pantomime dames and knockabout characters in outrageous costumes who sent the whole ideal up in a frenzy of laughter; and the man who dressed up in female attire and took himself very seriously indeed, wanting other people to think he *was* a woman. In fact, he was far happier dressed as a woman than a man. I wasn't either. I was amusing and attractive but, right from the start, the audiences have always known that I have never wanted to be taken seriously. It's all a glorious joke.

When we arrived in Singapore, we became a concert party in residence. We were often asked to present our shows and entertainments at other military bases for the Army and Royal Air Force personnel. We were typical of all concert parties, we had to do everything ourselves, from making our own costumes, to building our own scenery and providing our own props. But we found enormous pleasure in it all.

In 1976, Peter Nichols, the distinguished playwright, offered me the starring part in a new play he was about to stage in London with the Royal Shakespeare Company. He must have been aware of my concert party background in Singapore, because *Privates on Parade* has captured the concert party life to perfection. I am only sorry I had to turn the part down, but at that time I was booked solidly for two years in advance. The part I was offered was Captain Terri Dennis, which is one of the very best written for the modern stage, and Denis Quilley gave a truly marvellous performance in both the play and subsequent film version.

In December 1945, John Gielgud and his company arrived in Singapore as part of an extensive ENSA tour of the Far East. They had been presenting two plays: *Hamlet*, which Gielgud produced and in which he played the title role, and the comedy *Blithe Spirit*. After a short stay, they went on to visit Hong Kong and Rangoon, before returning home via India and Egypt. When they appeared at the Regal Theatre in Singapore, they presented a lecture-recital entitled: *Shakespeare in Time of War and Peace*, with John Gielgud playing a certain Scottish king opposite Margaret Rawlings. Gielgud was brilliant in the production. Superb. Later he came along to see our humble offering of *White Cargo*, and he paid me the highest of compliments after the show. 'I don't like men who dress up as women,' he said, 'but you make me laugh.'

He added: 'You must take it more seriously.'

With a patron and recommendation like that, how could I miss? Yet, during my time in concert party, I was rarely seen in drag. Most of my appearances were as myself, singing songs or acting in sketches.

I enjoyed my short time in Singapore immensely. I felt a great affection for the colony that had suffered greatly and was now slowly returning to normal life after three and a half years under the Japanese, if life could ever be that normal again. I was attracted to the city at once, perhaps because the name 'Singapore' when translated means: The

Lion City. Being born under the starsign of Leo, I have tremendous affinity with lions of all kinds.

It was easy to see why it had been dubbed the Clapham Junction of the orient. Singapore was never silent, never still. There was activity all the time, frenzied activity, wheeler-dealing at the highest and lowest levels. It was a hustling, bustling peninsular, a steamy hotbed for world trade, where traffic of all kinds coming from the east met traffic of all kinds coming from the west. They clashed head on – and two distinctive cultures merged, yet still managed to retain an identity of their own.

Singapore was a colourful swirl of cosmopolitan existence with a heritage that went way, way back. It was a total paradox. In parts, it epitomized the British Empire and everything it stood for – tolerance, fair play and a gentleman's word as his bond – personified by the imposing Raffles hotel. In other parts, it represented extreme squalor and poverty in an overcrowded society of shaky deals, cheating and villainy, with everyone out to make whatever they could at others' expense . . . in order to stay alive.

I found it all utterly irresistible and got totally engrossed in its romance. When I was off-duty I would go ashore and savour the marvellous culture of the east. I was enraptured by eastern theatre and performers, lavishly colourful and very expressive, though I could not understand a word. I was fascinated by the magnificent costumes and the intricate make-up. I had never seen anything quite like it before. It was all exquisite. I also found the legendary puppet artistry of the theatre of shadows compelling and sat there spellbound. Midnight Mass on Sunday was always an occasion. It was held in the open air, with candles burning brightly and a superb choir. That stands out very prominently in my mind.

Sunday morning Mass was always held on deck, followed by inspection. Even in the Navy, I was particular about my clothes, although all I had was the basic Admiralty issue – shorts, whites, blues. On one Sunday morning assembly, 1,200 seamen lined up in formation on the main deck, dressed all in white, apart from one solitary figure immaculately dressed in *navy and white*. *Me*. I thought it was a better colour combination and looked nicer, too. I was put on a charge immediately for being improperly dressed.

Singapore was a notorious city of bartering. You could buy and sell anything and everything in the shops and bazaars. We soon discovered that English cigarettes were in great demand: Craven A were a particular favourite and fetched high prices in the right places. As I didn't smoke, I was able to flog my naval ration, which usually amounted to ten packets of twenty cigarettes every three or four weeks, at grossly inflated prices. It was a good way of making money. The Chinese traders then substituted rubbish cigarettes for the real thing and, using an authentic Craven A packet as guarantee, sold them at even more extortionate rates. Some friends and I were duped in this way by one scurrilous Chinese shopkeeper. So, to get even, I made a similar switch myself in the next shop I visited, offloading the inferior tobacco I had just received into the eager hands of an unsuspecting trader. As I walked back to the ship with my friends, feeling very pleased with myself at my recent transaction, I heard scuffles and a terrific outcry going on behind me. A few words were shouted in Chinese and I soon realized I was about to be set upon by the shopkeeper I had conned, *and* several of his henchmen, all brandishing clubs and after my blood. I didn't hang around to plead my case. My friends and I ran back to base as fast as we could. The Chinese posse gave chase immediately, yelling and cursing as they ran, using what I can only assume to be the foulest of all oriental swearwords, and calling me a stream of choice names. So much for inscrutability. But we managed to make it back to the Jahore Causeway without mishap and, once inside the British base, they couldn't get me. The things some people will do for a cigarette!

My love affair with Singapore, however, came to an abrupt end when I was posted back to England. I hadn't expected to leave so quickly. HMS *Alaunia* remained in port, so I was transferred to another, much smaller, vessel, HMS *Loch Ruthven* – a 'Loch' class frigate. Its motto was 'ship-shape and Bristol fashion', because it had been built by Charles Hill & Son, the Bristol shipbuilders. It was tiny by comparison to my previous ship. In bad weather, it looked as if we would be swamped by the huge rolling waves that crashed on to the deck, as the ship dipped and rose in and out of the water. It didn't affect me at all, I have always been a very good sailor, but some of my fellow crew members were violently ill.

Being such a small vessel, there was no concert party entertainment on board, but we devised other forms of amusement to keep us occupied on the long, and often boring, journey back home to port.

We stopped off at Bangkok and later put into Ceylon, which I loved. The British Navy was showing the flag. I was so excited about visiting

Ceylon, because I was able at last to send home *tea* – large boxes of it – to all the family. In England, rationing was still very much in existence and tea was like a gem from the orient, and twice as precious. I also sent a few pairs of silk stockings, too, for my mother and sisters.

I had been away for well over a year when the *Loch Ruthven* dropped anchor in Portsmouth and I finally returned to England. It was good to be home again. Since our last stop in Gibraltar, I had been counting the days; I was longing to see the family again and to share my adventures and stories with them. I was sent on to my home base at Devonport, where I was left to content myself serving out my days in uniform in a country desperately trying to come to terms with peace.

4
'I shall call you Danny La Rue'

Everything seemed to stop so suddenly at the end of the war. It was a big anticlimax. The camaraderie had gone. The solidarity and to-getherness disappeared, to be replaced by an aching feeling of emptiness and apathy. No longer did we need to pull together against a common enemy. We had our own private battles to fight, left alone to fend for ourselves. The world was changing.

I was demobbed in 1947 at the tender age of twenty, feeling very uneasy at what the outside world had in store for me. In three years, I had seen parts of the world I hadn't known existed before. I had also seen enough of the world to make me an extremely tolerant human being and I had shared a special sense of belonging with my colleagues and fellow seamen. We had been brothers in arms. Now I was on my own, I didn't know what I wanted to do with my life. Concert party in the Navy had given me a taste for entertaining. I loved the applause, it gave me a tremendous buzz. But I didn't think I could make a career for myself in the theatre. Anyway, I didn't know where to start. I had no real ambitions. I didn't come from that sort of background. Al-though I was a bright kid, I wasn't academic. I lived for the day, and everything else was a bonus.

I went back almost immediately to my old job at J. V. Huttons in Queen Street, Exeter, and it didn't take long for me to get back into the same old routine: Mondays – all windows cleared out and re-dressed; the rest of the week – *titivate*. Yet it all seemed so staid and dull after all the excitement of national service.

For a time I joined the Exeter Dramatic Group, presenting shows at the old Theatre Royal where, besides a bit of acting, I doubled as stage manager. I still keep in touch with the company all these years later. They recently formed a big ensign group and asked me to become an honorary member. I was delighted.

Back in Kennford, of course, I still had the village dramatic society. But it wasn't enough to hold on to me this time. The boy had grown into a man. Exeter was becoming too small for me. I am by nature a gypsy, I love travelling, and I feel restless if I am anywhere for too long. I wanted to move on.

Then came a stroke of luck. Out of the blue, I was tentatively asked if I might like to consider a transfer to Huttons' London branch in the heart of Oxford Street. They would understand if I turned the offer down. It was just what I had been hoping for. How could I turn it down? This was it. I grabbed the chance with both hands. I was going back to London.

I revelled in the new challenge and before long it proved a very successful move for me. I loved the work and became great friends with the shop owners, Eileen and Barry Hutton, who took me under their wing. I became their protégé. For once I was utterly contented with my lot.

London hadn't changed. It was still very much the same as I had left it, slightly shell-shocked and bomb-torn, but no different. The theatre lights were back on in Shaftesbury Avenue and Charing Cross Road to light up the sky once more. The people, too, were just like I re-membered them.

The theatres, though, were the big attraction for me, like a beacon. I had been starved of this kind of entertainment for too long and I had an awful lot of catching up to do. I saw everything I could in town: Gracie Fields, Richard Hearne, Danny Kaye at the Palladium, Sid Field at the Prince of Wales.

I went to live with my sister in a large, red-bricked house over a restaurant on the corner of Earlham Street. It later made way for a block of offices. Joan had moved into the house in anticipation that the rest of the family would eventually return from the West Country and, by 1950, Mary Ann, Dick, Nancy and her two children, had moved back to London to join us under the same roof. It was the first time we had all been together since Ireland.

Our house was at Cambridge Circus and from my bedroom window I could see the Palace Theatre where a feast of shows were presented during that time, and the names of many famous stars were blazoned in coloured illuminations across its mighty façade. It was a warming sight. There was something homely about that theatre.

I loved *King's Rhapsody*, which had a lengthy run at the Palace from September 1949, with Ivor Novello, Olive Gilbert and Vanessa Lee. I'm sad I never knew Ivor. There was an aura about the man. He was a great British tradition and I looked up to him in admiration. Yet, he was surrounded by sadness and tragedy. Strange things happened to several of his shows, and some people thought the man was jinxed. At Sunderland, an assistant stage manager walked out of the theatre one afternoon and was never seen again. Then one of Ivor's leading ladies, June Bronhill, escaped death by inches when scenery fell on her during a performance. Not long afterwards, members of the company from another show were killed in a terrible car accident right outside Ivor's home.

King's Rhapsody itself was beset with problems. Illness attacked the principals in turn, and there was a spate of missed performances. Ivor himself became a changed man and often went into long and unusual silences, so uncharacteristic of the musical genius. He was taken ill in his dressing room one night in 1951 and three hours after curtain call, he was dead.

I am strangely superstitious. When I went into the Palace Theatre in my own show in April 1970, I flatly refused to occupy the number one dressing room because it had been Ivor Novello's. I wouldn't tempt providence, and took another room instead. The show proved to be one of my biggest successes in the West End. On opening night, Charlie, the stage door keeper who had been at the Palace for a number of years, came up to me after the show and paid such a great tribute. 'It's like having the guv'nor back,' he said, meaning Ivor Novello.

We had a very theatrical neighbour in Earlham Street: Pearla Ranzer. She was of Jewish descent; her husband was German and worked as a waiter. My sister had told her of my great love of the theatre and explained my background in amateur dramatics and naval concert party. Pearla asked me if I would like to join her theatre group at the YWCA at Tottenham Court Road, and added as a rider: 'We need good-looking men like you,' trying to tempt me further. She didn't need to bother, she couldn't keep me away.

The YWCA had a flourishing drama society after the war, run by Pauline Stewart. There were about fifty members, from all walks of life – shop assistants, bank clerks, insurance salesmen, professional people – and although there was a larger representation of women, nevertheless there was still quite a number of men, eager to show off their acting prowess. Nice people, all of them.

It was well-organized. We staged pantomimes, musical revue, sketches and plays. Having so many active members, there was always a healthy rivalry for parts whenever a new production was put on. Everyone in the society had to audition. It was good fun and fair because you could play the lead in one presentation, and have a walk-on part in the next. I seemed to end up playing sons, or the boy next door, or brothers in plays, never the romantic lead. I much preferred the revues we staged, like *Black and White* or *April Folly*. They were inevitably musicals and we could let our hair down and be funny. The only time I actually dressed in female attire during the period I was with the YWCA company was in one spring revue where I was called upon to play the back end of a cow in a sketch.

I was able to help out the society by borrowing a lot of material and clothing from Huttons. No one ever had clothing coupons to spare for amateur dramatics, that would have been taking the commitment too far, so my contacts in the fashion world came in very handy. For a production of Dodie Smith's play, *Call It a Day*, I supplied a length of blue Moygashel linen, which we used to drape over the french windows on the set to give the appearance of luxurious curtains. It looked very effective. Unfortunately, after the show was over, someone pinched it, and I had to go back to Huttons with a lot of explaining to do.

I also managed to bring along display pieces from the shop, to furnish the bare stage. It all helped, and raised my stock among my fellow actors sky high.

All the shows we presented were successful and well-received. We played to large and enthusiastic audiences at the Queen Mary Hall, though I suspect most of them comprised family and friends of the company. Still, no matter, we were dedicated amateurs, and I was developing into a competent actor. Whatever I did, I tried to make it the best I could.

During the late forties inspectors were sent round to visit amateur dramatic groups to see what they were up to and how they were coping. Perhaps they came on a morale-boosting exercise, or perhaps they were sponsored by the local council. I never discovered the reason. However, after one of our shows, I was approached by one of these so-called officers, a rather arrogant little man, too, and he proceeded to tell me off, for being too *professional*.

'You must remember, young man, these are *amateur* dramatics,' he said with a very condescending attitude. 'I didn't like your performance at all. You added far too much to the production.'

I was speechless. It made me think again.

Not long afterwards, I met up with a super young man called Tony

Thompson. We had known each other in the Navy. Tony told me he was down in London to try for a part in *Forces Showboat*, a touring all-male revue which was about to go out on the road. Ralph Marshall, who was presenting the show, was auditioning young men to dress up as women for the chorus and parade sequences, and Tony was confident of getting in. Knowing of my connections in the rag trade, he asked if I could help him out with some material for his frock. I was delighted to be of assistance, he was an old mate after all.

The auditions were being held at Mac's Rehearsal Rooms in Windmill Street and I went along with him to lend a little moral support. I also helped to pin him into his outfit and prepared his make-up. I was very clever with clothes.

Tony didn't get the job, but as we were leaving the audition, he turned to me. 'Dan, you go for it,' he said. 'You've got a marvellous face – you'll be wonderful, just what they're looking for. You can't fail, I'll put money on it.' His enthusiasm was infectious, but I argued with him. I had a steady job at Huttons, I was happy with what I was doing, and I certainly wasn't looking for a new challenge, thank you very much. It had never been my intention to go into show business, least of all dressing-up in a frock in an all-male revue. I was quite content to work in the shop during the day, to indulge myself with the YWCA drama group at night, and to visit the theatre whenever I wanted to. No ties. But the more he tried to convince me, the more I was being swayed by his conviction. When I seriously thought about it, I warmed to the notion. He was right, I thought. I'm young, I can afford to lose a couple of years and have a giggle going round the country. I'll enjoy it. I was talking myself round.

Using the same piece of material I had purloined for Tony Thompson, although in a completely different way, I borrowed his wig and returned nervously to the basement studio in Windmill Street to audition. I was surprised, Tony was right, I did look fantastic in all the gear.

When I went in, someone asked me if I could do anything.

'No,' I said. 'I can't do anything but look good and move well.' That caused a ripple of laughter. It was a good sign.

I walked out tenuously on to the floor in my makeshift costume, and Ralph Marshall immediately offered me a job in the chorus. It was as easy as that, I'd done absolutely nothing. So much for auditioning. No one was more shocked than me. I was totally unprepared. Now what was I going to do? How could I tell my family I was leaving my wonderfully respectable job at Huttons to go on the road and dress up as a tart for much less money than I was earning in the shop? I got six pounds and ten shillings a week, and out of that I had to eat, pay for my own digs, supply my own make-up, my own costume and find a glamorous outfit for the parade scene. Everyone I knew thought I was stark raving mad, but no one tried to talk me out of my decision. My family never queried anything. My mother wasn't over-ecstatic about the situation, but she never commented. In later years when I was struggling to make ends meet, the family didn't once try to put me off or stop me. I had their undivided support at all times.

All-male shows were very popular in Britain just after the war. Touring revues were staged all over the country, playing many of the top theatres as well as the smaller number twos and threes. They were invariably billed as ex-servicemen's shows, with men playing women. Really, it was only glorified concert party, given a fancy name and a bit of glamour. They were big companies, well-dressed and staged with good scenery, and included sketches, dance routines, songs and lavish production numbers. The shows were billed as family entertainment, but they flooded the market with a host of female impersonators. Still, the shows certainly captured the imagination of the public and played to very good houses almost everywhere. The shows were well-rehearsed and the entertainment value, in the main, was excellent. It was the type of production that could grace any summer season today, although as a show it would be far too big and expensive.

These shows were a revival of a production first presented during the First World War called *Les Rouges et Noirs*, later to become known as *Splinters*, with its origins in France. This had played a season in London's West End at the Queen's Theatre and for many years it toured the major provincial theatres with consistent success until the outbreak of the Second World War. One famous double act of female impersonators to come out of *Splinters* was Vic Ford and Chris Sheen.

Soldiers in Skirts, in which I later appeared briefly, was the longest-running of the contemporary all-male shows. It started in 1945 and toured through to 1952. However, *Forces Showboat* was by far the classiest and best of them all, playing the number one venues. It featured a cast of two dozen boys, and starred two brilliant female impersonators, who at one time were the very best Ugly Sisters in pantomime – Bartlett and Ross.

Terry Bartlett was the comic of the duo, a thin man with a broad Welsh accent, who specialized in fairly grotesque female impersonation, exaggerating everything. His partner, Colin Ross, was a total opposite. An elegant man, he was very ladylike in his ways, with a peaches and cream complexion and a very pretty face. I heard later that he didn't want me to join the company in the first place and tried to stop Ralph Marshall from hiring me. Colin thought I might be competition to him. Terry Bartlett didn't mind, he thought I was wonderful. But I learned an awful lot from them both.

A young Harry Secombe was the comic on the show, occupying the speciality spot in the first half of the programme. He performed his famous shaving routine, which consisted of a series of impressions showing how various people shaved themselves. A couple of years earlier, Harry had been one of the comics performing at the Windmill Theatre. Now he was on a salary of thirty pounds a week, which at that time was deemed a small fortune.

The show started its tour in the autumn of 1949 in Aldershot and for the next few months played throughout Britain. Another week, a different town. Not long after we had started, Harry and his wife Myra asked to see me, and then tried to make me leave the company.

'You're too nice a young man to do this kind of show with all these male artistes,' he said, and was deadly serious. 'It's not for you. Myra and I think you should leave. I don't think you are really cut out for show business. Take my advice, go home and get a real job.'

Many years later, Harry and I appeared on the same chat show together in Australia, and reminisced about our times in *Forces Showboat*. Towards the end of the programme, Harry was asked if he had any advice he would like to pass on to any young performers just starting out in show business.

'Don't ask me,' he said. 'I once advised someone to leave show business completely, and I think they have done quite well since. I was the one who told Danny La Rue to quit because I didn't think he could make it. So what do I know?'

Harry was actually right to be concerned in those early days. Some of the behaviour of my colleagues in the chorus line was outrageous. It was far too high camp for me. I was surrounded by boys who would literally have preferred to be women. They were happier as women; they lived in women's clothes for much of the time and they desperately wanted other people to accept them as women. They were so serious.

They loved dressing up. I could see the point of dressing up as a bird to get laughs, but not to be serious. I couldn't equate with that. Many of them got to the point where they could have been girls, there was no reference to their being anything else, until the end of the show when they took their wigs off. I always thought it was completely and utterly revolting to see a man's head in woman's make-up. On train journeys, however, they would sit in the carriages in sequin dresses, doing their wigs. I have never wanted to be a woman. My whole success has been that I created many beautiful women, but I never lost Danny. I have never had my own identity swamped. It is almost schizophrenic; there are two people. I couldn't take all the bitching and the weird chorus boys flying around in frenzies. They didn't behave like women at all. There was far too much envy and jealousy amongst their ranks, and there was far too much noise when they all got together. Their outrageous behaviour was very evident in their costumes, which were often totally over the top. The simpler I dressed, the more realistic I looked and I always, without failure, stood out from the rest of the chorus even though I never spoke a word. People have told me that when I went out on stage, they couldn't take their eyes off me. I was hypnotic. I was stunningly attractive. At that time, I was madly in love with Hedy Lamarr and I used to base my make-up and my clothes on her. I made my own wigs from bits of hair and used all my own hair with just a switch at the back. People were aghast. They couldn't tell I *wasn't* a woman. I created an illusion because I had a certain amount of style, which came from my mother.

After a few weeks on the road, I began to enjoy it all. It wasn't a chore any more. It started to take hold of me. I hated the behaviour and manners of some of my colleagues, but I loved the atmosphere of a packed theatre. I got a high from every performance; it was fun, it was exciting and by now I had finally succumbed – I *wanted* to be in show business.

It was hard work, though, and long hours. We moved around in those days, with so many variety halls to play you were rarely out of work. There were enough theatres in London alone for an artiste to work for a whole year and not play the same venue twice. But we never ate properly, we never had enough money and it was hard going unless it meant something to you, then it was dedication. You kept going on the blind faith that success was just around the corner, something would turn up shortly to make us all stars.

Some of the digs we stayed in were dreadful, yet we survived. I'll never forget rushing home to one set of digs after a show, absolutely dying for a pee. I could contain myself no longer as I reached the front door and flew upstairs to the bathroom to relieve myself. On the landing I pushed open the bathroom door only to be greeted by the landlady sitting serenely on the loo, knitting – her drawers round her ankles, and her hair piled high in rollers. She was so shocked when she saw me, she panicked, dropped the knitting needles and put her hands to her head to stop me seeing *the rollers*.

I didn't realize it at the time, but I was serving a very valuable apprenticeship out on the road – it is what helped to make me the performer I am today. I have no regrets. I would never give back one of those days for they gave me the experience one cannot buy. We once played to an empty theatre every night for a week. The stage can be a lonely place then, yet I was learning my trade and working my balls off. I learnt quickly.

We journeyed from theatre to theatre and every new town and city by train on Sunday mornings. Actors and fish always travel on Sundays, each needing to be at their destination for the start of a new week. 'Change at Crewe' . . . almost every other week it seemed. All railway tracks appeared to converge at Crewe. Besides being a station of such repute, it was also a meeting-place for the profession. A bazaar to swap stories, exchange experiences and to put the business to rights, with the smaller fry of the chorus, the supporting companies and speciality acts rendezvousing in the platform buffet, while the stars stepped out to the grander bars of the nearby Railway Hotel.

It was also a melting-pot for a million lies.

'How did you do last week?'

'Wonderful, we were packed every night.'

'How about you?'

'Capacity business, not a seat to be had in the house.'

'Never seen it so busy.'

'Marvellous audiences. Sensational reviews.'

'You should have seen it for yourself, don't take my word.'

And so the ritual went on, everyone playing the same game, keeping to the same script, and no one believing anyone. We'd all cried 'Wolf!' too often to be taken seriously.

We were all pros together in the *business*, bound by many rules of conduct. A select few, a family spread around the country. Always on the move. And then, we were all gone, rushing madly across the bridge to make connections for Manchester or Leeds if we were playing the number ones; Attercliffe or Byker if we were 'tatting' around the number threes. All with a common destination: 'to be on the green somewhere, first house Monday'.

Forces Showboat toured virtually every town and city in the country for the next fourteen months before coming to an abrupt halt in Bristol just before Christmas. It petered out after taking no money the previous week which meant none of us was paid. Some of the company were stony-broke, me included, and hadn't enough money to get home, until Harry Secombe's brother, Fred, came to our rescue and bailed us out with our fares.

Nevertheless, I had got the taste for show business, it was becoming a drug, and one failure wasn't going to deter me. I had chosen this way of life, and was anxious to see it through to a conclusion one way or the other. After *Forces Showboat*, I found it easy to pick up work, and I toured with several more all-male revues over the next three years. My looks were my passport; all I had to do was look glamorous, and very little else. Nothing was happening to me. I occasionally got the odd few lines to say, which gave me a few extra pounds in my pocket, but I wasn't progressing. I was stifled because I was still only part of the line-up, a pretty member of the chorus.

I appeared with Bartlett and Ross again in *Forces in Petticoats* and *Soldiers in Skirts*, which I joined for just a few weeks. *Soldiers in Skirts* was a number one touring show, but I detested it. I couldn't stand the decadent and degrading antics of certain members of the company offstage. They were worse than girls, and I just wouldn't accept the situation. It was pitiful, so I left at the first opportunity. An interesting incident happened, though, when we played the Wood Green Empire.

I had just come off stage at the end of a show when the stage door keeper told me there was a man asking to see me, and would I care to take coffee with him? I thought it a little strange and declined the offer. Why should anyone want to have coffee with me, particularly someone I didn't know? I was totally naïve. However, I changed my mind for some unknown reason, and was introduced to a large, rotund gentleman called Ted Gatty, who was full of fun. He was one of the doyens of our business, a star of late-night cabaret in the West End of London and old-time music hall.

'You know you are going to be a big star, don't you?' he told me over our drinks. I was shocked. I had never seen this man in my life before and here he sat, telling me how great he thought I was.

'I'm only a chorus boy,' I said in modesty. 'You don't know what you're talking about. You're mad.'

'I've seen this show several times now,' he explained. 'Nobody looks at anyone else when you're on stage. *They only look at you*. You've got it, you're a star. You have this marvellous charisma and presence. You don't have to do anything. As soon as you walk out, all eyes in the theatre go straight to you. It's uncanny. Mark my words well, you are destined for greatness.'

What could I say? At that moment in my career, I was still only playing minute parts. I was an extra, someone to make up the numbers on stage in the big production parades. A nobody, who wasn't exactly setting the world of show business afire with my scintillating personality. No one would give me the chance. Still, I admired Ted Gatty's bravado and we became friends from that moment. Later, he played an important part in my career and he certainly helped to make his prediction come true. He always saw in me what I couldn't see myself.

Although work was fairly regular, there were often odd periods of unemployment. I hated being out of work, it was undignified and definitely not part of my nature. So I took any job I could find to tide me over and bring in some much-needed money until the next tour came along. I washed dishes at Lyons Corner House in Coventry Street with Peter O'Toole, who was just as broke as I was, for ten shillings a night and a free meal.

I have always been prepared to do any kind of work, rather than sit back and do nothing. One Christmas, I worked in the sorting office at the GPO in Mount Pleasant and earned far more money over the period than I would have been paid in the chorus of a pantomime, about seven pounds a week. I also won a prize for my high-speed letter sorting. I think they were sad to see the back of me, I'd coped so well. Another occasion saw me working for Wall's ice-cream in the packing department. I hated the idea of not being able to support myself. My pride, however, would never let me return to work at Huttons when I was resting, even though I knew the owners well and I am sure they would have helped me out – that would have been like giving in and admitting I had been wrong all the time.

In *Misleading Ladies* I started to come into my own with lines and more substantial parts. I became what was termed a semi-principal performer. I was moving . . . slowly. Vic Ford and Chris Sheen were the stars of the show. They were not as talented as Bartlett and Ross, but, none the less, were very popular with audiences. However, with me in the production, it was like putting Laurel and Hardy with Raquel Welch!

The show featured a fashion sketch, *they all did*. It was a glorified excuse to dress up even more elaborately. In this particular one, I played the madame of the shop who was supposed to be middle-aged. I was in my twenties and looked it. Chris Sheen played the part of a little girl customer brought into the shop by the roué. He was twice my age and was supposed to be playing somebody much, much younger. It was a farce, like those terrible amateur operatic societies where the manager's wife plays the juvenile lead. But the stars were all-powerful and got all the best parts.

During this time, I met the man who was to become the single most influential person in my life, who guided me to stardom and nurtured my career for over thirty years. And we became inseparable.

I first met Jack Hanson in the Bear and Star public house in London's Charing Cross Road, opposite the Wyndhams Theatre. It was a pub where artistes of all kinds would congregate and spend the time of day together. When the pub closed, we moved on to the Express Dairy for tea and sandwiches, and to discuss how good or bad we all were.

Jack and I had an instant rapport and the highest regard for each other. He was a very intelligent and literate man. At the time of our meeting, he was production manager for Michael Codron and worked with Harold Pinter and John Mortimer in the early days. Jack was a brilliant stage manager, one of the best in the business, organizing tours. He had a tremendous knowledge of the theatre and did a lot to guarantee Michael Codron's success right at the start. I have a lot of admiration for Michael Codron, who was one of the most avant-garde producers in show business. I was extremely grateful to him for allowing Jack to work for me while still in his employ. Jack had vaguely heard of me when we were introduced.

Jack Hanson was a Yorkshireman from Leeds, straightforward and honest. He had dabbled a little in amateur dramatics himself in his younger days and had worked as a journalist on the *Yorkshire Post* before breaking into show business on the production side. He had a marvellous rich voice and a remarkable way with words. He had been a commando during the war and served at Arnhem. He flew gliders and survived three crashes, although he was severely injured in one and spent the next year recovering in hospital. Coincidentally, before he joined Michael Codron, Jack worked as a stage director for a touring all-male show called *Back to Camp*, with Ken Ryan and George Clark, which played the number twos and threes. He also worked briefly with a man called Arnold Taylor on a show called *Crazy Dames*. When Taylor went broke and packed it in, Ted Gatty came to the rescue. He and Jack ran the show between them.

Jack had a tremendous sense of quiet, we were a contrast in that way, and yet he had a wonderfully dry sense of humour, like my sister, Joan. When he laughed, it was infectious; he laughed like a child. He was sensitive and witty, everything you could wish for in a human being. I don't honestly know anyone like him.

I can't talk to anyone else like I talked to Jack. He had complete understanding. I loved his regard for people, he knew instinctively how to treat everyone from royalty to the man in the street. A splendid person with paramount taste.

He would often say to me: 'Dan, you realize you are a great star and better than most people. You are born out of your time.'

My mother adored him and looked upon him as her third son.

When Jack became my manager in 1960 and gave up such a superb job with Michael Codron, he took over my life completely, guiding, advising, helping me. I still made my own decisions, however. You can take all the advice in the world, but at the end of the day, it has to be down to you. I always made up my own mind because I hated having to blame anyone for the failures. I made mistakes myself and accepted full responsibility. I could never blame anyone else.

An artiste and his manager should always have a special relationship if they are to succeed in show business. They must be reliable and must trust each other implicitly, and know each other's moods and reactions. There can be no secrets, they must virtually think like each other, and know what the other is thinking. It's a two-edged sword: each working for the same good and through good times and bad. A close bond. They must be the best of friends and believe in each other completely and share a mutual respect and admiration if the association has any hope of succeeding. Jack and I had this special relationship for thirty-two years. At first, a lot of people thought he had created me. I believe I created me with Jack's help.

Someone once congratulated him after a show. 'Danny's very lucky,' he said. 'He must be so delighted and proud to have such a wonderful manager as Jack Hanson.'

'Oh, no,' said Jack in his deep voice. 'Jack Hanson's the lucky one. He is so delighted and proud to have such a wonderful manager as Danny La Rue.'

Christmas 1953 gave me the opportunity of appearing in my first pantomime, *Aladdin*, which Ralph Marshall presented initially for a five-week run at the Chatham Empire. The show starred Harold Berens and Gladys Hay from the popular radio series of the day, *Ignorance is Bliss*, and Marshall devised an unusual publicity stunt to launch the pantomime which the press received warmly. Instead of booking a conventional all-girl chorus line, he employed six girls – all southern beauty queens – and six boys in drag. I was one of them. The audience had to guess who was who: which were the girls, who were the boys. To be perfectly truthful, the boys looked a lot better than the girls, and *I* was the boy who looked the best, or so I was told. Harold Berens was very generous: 'Danny La Rue stood out a mile,' he said. 'The best female impersonator I have ever seen. Stunning, like Hedy Lamarr.'

When the *Daily Mirror* discovered our chorus-line ruse, they exposed it in the newspaper, and we picked up some superb publicity which enabled the show to run for an extra month. I was on twelve pounds a week for the season. Since then, Harold Berens and I have become fellow members of the Grand Order of Water Rats.

After *Aladdin*, I flitted from one show to another. I couldn't really settle. I loved the business, but I was never completely at ease in the all-male shows and I rarely associated with my fellow performers.

Tommy Rose was one of the classiest of all female impersonators in the profession. I first saw him at the Chelsea Palace and I hadn't the faintest idea then that he was a man. He looked sensational as a woman, and I admired his talent so much. He worked with a guy called Sonny Dawkes, who had a voice like Deanna Durbin. When I was booked to appear with Tommy Rose in a show called *This Was the Army* at the Collins's Music Hall in Islington, I was delighted. I was looking forward to it immensely until it started, and then I absolutely detested it. The boys in the chorus were unbearable; they were incredibly jealous of me. I couldn't take it any longer. I didn't even bother to hand in my notice, I left the same week I joined. I had had enough and made up my mind then and there to get out for good, to quit show business and find something else.

79

I could see no future for me in the profession any more. I wasn't enjoying it like before, and after all, I convinced myself, nothing was really happening to me. I was very good at what I did, and I loved the work, but I was doing everything I was told to do, like a silly chorus girl. There was nothing of my own creative mind.

I decided to go back to what I really thought I was destined for – the rag trade I knew at Huttons – if they would have me. I was welcomed back at J. V. Huttons with open arms, like some long-lost prodigal son returning to the fold. I had a very strong relationship with the Huttons. They had tried to make me change my mind and go back to work at the store on a number of occasions while I was trying to build a name for myself in show business. Each time I had resisted their advances; this time I was sure.

I am not conceited enough to think I would be wonderful at anything I simply turned my hand to. I am a very practical person, a bit selfish and I don't like to fail. But I found I had great flair for the fashion business and used my theatrical background and experience to my advantage. I soon re-established myself at the store and carved out a unique position, not only in window design and display, but also as a flamboyant and artistic salesman. I created my own special niche and the owners recognized my inventive mind. I loved it all: it was show business by another name.

Eileen Hutton was a lovely lady and she was very fond of me. I would do anything to help her. One afternoon I was working on a display when I saw her car pull up outside the store. She had obviously been away on a buying trip and I knew she would be loaded down with packages. I walked smartly outside to lend a hand and, as we exchanged greetings, I threw open the car boot in my enthusiasm to get the luggage. It was a mistake. Instead of being greeted by a set of dour luggage and parcels as I expected, I came face to face with six enormous live ducks who made a swift bid for freedom and flew out of the car and off in the general direction of Regent Street with me in hot pursuit. It took us a long time, but we eventually managed to catch them all and return them to their temporary home in the boot. Mrs Hutton had been given the ducks by a local farmer on her trip into the country. I think they were destined for the oven.

I got so depressed by the appearances of so many women in London. Poor darlings, they were struggling along, having to buy their clothes with coupons in the main, which were still very much in existence in the early fifties, and the fashions, like London itself, were dull and drab and gloomy. They needed something to brighten up their lives and bring a little colour back.

Huttons was a very ordinary store in the West End, open to the general public, without being pretentious or exclusive. We catered for everyone, but then so did a good many other similar shops. We needed to be different to create interest and attract customers. I was virtually given a free hand in the store, so I borrowed an idea from Christian Dior and used it to bring a touch of elegance and excitement into our customers' lives. It did the shop a power of good, too, through marvellous publicity.

I introduced fashion parades with mannequins during opening hours. Customers would be seated at tables enjoying a cup of coffee or tea, while my models paraded around them wearing the clothes that were readily available on sale in the store, which the public then had the opportunity of buying.

It was unique – unheard of in 1954 – and proved a great success. I became the first person to put on mannequin parades of this kind in a London store. Later, we did things on a much grander scale and had a stage with spotlights built on the first floor of the building. Here we staged much more elaborate shows that were advertised. As the models paraded around, I took charge of all commentaries on the microphone. I was performing again. The Huttons were very impressed with my efforts, and I thought at last I had found my true vocation in life. It had been ordained, or so I believed.

When we started our mannequin parades on the recently converted first floor, the hit American musical *Pal Joey* opened at the Princes Theatre, starring Carol Bruce. She was a big American star at that time and, through my theatrical friends, I managed to make contact, and put forward a proposition. To my sheer delight, she agreed to come along as my guest, to open our new room and launch our fashion shows. It started a trend.

Not long afterwards, Paul Raymond, whom I had known for a long time since his own days on the boards as a hypnotist, asked me to teach some of his girls in his touring show how to walk correctly and conduct themselves. I had to show them how to stand and how to walk down a staircase. It was a strange request, yet throughout my career, many people have been recommended to come and see me work, to watch how I walk, how I move about on stage, or how I talk and deliver lines and learn from me. I am tremendously flattered that I can give some-thing back.

Women, too, often come up to me and ask me to teach them how to walk correctly, or to find out how to acquire some other mannerism of mine that has caught their eye. They don't realize, however, that they don't have to learn. It comes naturally, after all *they are* women. I'm not. I have to learn these things myself by watching and studying the opposite sex so closely, therefore, I suppose, I am slightly better because I go to so much trouble.

Siobhan McKenna once brought several of her young actors from the Abbey Theatre Company in Dublin to see my work, so they could learn *timing*. 'You are the master of it,' she told me.

When Ralph Richardson was appearing in *What the Butler Saw* in London, he sent his co-star Coral Browne along to see me and to learn how to stand.

Ingrid Bergman once wrote to me saying she had never seen anyone walk down a staircase like I do, and added she wished she could do it herself. She was a regular visitor to my show at the Prince of Wales when she came to London in 1973 to star in *The Constant Wife* at the Albery Theatre.

At Christmas 1970, while I was appearing at the Palace Theatre, there was a tap on my dressing room door. It was Mary Hopkin, who was also starring in the West End alongside Tommy Steele in panto-mime at the London Palladium. She was very charming and told me that my director, Freddie Carpenter, had sent her. As she talked, I couldn't help but notice that she was watching my hands intently, she made me feel slightly self-conscious about them.

'I've been sent to see how you use your hands,' said Mary, smiling nervously.

I burst out laughing. She looked puzzled and embarrassed, poor girl.

'I really do think Freddie means for you to come and see my show,' I explained. 'Then you will be able to watch me working on stage, using my hands to create the right kind of expressions. Your hands are so important. They must be used correctly.' I put her right.

Some time later, Gracie Fields told me a similar story. A very great fan had told her once that she had the most expressive hands she had ever seen, and that Gracie used them in such a beautiful way – it was exquisite to watch. Gracie thanked the woman very much for her kind comments, and thought no more about the incident until she was on stage one night, in front of a packed audience, and suddenly re-membered the conversation. In that moment, she became totally aware of her hands and froze and just didn't know what to do with them any more. The more she tried, the worse it became and her hands turned into two great weights on the end of her arms. She had a complex about it for a long time afterwards.

I had been back at Huttons and out of show business now for quite a few months, enjoying every moment of my new-found zest for the fashion business. I was doing very well, too, when Ted Gatty re-appeared in my life.

I was actually working in one of the display windows when he tapped on the glass and asked if we could meet. It was good to see him.

'Can you do me a great favour, Danny?' he asked. 'Can you help me out with a show? I've taken a contract on the Irving Theatre in Leicester Square and I need eight bodies. I've already got seven, but one's dropped out and I'm short. Do you fancy coming in with me? Unfortunately, there's no salary, but we'll split the takings between us.'

I said 'no way' almost before he'd finished speaking.

'Look, Ted, I'd love to come along and help you, but I'm happy here,' I told him. 'It's a good job, steady work and very good prospects for the future. I love it and I don't really want to get involved with any more shows. I've had enough, I'm sorry.'

Ted persisted for several minutes, trying to make me change my mind.

'But I'll lose the contract if I can't find eight bodies,' he added finally. 'Go on, please, it's only for two weeks.'

I think it was the fact it was for so brief a period of time, and he was such a good friend, that made me change my mind.

'All right,' I said. 'I'll do it for you, but on one condition. Nobody must ever know I'm in the show and my name must never appear on the bills. There must be no mention *whatsoever* of Danny Carroll. I don't want a name on any billing, and I certainly don't want anyone from the shop to find out I'm appearing. The store must never know.'

'No problem,' said Ted, beaming. 'Leave it to me. And thanks.'

When I arrived at the Irving Theatre for rehearsals that night, there was a large poster on display and the name DANNY LA RUE caught my eye.

'Who's that?' I asked Ted Gatty, pointing to the name.

'You,' came the reply.

'Danny La Rue?'

'Yes. You *had* to have a name and billing,' said Ted. 'I didn't want to get you into any trouble at Huttons, so I made it up.'

'But why *Danny La Rue*?' I was intrigued, but I rather liked it.

'Well,' he said, 'you are very glamorous and very tall. In all your feathers and plumes, you are very nearly seven feet tall! You look wonderful in costume and you remind me of Paris, like the Follies. You are also long and lean like a lovely French street, so I thought I would call you Danny the Street – *Danny La Rue*.'

So Danny Carroll became Danny La Rue, courtesy of Ted Gatty. It had a certain ring to it, however. It was a glamorous made-up name for a glamorous made-up person.

I was back in show business . . . but for how long?

5
'But I can hang up my tits when it's hot'

The Irving Theatre was tiny. It was located above the Paramount Grill Indian Restaurant in Irving Street, leading out of Leicester Square. On a good day, the theatre held no more than seventy-five people. It was owned by the restaurateur, an Indian gentleman known as Mr Chowderry, whose Irish girlfriend was very fond of me. It was one of the first of the club theatres that sprang to life in London during the fifties, and Chowderry let it out at every opportunity to manage-ments and individuals who came up with the right kind of money, to stage revues and shoestring productions. At one time, Jill Gascoine appeared in a show there, and Victor Spinetti became a regular. The theatre also had a short career as a strip club. It was all pretty daring for 1954.

Ted Gatty had indeed booked the Irving to present an evening of intimate revue, called *Men Only*, with a talented all-male company. He compèred and ran the show, which featured several other artistes, including Tommy Osborne, Dougie Curry, and a piano-vocal duo called The Gay Bachelors – words had different meanings in those days. They wouldn't get away with a name like that today and still work! – and the recently created Danny La Rue. The pianist in The Gay Bachelors doubled up as the show's musical accompanist.

Men Only was a very clever and witty show, a class above many all-male revues on offer. In those days, boys simply kicked their legs in the air, danced and sang songs that everyone knew. We presented a show which had been specially written for us. It was totally original. No one else was doing anything quite like it in London. It was fringe before the fringe had been invented. It also proved to be the beginning of a whole new career for me.

Danny La Rue was launched not with money, but through the impact I made on other people. I stepped out of the chorus for the first time and found my footing immediately. Instead of merely moving well and looking good, I was given the chance to project my personality on stage and actually play to the audience. Now I not only looked stunning, I sounded witty and sophisticated, too. It was an unbeatable combination. I felt at home. I was doing things no one had ever done before.

We had a very talented man writing the shows for us. Larry Gordon, who was associated with the Television Toppers and the Black and White Minstrels in the early days, supplied a lot of the very topical and up-to-the-minute material for the revue, and wrote a wonderful number for Dougie Curry and me, called 'Harper's Bazaar and Vogue'. It was a satirical parody on the top models of the day, Fiona Campbell-Walter and Barbara Golen, and was hilarious. Dougie made our costumes himself, and together as models we looked so glamorous and very chic. The sketch received riotous applause from the audience.

Jack Hanson wrote a special solo piece for me in which I played the part of a psychiatrist's secretary, dressed in a pencil skirt, wide blouse, horn-rimmed glasses and short hair. Very prim and proper. Throughout the sketch, I sat on a stool and presented a very funny monologue, which revolved around the various kinds of people who visited the psychiatrist, and I discussed their intimate problems with the audience. Right at the end, I said, 'Well, thank goodness I'm normal,' and took a pipe from out of my cleavage, lit it, and walked off stage.

At first, we had quite a struggle to attract audiences for our shows at one pound a head, even though we only had seventy-five seats to fill. Ted Gatty had literally to pull them in off the streets. He would stand by the box office outside, and hustle punters inside with promises of, 'Come and see the lovely girls . . . plenty inside.' The title, *Men Only*, also helped to stimulate trade. Once the house was full, or as near as made no difference, Ted would rush back to the dressing room to get changed for his opening spot in the show with a warning: 'For God's sake, don't let them know you're all fellas,' he cried putting on his make-up. 'And don't take off your wigs. If they find out you are not *real* girls, they'll lynch me.' We used to get a mixed bunch of audiences this way, mainly tourists – French, Egyptians, Chinese – who couldn't understand much English anyway, except for the word 'girls'. It didn't matter so long as they paid.

Being an all-male revue, we also attracted a lot of gay audiences to see the show and on occasions the theatre would be taken over by the sweet smell and heady atmosphere of various brands of after-shave lotion. Sometimes it was overpowering.

Every evening, Tommy Osborne went down into the audience to

sing a number called, 'Is There a Man in the House?'. He came back quicker than we bargained for one night, shocked. 'There's more bloody make-up down there,' he said, 'than up here on stage.'

We were originally contracted to run for two weeks but, before long, word got round that the Irving Theatre was the place to be. We had become fashionable and everyone came to see us. In the end we played for over four months, and I regularly picked up £25 a week as my share of the pooled box office receipts. I kept on my job at the Oxford Street store; my secret was safe, no one at Huttons knew I was leading a double life and they certainly wouldn't have connected Danny Carroll with Danny La Rue.

As well as producing and presenting *Men Only* at the Irving, Ted Gatty also appeared nightly at Churchill's nightclub in Bond Street, where the cabaret was devised and staged by Cecil Landeau. He was an important impresario in British show business and had discovered several major stars like Audrey Hepburn, Eartha Kitt and Norman Wisdom. He also presented the biggest revues in London. Unbeknown to me, Ted Gatty had been telling Cecil Landeau all about Danny La Rue – 'You must come and see this man who is really remarkable to look at,' said Ted – and persuaded him to come along to the theatre. He arrived one night, unannounced, with Tennessee Williams.

It was our policy at the Irving that if anyone famous came in to see the show, they would be introduced to the audience from the stage by one of the company. We were absolutely thrilled to welcome celebrities to the show, and because I spoke quite nicely, it was down to me to make the welcoming speeches. So, in awe of Cecil Landeau, I stepped forward and made my announcement.

'Ladies and gentlemen,' I began. 'Thank you for coming to see our show tonight. I'd just like you to know that we have a great impresario in our audience this evening. Mr Cecil Landeau.' I paused and waited for the applause to die down. 'And also with us tonight,' I continued, 'is that marvellous man – *Tennessee Ernie*.'

I found Tennessee Williams to be a very charming man. Very gentle, very quiet, though his reputation was quite awesome. To me he was a modern-day Ibsen. I had difficulty sometimes in relating to him: some of his work is all tragedy. I always see light, and I should imagine he was a much-persecuted man. There is always light in life and, although there are dark passages, it is not all death and destruction. All these things are part of life, but they are not life itself. Maybe I'm frightened

87

and I hide behind tinsel and glitter, but I have done that for long enough and I am a happier person for it.

Cecil Landeau was very taken with me. He could see all kinds of possibilities for me and asked if I would like to work with him at Churchill's in cabaret. It was like a royal summons. Cecil Landeau was as revered in the busines as C. B. Cochran: one didn't refuse him. He booked me to appear at the Bond Street club for a trial period of two weeks. I stayed for over three years. But I was convinced I was going to be sacked on my very first night.

In the mid-fifties, Churchill's was the most important nightclub in Europe. It was owned by Harry Meadows, who presented a big and spectacular floorshow and cabaret, featuring showgirls, dancers and speciality acts like Ravic and Babs, Patricia and Neil Delrina, who were great favourites. Several of the girls doubled with appearances at the Talk of the Town. Jacqui Jones was there for a while, Josephine Blake and Anne Hart, later to become Mrs Ronnie Corbett. Aleta Morrison was the principal dancer with Terry Theobald and Johnnie Moreland. The club attracted a large international clientele. It was a frightening prospect for a young unknown twenty-seven-year-old who dressed in a frock – good as everyone thought I was – to make his first appearance in such a prestigious arena.

On my opening night, Cecil Landeau had arranged for me to perform a solo number and I was given a big build-up and introduction as I made my way out on to the tiny stage. And then . . . I completely dried up. I forgot every single word in the song and just started to talk about anything that came into my head. There was a stony silence from the audience. Nothing. It was a disaster.

I came off stage heartbroken. Trembling. My big moment and I had blown it. Terry Theobald was near by.

'Well, that's it. I've had it,' I said to him, spitting out the words. 'I have never been so embarrassed in all my life, and I'm obviously going to get the sack.' I was so disillusioned. Then someone grabbed my hand and shook it hard.

'Congratulations,' they said. 'You were wonderful.'

I thought they was taking the mickey and started to fight back. But they were totally genuine. I was a hit. A big success. But why?

I had never worked a nightclub before. I hadn't realized the audience had been overwhelmed by my presence on the cabaret floor. They had never seen anything like me before. Churchill's was a hostess club and usually the punters paid no attention whatsoever to the cabaret, it was simply a background disturbance and irritation. They were far too busy getting drunk or chatting up the hostesses to be bothered with any kind of organized entertainment. When I'd dared to interrupt them by coming out on stage, it was the first time, so I was told later, that any of the audience had ever watched or listened to the floorshow. I had made them sit up and take notice, I made such an impact. I soon learnt afterwards that the first rule for any new artiste coming to the club was to befriend the hostesses. They were the key to it all. If you didn't get in with them, they would natter all through your act and encourage members of the audience to do the same. I was learning fast.

With my contract to appear at Churchill's, I was holding down no less than three different jobs and I kept up this almost daily routine for several months. I still wasn't totally convinced that my future lay in show business, so I retained my position at J. V. Huttons as insurance. It was a tough and tiring schedule. I worked at Huttons from nine to five, followed by the show at the Irving Theatre until ten p.m., then on to Churchill's for late-night cabaret from eleven thirty. I was getting home at three in the morning and having to get up by eight, to start all over again. My sleep was limited to just a few hours each night. I thrived on it, and I was taking home over forty pounds a week for all my efforts.

The money enabled me to re-invest in my show-business career. I had glamorous new stage costumes designed and made up for me – nothing off the peg. The new outfits actually didn't cost that much. I found a mate who loved making clothes and wanted to do it for me. It was bascially down to the cost of the material. It also meant I could hire wigs from Stanley Hall at Wig Creations in London, who was kind enough to create new styles for me. Most of the time, however, I made my own wigs, or simply used my own hair with switches at the back. In the early days, I could not afford to pay for my wigs, but Stanley never worried about it. Given time, he thought I just might make enough money one day to settle his bills. He was a great support.

But the most important advantage the extra money gave me was that I was at last able to afford to have new material specially written for me by good writers. Larry Gordon was one of them. My colleagues thought I was insane. Ted Gatty used to tell me to save my money. 'I know you're good at what you do, Danny,' he said. 'But nobody has ever hit it big in a frock. Sure there have been a few big names, but no big stars.'

I kept on working at it. I had set my standards, I was determined to keep them high and to keep on improving them. I knew deep down in my heart, simply from the reaction I'd already received, that something was going to happen to me. The bubble would burst and I would be there. It was intuition I suppose, but I wanted to be ready.

Within a year, I established myself sufficiently in late-night cabaret to be able to leave Huttons for good. It was a wrench, and I still wondered if I had made the right decision for weeks afterwards, but I didn't look back.

Ted Gatty and I worked well together, although we were never a double act as such and still retained our own solo spots. Ted was a performer of broad range and did marvellous characterizations. He was able to work as a dame or straight. He wasn't particularly glamorous in female attire, weighing over seventeen and a half stone, but he did a superb impersonation of Sophie Tucker in his act. He had the bulk to go with it. It was a perfect contrast to me, and we were a great team.

At Churchill's we re-worked the 'Harper's Bazaar and Vogue' idea, reversing the roles Dougie Curry and I had originally created. This time we had an old model and her young counterpart. One was passé, the other was the model of the day, and we kept updating to include whoever was in vogue at the time. Later on, Twiggy became part of the same act. Ted and I also did a routine as a pair of hostesses, and a spoof on the 'Dance of the Seven Veils'. On the seventh and last veil, there was a large 'L' plate, for 'learner'. It was all good harmless fun, wickedly bawdy, a little risqué and filled with innuendo, but never blue or dirty. It was typical nightclub material. The audiences lapped it up.

One of our most famous routines was the mind-reader – Madame Loofah. Ted made a brilliant clairvoyant and I used to stooge for him. As Madame Loofah, he was blindfolded on stage while I was in the audience picking on customers.

'Madame Loofah, and what am I touching on this man's head?' I called.

'Dirt,' came the reply.

'Madame Loofah, what is this man holding in his hand?'

'I couldn't possibly answer that.'

It worked very well in the nightclubs and soon became a classic and well-loved routine. However, one night Ava Gardner walked out on our act in disgust. Ted and I were both on stage performing the same routine, when Madame Loofah went into a trance.

'I must have contact. I must have physical contact,' called Ted, and grabbed hold of my outstretched little finger which he proceeded to hold up high in the air. He felt it for a few seconds in full view of the audience, looked puzzled and said: 'I wonder whatever happened to Frank Sinatra?'

With that, Ava Gardner leapt from her table and stormed out of the room in a fit of anger, muttering something about never having been so insulted in all her life, only to return seconds later: she had left her shoes under the table.

As part of my own act, however, I presented several of my own characters and creations for the first time, including a Japanese geisha girl, a teenage rocker and a striptease artiste with suitable parodies written for me. They were the forerunners of my special 'ladies'.

Churchill's was the kind of club that attracted celebrities from all over the world. It was the place to go and the place to be seen in London. Film stars, playboys, sportsmen, the jet set, fairytale princesses and Middle Eastern sheikhs were all regular clients. It catered for the very rich and the very famous.

Yet, although it was a large and spacious club and looked splendid from the cabaret floor, behind the scenes was chaotic. The dressing room accommodation was non-existent. We all changed together on a set of steps which led to a room at the top of the landing. Whoever had the top step, was top of the bill. I stayed on step seven for a long time.

I first met Liberace at Churchill's and we became the greatest of friends for over thirty years. We had an instant liking for each other. When we met, it was as if we had known each other all our lives. Whenever Lee came over to England, I was always the first person he contacted. He stayed at my home on many occasions.

Errol Flynn came to Churchill's a number of times during his visits to England to film *Lilacs in the Spring* and *King's Rhapsody* for Herbert Wilcox and Anna Neagle. We got on well together and liked each other immensely. He was a charming man, and had this legendary quality about him that couldn't be defined. It was very easy to see how he had gained such a reputation for himself as a ladies' man. He had an unbelievable presence although he was already a little bloated by then with the ravages of excess. Yet to me, he was still the great romantic. It was wonderful to meet the man whom I had seen as Robin Hood when I was a boy.

A few years later when I had my own club, Jack Hanson came into my dressing room crowing like a schoolboy in excitement. 'You'll never guess who's in the foyer?' he said in glee.

It was Sean Flynn. He came over and introduced himself as Errol Flynn's son and said he was in town on his way to South East Asia as a war correspondent. We spent a pleasant few moments talking about his father and then he was gone. He never returned. Not long afterwards he was killed in Vietnam.

Whenever Dana Andrews came into the club, he was always drunk and spent every evening heckling the cabaret. Terry Thomas just talked the whole time, while Leslie Hutchinson – 'Hutch' – came in for his breakfast when he was over on tour.

Anthony Steel, who was then a huge movie star and a devastatingly good-looking man, tried to proposition me. He had arrived at the club with his wife, actress Anita Ekberg, and they seemed to be in fine spirits. Shortly after the cabaret started, however, Anita Ekberg stormed out of the club in a flurry. None of us could understand what had happened at the time. Perhaps the volatile couple had had another blazing argument. What we hadn't realized, although we found out later, was that Anthony Steel kept telling his wife that he found *me* very attractive. Naturally, she couldn't take that, so she left.

After the show, the movie star pursued me backstage.

'You're very interesting,' he said. 'Very interesting, indeed. Your lovely voice is a cross between Glynis Johns and Joan Greenwood.'

I couldn't understand what was going on. 'Are you sending me up,' I said, and with that I took off my wig. Anthony Steel's face went snow white and then slowly turned to ashen grey. His mouth dropped open and his eyes stared in disbelief. He had genuinely thought I was a girl. No wonder his wife had left him so abruptly.

A great favourite at Churchill's was the Maharajah of Baroda, who just couldn't keep away. He was a lovely, generous man and very popular. The Maharajah always encouraged us to sit with him and his party after the cabaret was over, and to share a few drinks together and some pleasant company and conversation. He was a charismatic man, yet very down to earth. When we tried to address him as 'Your Royal Highness', he would have none of it.

'Just call me *Charlie*,' he insisted.

There was an unwritten rule at the club that if ever we were raided by the police, which was a distinct possibility in those days with the licensing laws in such disarray, everything on the tables had to go on the floor – glasses, champagne, lamps, *everything* – no matter what the cost. They were Harry Meadows' instructions. At that time, the law said a person had to be found in possession of an alcoholic drink after licensing hours to be charged with the offence. Harry figured that if the evidence was on the floor the police would be hard-pressed to prove a point. Usually, we were tipped off before a raid took place. Harry had friends at Savile Row police station and, if they knew we were about to be hit, plans could be made for a speedy cover-up job.

But we were raided one night, without warning, in the middle of the cabaret. Everyone was searched, and Harry Meadows was taken off to the station for questioning and later landed up in court. He was charged with selling drinks after hours and had fallen into a carefully laid trap. A police officer in plain clothes had joined the club one evening as a member, giving his occupation as a journalist. He then made such a scene inside, demanding a drink after hours, that Harry gave him one just to shut him up. Of course, he was reported immediately, and that was that. Caught in the act by a copper. When the case came to court, Sir Lawrence Dunn was the magistrate and he threw it out, saying the policeman in question had gained membership and access to the club by deception, and he would have none of it.

Shortly before the raid, however, the police had been keeping Churchill's under surveillance, looking for signs of any suspicious activity. In the early hours of one morning, the Maharajah just happened to leave the premises by the back entrance, down the steps and straight into the arms of two waiting police officers who stopped him for questioning.

'Unhand me. Don't you know who I am,' he cried in a voice that pierced the dawn air. 'I am the Maharajah of Baroda.'.

'Yes, sir,' said one of the policemen, 'and I'm Charlie Chaplin.' When someone at the club was asked to verify the Maharajah's identity, they couldn't. They only knew him as Charlie and didn't realize his full title, and told the police as much. With that, the Indian prince was carted off to Savile Row still protesting his innocence. He was back in Churchill's the following night.

The Maharajah of Cooch Behar also came into the club from time to time and got on very well with everyone there. He wanted to give me a tiger and I naïvely thought he meant a tiger skin rug or something equally exotic. He didn't, he meant a *real* one. I had to decline as we had no facilities for keeping one at Earlham Street!

Besides the glamorous and famous, Churchill's also proved a magnet for the infamous, including several notorious members of London's underworld. But they were always polite and always respectable whenever they came into the club for a night out with their friends. You would only find out their true identity if they were ever arrested and featured in the papers. On several occasions the club played host to murderers and gangland hit men, but we never knew. I also heard terrible stories about protection racketeering, but I think that only took place in the sleazier clubs. Certainly, I never came across it at Churchill's.

The club seemed to attract the great eccentrics, too. There was one particular customer who came into Churchill's in full evening dress, top hat and tails, and then proceded to shout 'bollocks' and other obscenities at the top of his voice throughout the cabaret. I remember Ted Gatty asking him if Noël Coward wrote his scripts. But, after the show, he sent champagne round for the company together with a note of apology.

When the Dairy Show was on in London, the place was filled with farmers up from the country, who were often paralytic. They had only come to ogle the girls and were so drunk they didn't even know what day it was. We had some rough houses during those few days. Ted and I used to go out on stage and do three or four minutes fill-in to allow the girls to change for their next number. But the audience made so much noise, we would start talking complete and utter gibberish to each other *and* to the audience, making up any stupid words that came into our heads, and suitable noises as well to give the conversation expression. No one knew the difference, or cared. At the end of our spot, we walked off to tumultuous applause.

Working with Ted Gatty, who was a very experienced entertainer, I was able to learn so much about the business. When I first started out, I worked very straight, almost like a leading lady. I created a remarkable illusion of glamour to which the customers warmed. It was pure fantasy and very shallow. It wasn't enough, there was no depth. Necessity soon taught me how to develop, and then how to cultivate, comedy back-chat and ad-libs. I needed to be able to deal with hecklers to survive in the clubs, particularly dressed up as a tart. And it was in that way that my catchphrase, '*Wotcha, mates*', evolved. In the end, I had enough material to suit almost every situation that might arise. I was never thrown out of my stride. It all added to the charm of the character I was creating. I never tried to hide Dan, though. I went a step further than the broad dame and made the broadness of such great comedians as Norman Evans attractive and gave it a glamorous shell. I think I am clever: to get belly laughs when you're glamorous is difficult. That quality came from the clubs.

I was on stage in the middle of the cabaret once when I noticed one of the hostesses was trying to captivate a boyfriend, who was paying far more attention to me than to her. It was too much for the poor girl to take, so in an act of sheer desperation – and in front of a packed club – she pulled down her shoulder straps and produced her boobs for everyone to see.

'Look,' she said to the wayward boy, '*these* are real.'

'Yes, darling, they are,' I called from the stage. 'But I can hang up my tits when it's hot.'

We worked with some delightful girls at Churchill's. Pat Raine was the first coloured girl I'd come across who put henna on her hair. It looked fantastic, but I honestly thought she wore a wig. She was a very talented girl. At the end of the cabaret, it was customary for the entire company to appear on stage together to take a final curtain call, and Pat would stand in between Ted and myself as we walked out to face the applause. As we were taking our bow, someone yelled from the audience: 'You're all a load of lesbians.' I turned to Pat. 'Quick, girl, take off your wig and show 'em it's a fella.'

There was another, very young, very naïve dancer, who was doubling at the London Palladium. She came into the club one night, bursting with excitement. She couldn't contain herself, and told us that Robert Nesbitt, who was producing the London Palladium show, wanted to put her into a singing quartet with two other boys and a girl, and to give her a featured spot in the show.

'But they want suggestions for a suitable name to call the group,' she told us. 'Any ideas?'

Quick as a flash, Ted came up with a name. 'How about the Four Wankers?'

'That sounds terrific,' said the girl in all innocence, completely oblivious to what it really meant. 'I can't wait to tell Robert Nesbitt, he'll love it.'

The next morning when she presented her suggestion at rehearsals, she couldn't understand why everyone fell about laughing. No one bothered to explain to her.

'I think it's a wonderful name,' she told us that evening. 'It would look fantastic up in lights. I can see it now – THE FOUR WANKERS.'

As our reputation grew within London's nightlife community, Ted Gatty and I had many offers to appear in other clubs all over London and, whenever we were able, we did perform in other venues. It was quite lucrative, too. Billed as Danny La Rue and Ted Gatty, we doubled at the 21 in Chesterfield House, Mayfair, which was run by Harry Meadows's brother, Bertie, and went on to the venue after we had completed our spots at Churchill's. We had a gentlemen's agreement.

The 21 was far more exclusive, frequented by debs and guards officers, although, on many occasions, we had to work to an audience of less than ten people. It was a gambling establishment, but despite its grandeur, the club possessed no dressing room facilities at all. So Ted and I had to travel across town by taxi, fully made up and dressed in our cabaret costumes. One night we had great difficulty in getting a taxi. We were out of luck and had virtually minutes to spare before we were due on stage at the 21. There was a young boy, well-known to us all by reputation, who used to tout for business, dressed in drag, in Bond Street in his car. He cruised up and down the road looking for trade. We saw him on this particular night, and in sheer desperation, flagged him down and asked him to take us to the 21. His eyes lit up, he hardly believed his luck had changed. But he dropped us off in a huff after learning our true intentions, and went back on the game. But it solved our problem.

The Keyhole Club in Mason's Yard, off Duke Street, St James's, was another cabaret room that booked us. It was tiny and not very salubrious. It attracted the wrong kind of people. There was a young Greek girl singer appearing on the bill with us and halfway through her act a member of the audience rushed up on to the minute stage and started fondling her breasts, and then sat down again as if nothing had happened. The poor girl screamed and ran off. It was all very off-putting. Ted and I thought we might be next in line for the treatment, so we rushed through our act and kept moving all the time.

Our début appearance for Carl Hyson at the Cascade Club, formerly the Bagatelle, in Mayfair Place, was as a replacement for Shirley Bassey. She had been booked for a week's cabaret at the Cascade and on opening night caused a minor sensation. Her reception was tumultuous. The audience wouldn't let her leave the stage. A new star was taking

above In 1954 I introduced fashion parades with mannequins into Hutton's to create interest and attract customers. They proved such a success that the first floor of the London clothes shop was converted and refurbished especially for this purpose. The unique event was launched by the lovely Carol Bruce (*seated, left*), who was in London at that time, starring in the musical *Pal Joey*. (*Kent News* Pictures)

left Outside J. V. Hutton's, the Oxford Street store where I worked as a window dresser and designer, with owner Eileen Hutton (*left*) and American musical star Carol Bruce. (*Kent News* Pictures)

top Ted Gatty (*second left*) and I share a drink and a joke with the customers at the exclusive 21 Club in Mayfair, which was run by the dapper Bertie Meadows (*far left*). The club had no dressing-room facilities for artistes, so Ted and I had to travel across London from Bond Street by taxi, fully made up and dressed in our cabaret costumes. (John Heddon)

bottom Cabaret time at Winston's in Clifford Street with a very talented company, including a young Barbara Windsor (*holding Aladdin's lamp*) and Amanda Barry (*third from the left*). (Lewis Photography)

above Ronnie Corbett and his wife,
Anne, are my closest friends in
show business. I first met Ronnie
at Winston's Club, and we
worked together for many
years at my own night
club in Hanover Square, where
this picture was taken. In my
opinion, Ronnie Corbett has a great
comedy talent and a marvellous
personality. (*East Kent Times and
Broadstairs Mail*)

right and overleaf My career in West End
cabaret can be charted in these three
programmes for Churchill's, Winston's
and my own club, Danny La Rue's. I
spent eighteen very happy and rewarding years entertaining London's late-
night audiences from 1954 to 1972.

DANNY LA RUE

CHURCHILLS CLUB

BOND STREET
LONDON

above We presented a special dress rehearsal of *Come Spy with Me* in aid of charity, at the Golders Green Hippodrome, just days before our West End opening in May 1966. The Master himself, Noël Coward (*left*), came along to see the show with Rudolph Nureyev and joined Barbara Windsor and myself backstage afterwards for drinks. Both Coward and Nureyev were great patrons of mine and were frequently seen at Danny La Rue's. (Rex Features Ltd. Photo: Ben Jones)

left I found Judy Garland utterly irresistible and charming. I idolized her. Quite simply, there has never been a talent like hers. Judy was a regular visitor to my West End club and often took to the stage to join in with the company and give an impromptu performance.

above One of Mark Canter's magnificent creations for *Danny La Rue at the Palace*, designed in beaded pink lace and tulle, with a twenty-foot-long train made entirely from ostrich feathers. It looked stunning. I am superstitious about lions, being a Leo: when you turn this photograph upside-down the features in the elaborate head-dress give the uncanny illusion of a lion's head. (Tom Hustler)

This spectacular dress, with its mirror-studded train, was designed especially for my London Palladium pantomine in 1978. It cost £7,000 to create.

The Merry Widow Twankey was a marvellous part to play in *Aladdin*, first at the London Palladium and later in Bristol and Birmingham, where the show established itself as the most successful pantomime ever staged in the provinces. Mark Canter designed all the costumes.

My very own special tribute to a highly talented Hollywood legend, Betty Grable. We first met in 1969, when she was in London to star at the Palace in *Belle Starr*. Betty never stopped for a moment trying to persuade me to work in Las Vegas. (Ray Mantell Photography)

right A royal tribute to another remarkable lady: Princess Anne gets the La Rue treatment in *Danny La Rue at the Palace*. (Tom Hustler)

below My mother, Mary Ann, was a great lady and a wonderful friend. She had a hard life but, throughout it all, retained a marvellously dry sense of humour and a sharp wit. She had a smile that could light up a dark sky on a dreary day.

off. She had class and magnificent talent written all over her. The following day, however, Shirley collapsed, and had to cancel the evening performance. Ted and I were asked to go on in her place.

How can you follow someone like Shirley? We were absolutely petrified at the prospect. She was such a great star, but we had to try. The packed audience, who had paid ten pounds for a ticket, a small fortune in those days, were very hostile towards us at first as we started our act. When we finished, we left the stage to a standing ovation. Commenting on our performance afterwards, one newspaper correspondent wrote: 'Rarely have I seen a substitute act receive such an overwhelming and sincere reception. Within minutes, Danny and Ted captured and held everyone's attention.'

After that triumph, we became a regular attraction at the Cascade, which was a high-class Mayfair club. The management there wanted to impress their customers when the club changed names. They spent a vast amount of money on designing and creating a fantastic illusion that had been custom-built. On display in the main room was a huge glass cabinet, which featured a spectacular water cascade inside. It looked stunning. The cabinet was filled with hundreds of tropical birds of all colours and kinds. It was a breathtaking sight and a great talking-point among the clients and symbolized the name perfectly – the Cascade. There was a snag: the noise of the water falling constantly and the din of the birds combined together was utterly overpowering. Nothing could be heard above the racket, even the cabaret in full swing. It didn't last long.

Each summer, Ted Gatty left Churchill's to appear in old-time music hall for the season at the Sunshine Theatre at Dreamland in Margate, which was always successful. He was probably the best chairman of old-time music hall I have ever seen.

However, watching Ted's success away from the clubs made me think. I started to get itchy feet myself and was on the look-out for ways that I might follow his lead and diversify my own talents into other directions in show business. I hated to think that my own career might start and end at Churchill's. I didn't want to stand still, there must be something else I could do. Another great mate of mine came to the rescue and solved the problem.

Davy Kaye was one of the big stars of West End cabaret, appearing nightly at the Embassy Club. He was something of an impresario as well, it was another string to his bow, and he booked pantomimes and odd shows for Joe Collins, father of Joan and Jackie. In 1956, Davy approached me and asked if I would like to appear in pantomime myself that year. He had seen my own reputation growing in London nightclub circles and thought I would make the perfect Ugly Sister in the pantomime *Cinderella* he was presenting for a double season at the Regal, Gloucester and the Regal, York. It was just the right kind of career move I was looking for to extend my range. But at first, I turned him down. I refused. 'I won't play "ugly",' I said. 'It's not in my nature.' Still, Davy persisted.

'I'll do it if I can be a caricature,' I said. 'I'll be glamorous on the outside, but very ugly on the inside.' We compromised. After all, if you can get really good belly laughs by looking beautiful, why try to get them by dropping your drawers or having custard pies thrown in your face?

My fellow Ugly Sister was Alan Haynes with whom I'd worked at Churchill's in Ted Gatty's absence. We'd done bits and pieces together so we knew each other's work. Alan filled in during the summer and we did seem to work quite well with each other. We were paid ninety pounds a week between us for the season.

It was a new challenge for me. I had never done anything like it before. But I realized that the only way I was going to learn the business and progress further in my career was by taking different kinds of engagements. It was too easy to get stuck doing the same kind of job every day. I relished the experience, but was very apprehensive at the prospect.

I was bizarre. I based my Ugly Sister characterization on a cross between Marilyn Monroe, Jayne Mansfield and a totally exaggerated Diana Dors, whom I had known from Churchill's. She was a frequent visitor. It was big, brassy and brave – all legs, hair and large boobs. It was very glamorous, but totally over the top. The costumes were equally outrageous. I had one dress with a hat that was like a grass verge and a sign saying 'Keep Off the Grass'; another turned me into a Belisha beacon; in a third, I was a soap box. Alan Haynes was a complete contrast to me. He worked 'ugly' and grotesque on purpose as a catalyst to my 'glamour'. It all worked splendidly well. We clicked together instantly. My wickedness came from within me. The audiences were puzzled how such an attractive person could convey so much cruelty. I was the very first Alexis Carrington and it started a new trend: the Ugly Sister who *wasn't* ugly.

Cinderella really was a superb pantomime. Edna Savage, who was then quite a big star, played the title role with Lorrae Desmond as Dandini. Lorrae has now emerged as a big star in Australia, where she is seen regularly on television in *A Country Practice*. Davy Kaye played Buttons, and Dailey and Wayne were the Broker's Men. It was quite an eye-opener for me to walk out on stage for the very first time in a featured role in a major pantomime, knowing that so many people in the cast relied on me to give them their cues and *not* to make a mistake. It was a big responsibility. On opening night, I broke every tradition in the history of the Ugly Sisters and stopped the show. The same thing happened every single night.

Davy Kaye acknowledged my impact: 'Danny looked sensational. He was the prettiest, the most glamorous and sexy Ugly Sister I have ever seen. Unbelievable.' At the end of the show, he told the audience: 'Tonight we have seen one of the greatest dames in show business. This man, Danny La Rue, is going to be a great star.'

I took to pantomime immediately, and loved everything it stood for all the time I was involved. It was completely different to my normal working style in the clubs, but it was something new and exciting. *Cinderella* took my career off in another wonderful direction. Until then, Bartlett and Ross were recognized as the best Ugly Sisters in the business, now Alan Haynes and I were after their crowns. It's interesting to note, however, that Bartlett and Ross were a confirmed double act. Alan and I weren't. We worked together only in pantomime and separated otherwise. I never wanted to be anything other than *Danny La Rue*.

The following Christmas, we appeared once more in *Cinderella* for Joe Collins at the Finsbury Park Empire with Dave King . . . and it happened all over again – I stopped the show.

Tom Arnold was looked upon in the business as the greatest pantomime producer in the country. He presented the biggest and the best Christmas seasons at the number one venues, and had heard the reaction I was getting and wanted to see for himself this glamorous Ugly Sister. He came along to Finsbury Park and saw me working. At the end of the show, he offered me a five-year contract to appear in his pantomimes. Tom realized then I had become a kind of cult figure in the West End. He could see my potential and shrewdly wanted to exploit it in the provinces. Tom was a straight-talking Yorkshireman who knew the business inside out, and as such got on famously with Jack Hanson. It was the start of a long and happy association.

The contract with the Arnold office had been arranged and negotiated by Hyman Zahl who had become my first agent the year before. We met in Shaftesbury Avenue one day, shortly after my first panto season. He'd heard all about me and asked if we could meet at Foster's in Piccadilly, which was the biggest theatrical agency in the country and was responsible for bringing all the top-ranking American stars to Britain for engagements and tours. They had the finest reputation in show business.

At our arranged meeting, Hymie told me that Alan and I were going to be bigger than Bartlett and Ross and he would like to represent me. We came to an agreement, and I have been looked after by the Zahl family ever since; first by Hymie and, when he died, by his brother Sonny. Today, Sonny's wife, Ann, is my agent. She has guided my career meticulously and become a great friend and mentor over the years. A large part of my success can be credited to Ann. I have never signed a contract with the Zahls, it was all done on a handshake.

I did not return to Churchill's after completing my first pantomime season with Davy Kaye. There had been a terrific upheaval at the club some months before. Harry Meadows and his partner, Bruce Brace, who was the general manager, had parted company after a bitter argument. Bruce stormed out of the Bond Street establishment and the feud became the talk of West End nightlife.

Meanwhile, Bruce had managed to find suitable backers and opened a club of his own in Clifford Street, off New Bond Street, which was virtually opposite Churchill's and in direct competition. Bruce defiantly called his new club, Winston's. Harry Meadows was furious. Bryan Blackburn was writing and producing the shows.

While Churchill's had presented a feathery cabaret of variety, Bryan wanted to stage intimate revue at Winston's, and he had assembled a quite spectacular company together, including Barbara Windsor, Barbara Ferris, Fenella Fielding, Judy Collins and Amanda Barrie. However, the initial show was not well-received. In fact it was a bit of a disaster and ran for just six weeks. His next effort was better, running for nearly half a year, but Bruce Brace wanted instant success and was getting impatient. He realized he needed someone who would bring in the customers and build up Winston's into London's premier nightspot. He turned his attentions to the 'fella in a frock' over the road.

When Bruce Brace brought Barbara Windsor over to Churchill's to see me working with Ted Gatty, and explained his plans to put me into a new show at Winston's, the bubbling blonde tried desperately to make him change his mind. She told Bruce she didn't think it could possibly work. Fortunately, he took no notice and signed me up, and I transferred to Winston's at the beginning of 1957. Barbara had become like the Queen Bee at the club, loved and much-respected by the audiences, and she thought I would come in and take it all away from her. It was the last thing I wanted to do. She had so much talent in her own right, which she later went on to prove. We hit it off immediately and worked together so well. Barbara Windsor has remained a dear friend. She is also the first to acknowledge that it was through me that she realized her own true potential as a comedienne, and a great one at that. Instead of relying on a glamorous look, she started to play it for laughs on stage with great success.

Bryan Blackburn wasn't over-pleased with my arrival at Winston's, either. He was responsible for putting all the shows together in the early days and had never written for me before. When Bruce Brace brought me into the show, Bryan was quite annoyed. He hadn't realized that I was quite capable of adapting to anything he wanted me to do and I fitted into his shows with ease. I think at first we were both sizing each other up. We certainly underestimated each other's talents.

Bryan wrote some very funny material, very topical and satirical, in fact we were presenting a kind of *That Was The Week That Was* long before it ever appeared on television. He has been writing for me ever since, besides writing for all the top names in British entertainment. He is quite rightly regarded as one of our best scriptwriters.

A combination of Blackburn's clever writing skills, a witty and original revue, and a glamorous 'fella in a frock', soon put Winston's squarely on the nightlife map of London, and established its name and reputation in a matter of weeks.

We had a complete cross-section of audiences – foreign tourists, socialites, debs. Businessmen escaping from their homes came up to town for meetings and stayed on for a night out at Winston's on company expenses. It was much the same everywhere else in the London clubs. Yet, we seemed to attract far more celebrities than the others, and soon took over the mantle as London's glamour club from Churchill's in the days when the likes of Bing Crosby, Darryl F. Zanuck and Victor Mature would come in and rub shoulders with members of the British aristocracy, the nouveau riche and hard-bitten criminals. Bruce Brace took money off anyone and everyone.

Every visiting star to London came to Winston's. I met Judy Garland there for the first time who was to become a great lady in my life, and Nat King Cole. Dennis Price came in one night so drunk he could hardly stand and staggered to his table. Halfway through the cabaret, he collapsed from the effects of too much alcohol and went to sleep sprawled across the three steps that led to the stage where we were performing. He went out like a light, and we just left him there, performing the cabaret around his outstretched body and making sure no one stepped on him.

It never fails to amaze me what actions some people will get up to once they have a few drinks inside them. At Winston's we had our fair share of drunkards who often behaved so badly they had to be physically ejected from the club. Others given new confidence by the alcohol became monsters and said and did things I am sure they would have been horrified by in normal circumstances. Barbara Windsor often became the target of some outrageously lewd heckling from certain sections of the audience. One night, she was pelted with ice cubes throughout our entire cabaret performance, which went everywhere, showering the stage with water and making it treacherous underfoot. She was furious, but smiled serenely. When the ice tirade continued, she snapped at the person in question: 'Who do you think I am, Sonja Henie?' The whole place was in uproar.

Another time, we were only into our opening number when a guy at a nearby table started on Barbara.

'Cor, I fancy that little blonde bit with the big Bristols,' he said in a loud voice so that everyone in the room could hear him. 'Cor, I'd like to give 'er one.'

I stopped the show and challenged the troublemaker.

'How dare you,' I said. 'Have a little respect for my friend. Don't talk to her like that, she's a lady.'

'Oh, yeah,' came the reply. 'And what are you going to do about it, anyway?'

'Don't be fooled by the wig, mate,' I added and hit him. He made the mistake of underestimating me. I honestly don't think he realized I was a man.

I always felt very protective towards the girls and I got into several scuffles at the club defending their honour. People had no respect or manners, which made me so annoyed. Dignity is everything. Ronnie Knight, Barbara Windsor's first husband, came to my rescue one night when a crowd of punters ganged up on me.

The lovely Janet Howse, who was a delightful addition to our cabaret company, and who died so tragically young, could look after herself. When someone shouted obscenities at her during the show, she carefully left the stage, went up to the table in question, and emptied the entire contents of an ice bucket over the head of the offending foul-mouthed customer with great style, and then returned to the stage again.

Barbara Windsor became known as the chip lady. Every night we used to arrive at the club at around midnight, to go on stage at one fifteen and chances were everyone was starving by the time they got there. We all changed together in a very small dressing room near to the kitchen and next to the freezer. When the coldstore door was opened, the smell was unbearable. It was appalling in such a cramped room. But at most times, the aroma coming from the kitchen made us even more hungry.

The chef was a maniac, he was always in a temper, cursing, throwing things at people and chasing the waiters with an axe. No one was safe in his company, but he had a weakness. *Tits.* He was crazy for knockers, the bigger the better, and he spent a fair amount of time ogling the showgirls as they changed. It didn't take me too long to discover his weak spot and turn it to our advantage. I used to make Barbara sidle up to the chef, flashing her boobs at him. Then, at an appropriate moment, she would ask him for some chips for us to eat. It worked every single time. After all, she had the best equipment of us all; I only had dunlopillo.

'Oh, yes, Barbara,' said the chef, eyes popping out of his head on stalks, his mouth drooling. 'Anything you want . . .'

Barbara used to leave the club at regular intervals to go off and pursue her career elsewhere. She had been in the business since she was twelve and was itching to do other things. On the first occasion, she was offered a small part in a new show called, *Keep Your Hair On*, which was an important step in the right direction, as it was opening in the West End. On her last night at Winston's we decided to give her a special send-off. At the end of the cabaret I made a little speech.

'Ladies and gentlemen, we are sad tonight to say that one of the members of our company, Barbara Windsor, is leaving us to go off into new pastures. And we're sure you'd like to join with us in wishing her well for the future.' A round of applause was followed by a chorus of 'For she's a jolly good fellow', and Bruce Brace emerged on stage carrying a splendid farewell cake . . . And off she went.

Barbara rehearsed for three weeks before the show opened at the Lyric Theatre . . . it closed shortly afterwards. Back she came to Winston's for a further spell. Nine months later, she was offered a part in another show. On her last night at the club the same thing happened. I made a little speech.

'Ladies and gentlemen, we are sad tonight to say goodbye to a delightful member of our company, Barbara Windsor, who is leaving us for pastures new. I'm sure you'd like to join with us in wishing her all the best for the future.' Another round of applause, another quick chorus of 'For she's a jolly good fellow', and Bruce Brace appeared again with another farewell cake . . . And off she went again.

Four weeks later, the producers of Barbara's new show realized she was totally wrong for the part and they fired her. So back she came to Winston's for another spell. Nine months later, she was offered a part in *Fings Ain't Wot They Used t' Be* at the Theatre Royal, Stratford East, by Joan Littlewood. As she told us all the good news, Barbara turned to me and beamed: 'Do us a favour, Danny,' she said. 'Don't make a fuss this time, just let me get off. And don't you dare give me a cake.'

We didn't. Barbara Windsor never returned. The show was a big success and she went on to become what she is today, one of Britain's best-loved stars.

In 1965, however, she starred in the ill-fated Lionel Bart musical *Twang*, which proved to be one of the West End's most spectacular disasters. On opening night at the Shaftesbury Theatre, the audience howled its disapproval. Actually, it wasn't a great show, but it deserved better support. Lionel Blair tells a lovely story about the evening. Amidst all the booing and jeering from the first-nighters, a lone voice was heard from the Circle shouting back at them: 'If you don't like it, get out. They are artistes down there, doing their best. Give them a chance . . .' It was *me*, protecting Barbara's honour again.

I actually thought of leaving Winston's myself once and had given in my notice to Bruce Brace when Liberace stopped me. He'd been to see the show and talked me out of my decision.

'Danny,' he said, 'you are going to be very big in show business. Stay here, this is your domain. Wait and see.' I stayed and his prediction came true.

At the same time, I had a mad affair with a young girl, and would probably have got married. But, unhappily, she was killed in a plane crash. That was the only time marriage entered my head. My career started to take off in a big way shortly afterwards, and I became married to the profession. Show business was my mistress. Since then, I have seen so much tragedy through broken marriages. Show business is probably the worst business in the world in which to be married, especially if you are successful. I've found a lot of my contemporaries have been *divorced* two or three times and families have been split up with great bitterness. I don't think I could live like that. I find it very sad when two partners in life struggle so hard together at the beginning and then one makes it to the top and succumbs to all the temptations. Success is dangerous, it takes you into another world. It separates you from people. It alienates you from friends and family, if you are not careful. I don't think it was ever intended I should marry, I was becoming too successful.

The revues at Winston's were first-class and, before long, people came to the club just to see the floorshow. It was the most original show in town. We introduced new productions three or four times a year, which were always well-dressed. Looking back, it was incredible. It couldn't be done today, the cost would be prohibitive.

We had a wonderful stable of thoroughbred artistes in the Winston's companies, many of whom have gone on to bigger and better things. Ronnie Corbett was introduced to the club by Digby Wolfe and became one of the best comedy actors I have ever worked with. We sparked well together on stage; it was a winning combination and we had a long and successful association together. Ronnie met his wife, Anne Hart, at Winston's and I am godfather to their daughters, Emma and Sophie. The Corbetts remain among my closest friends in show business. Maggie Fitzgibbon was another. She now has a lovely farm in Australia and entertained me there splendidly on one of my tours. There were others – Clovissa Newcombe, Jenny Logan, Valerie Walsh and Victor Spinetti. Winston's was a marvellous training ground.

I learned later that many of the people who came into the club were there to see me. *I* was the main attraction. They were fascinated by me, and I was emerging as the darling of the West End. My own reputation was much bigger than I ever realized or imagined. Instead of going home after the show, I mingled with the customers and soon built up an amazing following. Bryan Blackburn was writing some marvellous material for me and we sort of grew together. It was at that time I introduced my 'ladies' into the act. I had the original ideas, and

Bryan wrote special parodies for me as glamorous point numbers for the club. They have developed tremendously ever since. I could go nowhere today without them.

Lady Docker, who was never out of the newspapers, was one of my first. She loved it, but she was a little bit peculiar. Anyone who has their car gold-plated must be a trifle eccentric. The car incident made every paper and we did a marvellous parody on it: 'I've had everything plated in my time, but never a streamlined Daimler.'

Liz Taylor was another 'lady', and there was Zsa Zsa Gabor, Mae West and Marilyn Monroe. Any star in the news was an instant target. I met Monroe for the first time with no clothes on. She was in England, shooting *The Prince and the Showgirl* with Laurence Olivier. She came for a fitting at Berman's – the world-famous theatrical costumiers, who supplied all the clothes for the Winston's floorshow – wearing a fur coat and nothing else. I didn't know her well, but got to know about her life later after she died through my great friendship with Betty Grable, who was one of Monroe's closest friends. She told me Marilyn never wore underwear because she thought it spoiled the line of her dress. Betty, Lauren Bacall and Marilyn Monroe used to go out together. One day, Betty Grable went to call for Monroe and got no reply from the doorbell. She rang for several minutes, but still no reply. Fortunately, she had her own key to the house and let herself in. She found Marilyn with her face under a hair-dryer because she had heard hot air was good for it.

Sabrina came in for the La Rue treatment, too. She had a broad Lancashire accent, which I captured perfectly. Her real name was Norma Sykes and she had been discovered by Arthur Askey. When she came into Winston's to see the show, she was appearing at the Prince of Wales in revue with Arthur and Dickie Henderson. She hated seeing herself parodied on stage. 'I don't talk like that,' she said in exactly the same accent I was using on stage, and walked out of the club very distressed. She was one of the few ladies who ever objected. She didn't see it as flattery, she thought I was taking the mickey in a nasty way. She missed the whole point of the joke.

We also prided ourselves on our topicality and presented parodies and sketches of all the major news events. We staged our own Wedding of the Year when Princess Margaret got married, while Toni Palmer and I did a wicked take-off of Mandy Rice-Davies and Christine Keeler when the Profumo affair blew up in 1963. No one was sacred and if there was a theatrical or political scandal in the papers it provided us with marvellous late-night material. A few people complained and thought our send-ups went too far, and that we had no right to attack the private lives of the famous. But I have firmly believed that if a person chooses to be in the public eye and becomes a product of the people then they must behave themselves accordingly, or accept the consequences.

After the cabaret had finished for the evening, Toni Palmer, who was my leading lady for many years in the West End, often went out into the audience for a quiet drink, and several times people came up to her thinking she was me. I was horrified at the prospect that people would actually think I would sit in the main room of the club dressed as a woman. The whole success of Danny La Rue has been built up on *two* people: Danny the person and Danny the artiste. They never meet. When I walk out on stage, I am another person. The costumes, the make-up, the wigs are tools of my trade and they are hung up and locked away when the dressing room door is closed behind me, and Danny the person emerges. People respect me for it.

I know that if I dressed and acted totally like a woman, which is one thing I would never do, I would immediately alienate the men in the audience who might find me tasteless and embarrassing. I have always played the part as a man dressed as a woman and I am very aware of the girls in the show alongside me. It is all a joke, really, a send-up, which the men in the audience identify with, and can feel completely relaxed about because this is a man, telling male gags, who just happens to be stunningly dressed. The women in the audience love the glamour and the fabulous costumes. But I have never wanted to do the uncanny impressions – 'Good heavens, that's never a man, is it?' – I love destroying that illusion.

When Bryan Blackburn moved on from Winston's, I ended up producing the shows myself with a young man from Leeds, Barry Cryer, writing the scripts and occasionally taking part in the shows as well. I'd seen him in revue at the Fortune Theatre, and I was so taken with his clever writing that I invited him to join me. Barry became a vital member of our company for several years and I introduced him to his wife, Terry Donovan, who had appeared with me in pantomime and later at Winston's. I am godfather to their daughter Jacqui.

Even though I was becoming the star of London's late-night cabaret scene, I was still living in Earlham Street at Cambridge Circus and I stayed there quite a while. My brother, Dick, had moved out when he married in 1950, but the rest of the family stayed together. It was convenient for me, too. Working first at Churchill's and later at Winston's, I could walk to and from the clubs. On my walks back home in the small hours of the morning, I got to know many of the ladies of the night who patronized Soho – purely as friends I hasten to add. There were some warm-hearted, colourful characters, dressed to the nines in white fox fur. Fifi from Shaftesbury Avenue was my favourite – a lovely girl, she seemed. There was a kind of romance about the girls, they were part of the whole Soho scene, now sadly gone. I missed them when I eventually left home, and Jack and I bought a flat in Elgin Mansions, Maida Vale.

I made my television début in 1958 while still working at Winston's. It was arranged by Hughie Green, who was then producing and presenting a series of magazine programmes for Jack Hylton at Rediffusion, as well as compèring *Double Your Money*. He had an idea to feature an all-woman programme within his series and had put the show together and booked several guests. Hughie and I had known each other for some time. He had seen me at both nightclubs and greatly admired my work. He had often said he would put me on television one day if the right vehicle came along. This was it, and he asked me if I would go on the show as one of the women. He explained to me exactly what he wanted me to do. I had no objections providing I could do one of my own numbers. Hughie agreed.

The show was live, in front of an all-female audience. Hughie introduced his first guest, the television cookery expert, Fanny Cradock, and then deliberately tried to antagonize her.

'Tell me, Fanny,' he began, 'don't you think women today have far too much to say for themselves in everyday life . . .?'

Even before he finished the sentence, Fanny was at him. She was fuming. 'I am amazed,' she replied with venom. 'How dare you say that. I thought you were a more intelligent man.'

Hughie interjected again. 'I'm awfully sorry, we seem to have got off on the wrong footing. Well, let's pause for a few minutes and meet our second guest.'

I was on. I looked incredible in my costume and I had the audience spellbound watching me. At the end of my song, the applause was unbelievable. I took my bow and joined Hughie and Fanny. The argument continued.

'Don't you think women have too much . . .?'

Fanny was champing at the bit, accusing Hughie of being a tyrant and not giving women any credit at all. She told him he was an ignorant man and didn't know the facts. Anyway, women had as many rights as men.

And so it went on with Fanny getting more and more heated as Hughie goaded her with a series of inane remarks. At the end of the bombardment, she turned to me for support.

'Now this is a very beautiful young lady,' she said. I smiled. 'Tell me, my dear, what do you want to do as you grow older? Do you want to be at the disposal of any man?' She anticipated my reply. I didn't disappoint her.

'Well, when I get older,' I said in my full 'wotcha, mates' voice, 'all I want to do is sit back in my easy chair and smoke my pipe.' It caused a sensation. When Fanny realized I was a man she nearly had a heart attack. Hughie was beside himself. He had gambled on a clever idea and it had come off. He had also created a television first by putting me on the screen. It is an achievement of which he is very proud.

'In all the years I did the original *Opportunity Knocks*,' he said, 'and I used to see over nine thousand people a year, I never found one artiste worthy of putting on television who even measured up to what Danny did. We saw many similar acts, but none of them had Danny's taste, his charisma or his incredible talent. And we often used to remark on that at the start of each new series – "This year, are we going to find the new Danny La Rue?" – we never did.'

On that first television show, I was introduced to a legend. I had known of Josephine Baker's reputation for a long time, but had never met her. She was making a rare television appearance herself, in fact I believe it was her first since the war, so she was hounded by the press. She had seen me in rehearsals and, when the cameramen persisted, she pointed to me deliberately.

'Don't photograph me, photograph him. He is going to be a big, big star.'

From then on, we saw each other whenever we could. I would visit her in Paris, she would come over to London to see me. I admired her so much, and several years later, I paid my own special tribute by including her as one of *my* 'ladies'. When we met, she had turned sixty and she wasn't the most beautiful of women. Yet, on stage, this elderly lady disappeared to be replaced by a glamorous vision. She had superb legs and a marvellous body. We were kindred spirits; we both created amazing illusions.

During the spring of 1987, the administrator of the Theatre Royal, Stratford East, wrote to me, telling me the company were staging a new show on the life of Josephine Baker called *This Is My Dream*, with Joanne Campbell playing the title role. A few years before, I had donated several of my costumes to the theatre company's cause to help them out. He was now asking if I might like to help them once more. I was delighted to be of assistance. I saw the show in rehearsal, and was so impressed with Joanne Campbell. She captured Josephine Baker as I knew her, to perfection.

By the sixties, I had established myself as the star of Winston's and I realized I had become a major attraction in London. Each Christmas, I took leave of absence from Clifford Street to go into pantomime for Tom Arnold. It was always *Cinderella* – well, at least for several years – with Alan Haynes as my partner. We went to the Manchester Palace in 1958 with Bob Monkhouse and after a sensational opening night, when I was hailed as 'the most beautiful woman on stage' by one local newspaper reviewer, Bob sent me a telegram: 'You've stolen my pantomime. Can I have it back, please?'

The following year, we played the Newcastle Empire with Bobby Thompson, and with Glenn Melvin and Danny Ross – both successful radio stars. But on the day of the dress rehearsal, Melvin and Ross disappeared, they walked out of the show, leaving us stranded. The pantomime had to be hastily re-written at the last moment and we opened without them. No one was any the wiser.

Then, for the next three years, Alan and I worked with Lonnie Donegan at the Theatre Royal, Nottingham (1960), the Birmingham Hippodrome (1961) and the Leeds Grand (1962). All number one venues, and each one played to record-breaking business.

Back in London, it was rumoured that I would at last be given a partnership in Winston's by Bruce Brace but, when that failed to materialize, I started to look around for other things. I felt let down badly. I had been at the club now for over seven years, so long in fact that I had become *Winston's*. It was time to move on. This time I approached Davy Kaye with a proposition.

'Look, Davy,' I said, 'you're at the Embassy Club, I'm at Winston's, and between us we've got the West End cabaret scene sewn up. With our knowledge, we can't fail. Why don't we go into partnership together and open our own club?'

He turned me down. He admits now it was out of loyalty to the Embassy Club, but acknowledges it was a big mistake. 'If we'd gone into business together, we would still be the kings of the West End,' he has told me on a number of occasions since.

I had an idea in my mind, but I had to look elsewhere for support. One night after I'd finished on stage at the club, I was having a pee in the toilet when a regular customer came in and joined me. We started talking as we went about our business. His name was David Lowes, a self-made millionaire.

'Your shows are bloody marvellous,' he said. 'I entertain clients down here all the time because of you and your show.' He hesitated for a while, choosing his words carefully. 'Why don't you open your own club? I'll come in with you,' he said it quickly. 'If you can find the premises, I'll find the necessary finance.'

I thought he was taking the mickey out of me, that the drink was talking instead of him. But, I found he was deadly serious. He had the business know-how and connections to turn my dream into reality. It was a genuine offer.

6
'I didn't recognize you with your clothes on'

'Dear boy, you could say *fuck* and no one would blink. Others would make the word sleazy, but you give it style.' Those were the first words Noël Coward said to me on seeing me in cabaret at my club on 5 August 1965. It was his way of reacting to the rumours that I had got a reputation for being risqué and very naughty on stage. He never said anything he didn't mean.

Noël had immense presence and wasn't particularly fond of female impersonators and said so on many occasions. But he thought I had enormous style and was the only one of my kind who was not embarrassing.

He had come to the club for the first time on that night, after attending a performance of John Osborne's play, *A Patriot for Me*, at the Royal Court, which, according to his famous diaries, he detested: 'The "drag" scene is so embarrassing that we could hardly look at the stage. After this curious experience, we dined well at the Empress (thank God) and went on to Danny La Rue's. He also was in "drag", in fact it was a big "drag" evening, but he was also witty and utterly charming and the whole show completely enjoyable. It finished with a long musical and vocal tribute to me, beautifully done.'

We were good friends and he influenced me a great deal. He had such great charisma and elegance. He inspired so many people. Noël came to several parties I held at that time. He loved parties. On the first occasion, the guests all congregated around the piano awaiting the master's arrival. Ronnie Corbett was playing when Noël came into the room, and immediately went into a number from *Bitter Sweet*: 'Someday I'll find you . . .' When the song was over, someone suggested that perhaps Noël would like to play for us all. We cheered. He looked coy and embarrassed, but smiled as he sauntered over to the piano and sat down, flicking his hands behind him as if he was wearing imaginary tails and the full regalia. He looked up and said: 'I really do wish I knew something I could play. Could someone hum a tune for me?'

We met again a few days later at another party, given by Billie

More, Kenneth More's ex-wife, and he was very apologetic at not having given me a house-warming present on the last occasion.

'Please accept this,' he said, taking a package wrapped in the union jack – typical Coward – from behind his back. It was one of his paintings.

Noël was a regular visitor to my club in the sixties and he always sat at a table in the front, near to the stage. He went backstage one night after seeing Anne Hart and Toni Palmer perform a superb version of his own composition, 'Mad About the Boy', full of congratulations. 'It's the best I've ever seen it done,' he said to the girls. Then he turned to Anne and brusquely told her that her lipstick looked awful and she should change the shade immediately. But he did it in such a business-like way that no one could ever take offence. Anne took his advice. He had that effect.

Noël Coward was just one of the many people who came to my club during the eight years of its existence from 1964 to 1972, from royalty to Hollywood and the man in the street. They all helped to make its name become legendary; it exceeded all my wildest dreams.

After our initial meeting in the gentlemen's toilet at Winston's to-wards the end of 1963, David Lowes and I met for lunch the following day to discuss plans and plot strategy for the new venture. I knew that Paul Raymond was unhappy with the way things were going at his Bel Tabarin Club in Hanover Square and it was up for grabs to the right offer. It was a very classy club, and Paul's pride and joy, but was not proving to be the success he had hoped for. I contacted him about the possibility of my buying the lease and opened negotiations to purchase. Within a month, we had agreed to buy, although Paul almost put me off the sale on a number of occasions. Quite honestly, he didn't think I could run the club. It was his vanity – if he couldn't make the place work, no one could.

Mervyn Conn had also tried to run a club on the same site, called the Riviera, for a couple of years before Paul, without too much success. Before that, it had been the Blue Mediterranean. It had become a white elephant and there were a lot of people in the business who thought I was making a big mistake and that I was destined to follow the same path to disaster. I was quietly confident in my own ability. I have never done anything like it before, so I was naïvely unaware of the pitfalls.

The deal was completed while I was appearing in pantomime at the

Pavilion, Bournemouth with Stan Stennett. I told no one about my new venture until I'd signed the contracts, then I threw a huge party.

I returned to Winston's to hand in my notice to Bruce Brace, who was upset at the prospect of losing me. He knew what I was going to do and tried to talk me round. 'You realize it can't possibly work and be a success,' he said. 'What do you know about running a club in the West End?'

He was right, for the wrong reasons. He was shrewd enough to know that I was the big attraction at his club and, without me, Winston's would be lost. But he had also hit a soft spot. What *did* I know? I wanted to try and I had a completely different attitude to nightlife in London than he did.

Jack Hanson and I put up everything we had to buy the club, while David's firm in the north of England acted as guarantors at the bank. We were in business and on a hiding to nothing. Already the traditional nightclub business in London was dying out. New clubs and owners sprang up almost weekly. Mervyn Conn and Paul Raymond couldn't make the club a success, why should I be any different? My only experience came from working for ten years as one of the most successful artistes in London cabaret and that would all count for nothing in a very short space of time if it all went wrong. I was certain we could succeed. We had to. We also needed a name for the club and we played about with several ideas. It was Jack Hanson who suggested *Danny La Rue's*.

'You're a great star,' he said. 'From now on your name should always appear *above* the title.' It was a very clever notion because every time the club was mentioned so, too, was my name and it had a very friendly ring to it.

Once we had become a great success, Paul Raymond came in often. He was delighted with the way things had worked for us and told us so. Paul has become a very successful man in his own right, yet he has such a marvellous quality in that he has no envy of anyone else's success. He's not that type of man.

Before we could open up officially we had to make the club beautiful. Most other nightclubs in London were simply rooms that happened to present cabaret. I was determined my club would be different, well-designed and custom-built for entertainment. The room was actually pallet-shaped, seating no more than two hundred, with a curved back wall and a circular stage at one end. The tables were on terraces. I had it completely re-decorated in pale grey, with orange and purple on black velvet walls. It looked tasteful and stunning. My brother, Dick, had a lot to do with the decor.

I can remember telling Liberace all about Dick, that he was a superb interior decorator and designer, and I gave him such a build-up that I'm sure Lee expected to see someone in a velvet jacket and large floppy hat. Dick arrived and, as he heard my glowing recommendation, he said in his singalong Irish brogue: 'I'm Dick, I only paint walls.' Lee loved him.

One of the club's startling features was a white marble floor, which, although small, looked unbelievable. We also had a gold-leaf ceiling over the cabaret floor. Richard Pilbrow kindly advised me on the lighting as a club-warming present.

Jack and I went to a lot of trouble to get the very best of everything. We scrimped on nothing and looked to find the right kind of people to help with the day-to-day running and management of such an establishment. I was going to run it myself, with Jack's help, but we required the best back-up team we could get. We found it, too. We brought in specialists to do the catering, and employed a marvellous chef called Bill, who came from Yorkshire. He completely belied the image of a first-class, flamboyant chef. Bill kept his teeth in his top pocket, and he would drink anything he could get his hands on. But he was a superb cook and could turn his hands to any culinary creation. I really do believe that one of the reasons we succeeded was because we served up the best food in any nightclub in town. Experience had taught me not to neglect such an important item. Bill loved the club, he cried like a child when we were forced to close down.

We looked after everyone whom we employed. My waiters were paid two pounds a week more than anywhere else, and they were very loyal. Our head waiter was called Miguel and later became head waiter at the Inn on the Park hotel. We had an incredible team. In eight years, we lost only one musician and two of the staff.

I took Bill Beim with me from Winston's to manage the club, and he talked me into hiring hostesses for a while. But I didn't like it and got rid of them as quickly as I could. It wasn't what I was after. I wanted a family club where people could come in and enjoy themselves with their wives and relatives. I was tired of seeing men come into clubs with young girlfriends on their arms while their wives waited at home. I wanted to change all that. I didn't want a nightclub as such, more a late-night theatre club. I wanted a place to which people would be proud to bring their mothers.

My ultimate aim was to have the best nightclub in London, which meant staging the best floorshow in town. Reputation counted for everything. I recruited some more old mates from Winston's to join my revue company, including Toni Palmer, Valerie Walsh, Janet Howse, Mary Preston, Clovissa Newcombe and, of course, Ronnie Corbett and Anne Hart. Sheila O'Neill and David Toguri, two of the best dancers in London, made up the numbers. I devised and produced the shows myself, which Barry Cryer, and later Bill Solly and Bryan Blackburn, wrote for me. They all did a splendid job. We had people queuing up to join the company and, over the next eight years, we had some marvellous people on board, like Peter Gordeno, Cheryl Kennedy, Rod McLennan, Jenny Logan and David Ellen, whom Freddie Carpenter discovered in pantomime in Edinburgh in 1966. He has been my leading man ever since.

On the night the crowd from Winston's left the Clifford Street club to join me at Hanover Square, they organized a big farewell party for themselves at the club immediately following the cabaret. Unfortunately just before they were due to celebrate, the place erupted like a Western movie. Tables were turned over, bottles smashed, chairs hurled through the air as a full-scale fracas ensued. Barry Cryer and the rest of the company just crept out unseen. It was an inauspicious ending.

It had been my original intention to open Danny La Rue's on St Patrick's Day, 17 March 1964, but it just wasn't possible. Instead, we opened a few days later on a Saturday night in March. I can remember it was very cold. We had two opening nights and both were packed with celebrities. At one, Alma Cogan brought the Beatles along, and they had to stand, I just didn't have a table for them. I knew then we were on to a winner. They patronized the club regularly. One night Lord Snowdon's mother, the Countess of Rosse, asked: 'Who's that man with the hook-nose?' It was Ringo Starr.

Within weeks, we were the talk of the town, and packed every night. If you were ever in London, you had to go to Danny La Rue's, if you could get in, of course, and before long, the club established me internationally *without* ever travelling. All the visiting celebrities from all over the world were brought to my club. It was fashionable. The Americans loved me, they had nothing quite like me back home in the States.

Besides attracting a wide clientele, it also became the place where members of the show-business profession went to relax after a show, in safety and in comfort. They knew that if anybody had a few drinks too many, and made a fool of themselves, *we* would protect them. We were fellow pros and we prided ourselves in that, *and* giving good value for money. Our prices for food and drink were very reasonable. We charged a pound entrance fee, although members of the profession came in free. We also had a nominal membership subscription and, within a few years, we had attracted over 13,000 members. Admission to our New Year's Eve function had to be by ballot.

Danny La Rue's became successful for one very good reason. It was the only club of its kind where Betty Smith from Harrow-on-the-Hill could sit next to Betty Grable from Beverly Hills, or Diana Dors, or Ginger Rogers, and that was so important to me. I didn't want the club to become exclusive to one breed of society. With my Irish background, and my sense of struggle, I never took anything for granted and I wanted to share my success with everyone. The club played host to members of Europe's royal families as well as families from Royal Tunbridge Wells and the suburbs. It had a magic atmosphere and an appeal all of its own. Strangely enough, everything came together as one: it was the right time at the right place.

The early sixties saw the emergence of a whole generation of new performers who revolutionized show business and, in many cases, quite rightly. But they aimed for street credibility, which offended a lot of people. We retained the glamour, the glitter and the razzmatazz of show business and helped people to escape from the reality of a troubled world, at the same time giving them a bloody good belly laugh. We also gave dignity back to the sixties at a time when society was in danger of running riot. Besides, it was one of the few nightclubs in London where you could go and not see brassy girls strutting around flashing their tits in your face.

Several other things helped to get us established. Peter Hepple, who is now editor of the profession's trade newspaper, the *Stage*, had been a friend of mine from the days at Churchill's. He had followed my career from the Irving Theatre and had been very supportive, writing articles and reviews for various publications over the years. He was very knowledgeable about London's late-night club and cabaret scene, so I asked him if he would look after the public relations side of the business and promote the club through the media. The press had always been very good to me in the past. Peter agreed and did a very professional job. He helped to launch the club and invited many of his colleagues from Fleet Street to our opening nights.

Ramsden Gregg, from the *Evening Standard*, got so drunk he couldn't review the show, and had to return on the Monday. He was very apologetic, and guaranteed a glowing piece in his newspaper the following day. He kept his word. It wasn't a very long piece, but it was there none the less, and it all helped. *The Sunday Times* did a superb four-page colour spread on the club in their magazine supplement within six months of opening, in which they proclaimed: 'Through sheer force of talent, amiability and business acumen, Danny La Rue has succeeded in making drag respectable.' I hate the word *respectable*, it's a very bad hangover from Victorian days, but it all kept the momentum going.

Shortly afterwards, Peter Hepple arranged for the club to be featured on networked television in a documentary series called *Tempo*, made by ABC Television, which projected us nationwide. The show went out on a Sunday afternoon and gained enormous publicity.

It was through Peter that I first met Princess Margaret. He had been introduced to Sir Harry Shiffner, who was involved with the Dockland Settlements of which Princess Margaret was patron, and asked him if he would help provide some artistes to appear at their annual ball at the Savoy Hotel. Peter suggested me. Sir Harry hadn't heard of me, but was amenable to the suggestion. The next thing I knew was that Princess Margaret was intrigued to see me so, instead of me doing a solo spot, we arranged to take the whole show there and hired a special mini-bus to carry us all. It was worth it. The show was a big success and Princess Margaret became a very good friend *and* came to my club on many occasions.

One night, I was just about to start the cabaret when Jack came backstage very insistent that I shouldn't go on yet, and that the show be held for a few minutes longer. 'We've a party of VIPs coming in shortly,' he said. 'Please don't go on yet, only a few more minutes.'

I waited a little longer. We always kept to the same format. The company opened the show, and then introduced me and I joined them on stage. We were supposed to start at one fifteen and by one thirty I was getting restless.

'I'm not waiting any longer,' I told Jack and gave instructions for the revue to start. The room was packed. The audience had been waiting for a long time. It was bad manners to go up late.

So we opened the show slightly behind time. Just as I joined the company on stage, I noticed through the darkness, a party of people picking their way to a table.

'Good evening,' I said and waved to a lady in the party. 'Sorry, darling, I didn't recognize you with your clothes on.' The place fell apart. I got a huge wave of laughter and applause.

As I came off stage, Jack was waiting for me.

'That went well,' I said.

'Yes,' he said, '*hysterical*. Do you know who that was you were talking to?'

'No.'

'Princess Margaret.'

It was her first visit to the club, but certainly *not* her last. I was invited to join her at her table after the show and found her humorous, witty and highly intelligent. But you always knew you were in the presence of a princess. I think she would have made a wonderful performer in other circumstances; she seemed a natural for the stage. She became a great fan.

The Princess and her party always used to come into the club through the back-door entrance, which led directly through the dressing rooms. Nightclubs are notoriously bad at providing adequate dressing room accommodation. Mine was no exception. We had two. One very small one, exclusive to me, which I shared on occasions with my dresser, Jimmy Hunt, and a communal room in which everyone else in the company changed together. It was nicknamed 'Night Train to Munich'.

One night, there was a tap on the outside door. It was Bryan Forbes and his wife, Nanette Newman, Peter Sellers, and Princess Margaret and party. We weren't expecting her. The door was opened and the Princess made her way gingerly through the changing bodies in various stages of undress, and passed various pleasantries with the company before asking if I was in my room.

I was totally unaware of what was going on. My door was shut and I was attempting to get ready for the night's show. Jimmy Hunt was waiting outside, almost on guard. When he saw Princess Margaret going through the ranks, he hammered on my door violently, and shouted in a loud whisper, hoping only I would hear him: 'Danny, it's Princess Margaret. Quick.'

'Piss off,' I called back, and threw open the door to see what was going on, only to come face to face with the Princess. I was naked.

'Hello, ma'am,' I said, not knowing whether to bow, curtsey, or cover myself up. She was charming, as usual.

We met again at several royal functions. She worked so hard – still does – and I admire her tremendously.

I was appearing in the autumn show at the Coventry Theatre once when I was invited to attend a dinner in aid of Barnado's, of which Princess Margaret is President. When I arrived, she made a High Sheriff move from her table so that I could sit next to her. After dinner, there was a charity auction to raise money for the cause, and Her Royal Highness admitted to me that she found it very boring. 'What we need are a few laughs,' she said. 'You go and do it.' A royal summons if ever there was one. So I did.

One of the items on offer was a photographic session with a local photographer. As I was about to auction the lot, I said: 'I'm not actually allowed to tell you who the photographer will be. It's hush-hush.' Everyone thought it was Lord Snowdon, and I made a small fortune for that particular item. Princess Margaret said she admired my resourcefulness.

I later had a marvellous session of my own with Lord Snowdon. It was for a spread in *Vogue*, and he photographed me brilliantly as Marlene Dietrich. You would never have known the difference.

Princess Margaret and Lord Snowdon came to the club to celebrate their wedding anniversary. I was flattered that they should grace my club on such a notable occasion. Whenever royalty was in, I made it a rule never to have a photographer on hand. But, on this occasion, someone had secreted a camera into the club, and took a picture that intimated Lord Snowdon was on his own on his wedding anniversary. It made the front page of a Sunday newpaper with a suitably snide caption. Lord Snowdon was offended. He knew I had nothing to do with it, he knew my ruling, but I still had a lot of explaining to do.

Princess Margaret was just one of many members of royalty who honoured me with their presence at my club. We became quite prestigious.

One evening Louis, my *maître d'hôtel*, tapped on my dressing-room door to tell me King Hussein of Jordan was in the audience and wanted to see me. I was a long way from being dressed and ready to receive royalty. I only had a sweater and a pair of slacks with me and felt improperly dressed to meet a king. So I told Louis to offer my apologies and say I would be with His Royal Highness in five minutes, giving me time to get changed into something more suitable.

Ten minutes later there was another tap at the door. It was King Hussein himself. I was embarrassed. 'If the mountain won't come to Muhammad,' he said, 'then Muhammad must come to the mountain.' He was an enchanting man, which the world must know judging by his diplomatic endeavours over the years.

Princess Grace of Monaco was a dear lady. She had a joyous belly laugh that filled the club. She always sat at the same table in the corner and used to explode with laughter at the jokes. I met Prince Rainier and Princess Grace at a party given by Paul Gallico at his home in Antibes in the south of France, with Billie More, who later brought them to Hanover Square. Paul was a great friend and host and introduced me to Their Royal Highnesses with whom I became very close. They wanted me to go to the palace in Monaco in November 1968 to celebrate the Princess's fortieth birthday, but I reluctantly had to decline because it would have meant travelling by air, and at that time I still hadn't flown. I think the Prince was slightly upset by my refusal. However, on one occasion when I was in the south of France on holiday, I received a royal invitation to take tea with the Princess. When I arrived at the palace, I fully expected to be shot at any minute. It was a very grand place. I had an escort of a dozen ceremonial guards in full dress uniform and plumes to meet me. I was ushered through the gates in double-quick time. Princess Grace was waiting for me and I was taken up to her room by lift. She was absolutely enthralling. We spoke for hours and she was very interested in everything I was doing and we talked and talked about the business; it was the old show-business trouper coming out in her.

Prince Rainier had seen me in my West End pantomine, *Queen Passionella and the Sleeping Beauty*, at the Saville Theatre in 1969, and had come to my dressing room after a performance. While we were talking, the telephone rang, I excused myself and answered it. It was Millicent Martin, who wanted to come backstage, too, to meet me. I explained my predicament to His Royal Highness and he was very understanding. 'I've seen her on television many times,' he said in his perfect English. 'Please let her come, I'd like to meet her, too.'

When Millie arrived, she was with two American friends, and I made hasty introductions. We were chatting, drinking champagne, and generally getting on well together when I noticed one of the Americans sidle up to Prince Rainier.

'Your face is very familiar,' he said to the Prince. 'I'm sure I've seen you on television somewhere – you're a famous actor aren't you? I can't quite place the name.'

I was horrified and so embarrassed for the Prince, and moved in quickly to rescue the situation immediately.

'I'm sorry,' I said. 'My introductions must have been garbled. Let me start again.' I turned to the American. 'This is His Royal Highness Prince Rainier of Monaco . . .'

The poor man sagged at the knees and went paler and paler. He reached for a chair to support himself in his total embarrassment. If the ground had opened up, he would have willingly leapt head first into the crevice to get away. Millie went hysterical; Prince Rainier burst out laughing.

'Don't be embarrassed, please,' he said. 'I was very flattered to think you thought I was a famous actor.' He smiled reassuringly. A lovely man.

Royalty definitely had a soft spot for the club. We would often be visited by Arabian princes with exotic names and sheikhs, whose personal fortunes from the oil revenue ran into millions. One sheikh turned up at the club in a massive limousine with a real live panther sprawled across the back seat.

Religion forbade many of them to consume alcohol, so I served them milk instead, in champagne glasses, from an ice bucket. They insisted on paying champagne prices for their drinks, which they were charged in all the other West End nightclubs as a matter of course. I wouldn't think of it. I made them pay only the current rate for a bottle of milk which was eight pence. They returned in kind by sending champagne to the company. One thing I would never do was fake or fiddle. Each one of the sheikhs who was served with milk was fabulously rich beyond compare and money made no difference to them, but it did to me, and they respected me for it.

Soon after the club's opening, I got a frantic telephone call from Joan Littlewood. I was in the bath at the time, so Jack Hanson took the call. It was six o'clock in the evening. *Oh What a Lovely War* had only recently opened at Wyndham's Theatre, but was already a huge success. That particular evening, however, Avis Bunnage, who was appearing in the show, had been taken ill and couldn't go on. Joan wanted *me* to take her place and sing an old music hall number. The curtain was due up in two hours. I held the conversation through Jack and told her I couldn't possibly do it, not in the time, I didn't even know the show or the song in question.

'Don't worry,' she insisted, 'you'll be marvellous as usual. The record's on its way to you by taxi and you can always ad lib if you forget the words. See you about seven.'

While I shaved and hastily got ready, Jack played the song, 'On Monday I Went Out with a Soldier', over and over again in the time available. At eight o'clock that evening, I went on stage unannounced and sang the song word-perfect . . . and added one or two lines of my own for good measure. I appeared in two further performances until Avis returned, by which time news had spread in the profession and all the staff from neighbouring theatres would creep into Wyndham's just to watch me perform. A great compliment from the business and a unique situation for a man to take over a woman's part. It was the forerunner, in a way, to a much more substantial female role I would play on the West End stage in a few years time.

Joan Littlewood was a great admirer of mine, and I had a lot of respect and love for her. Her theatre at Stratford East from where *Oh What a Lovely War* originated, was really a form of cabaret. Several members from my companies appeared there, including Victor Spinetti, Toni Palmer and Barbara Windsor.

We introduced an innovation to Danny La Rue's. Saturday night became 'family night' in an effort to attract the family audiences to clubland, which had always been one of my intentions when I first opened the club. It was unheard of in the West End, but I don't think anything has touched its success before or since. We encouraged birthday nights and anniversary parties.

Cilla Black brought her parents in one night and, at the start of the show, I introduced her to the audience from the stage. Cilla later told me it made her parents' night that their daughter had been recognized in a posh West End nightclub. Towards the end of my act, Cilla's dad leant over to Cilla's husband, Bobby, and pointed to the stage. 'Don't tell the girls,' he whispered, 'but that girl on stage is really a *man*.'

When Liza Minelli was engaged to Peter Allen, in 1966, she held her party at my club. I liked Liza very much indeed, a great talent – but there could never be anyone to touch, or compare with her mother, Judy Garland, whom I idolized.

We had been friends since the days of Winston's and we adored each other. She was a one-off. Nobody has matched the talent of Judy. For me, of all the stars, of all the women I have known, I think she was the greatest of them all. She had everything. She could tear your heart out with a song; she was a great actress and a wonderful comedienne. But she was so vulnerable. When she smiled, the room lit up and glowed.

Judy was a frequent visitor to the club. One night I introduced her from the stage during the show and took the microphone over and offered it to her to sing a few bars. She ended up singing three complete numbers, while I just sat down at her table and let her get on with it. It was wonderful to watch such a great artiste perform. Another time, we were presenting a musical version of *Hello Dolly* on stage, and Judy went crazy over the red dress I wore. She just had to try it on after the show. She was so tiny, it swamped her, and there was this little head sticking sheepishly out of a great mountain of material. But Judy was like that, she loved the carabet and would often join in with the finale.

One evening, while performing a musical tribute to Garland, when Toni Palmer came on stage to sing 'The Trolley Song', within seconds of the orchestra striking up the first few bars, she was joined on stage by Judy Garland and Liza Minelli, and they finished the number between them. Sensational.

Yet there were some tragic moments, too. Judy came into the club one night looking very drunk – although I didn't think she was well – and she did something she would never have done in normal circum-stances. We were in the middle of a number when she walked straight across the floor in front of us and stopped. Her make-up was running and she had been crying. A lady at the front table burst into tears. I think she had an illusion shattered. She could remember Judy singing 'Somewhere Over the Rainbow'; she had remembered the glamorous star of so many movies, and here was someone who looked so pitiful. She did look a mess: her tights were ripped and bedraggled and her make-up was appalling. She had actually made up her face from a tin of child's paints at a friend's home, which had blistered her lips. She was like a child herself, she looked no more than twelve years old. When she staggered into the club, I was on stage in the middle of a Gibson Girl routine, wearing a heavy black velvet outfit and large picture hat, but I bent down with great difficulty and picked her up in my arms. She was then like a sparrow. She used to fluctuate from being tubby one minute to being on a crash diet. I carried her backstage to the dressing room where we had to scrub her face and generally clean her up. I sat her on the dressing-room table and told her to be a good girl and to stay there. She did, for over two hours, chatting to the boys and girls in the show. Like me, they, too, were captivated.

I found Judy Garland utterly irresistible and quite charming. Sometimes she could be irritating, but there has never been a talent like hers. She made so many comebacks, but when you are emotionally disturbed, your career must suffer. Her talent *never* went downhill; she abused her talent.

Towards the end, she told me she had become too frightened to go on stage. The last time I saw her performing was at the Talk of the Town in 1969. By then, she had started to fall apart. We all went to the first night. The show was supposed to start at eleven, but didn't. The place was packed with people who adored her. The audience was on her side from the start but, after an hour of waiting for her to appear, even their patience ran dry and they started to slow handclap.

When the show eventually started, Judy came on looking pale and drawn. She was agitated and walked round the stage a couple of times and then dried up. When she saw me, she came over and knelt down beside me. 'Danny, help me, I can't go on,' she whispered, but she had forgotten the microphone was still on and the audience had heard every word. Judy was in another world. 'Help me, Danny, please.' I had recently recorded 'On Mother Kelly's Doorstep', which was proving a big success for me, so I climbed up on stage and told the musical director, Burt Rhodes, to play the song in B flat. Judy sat on the stage watching as I performed and got the audience to sing along with me. It gave her valuable breathing time to compose herself. When I had finished, she picked up the microphone and carried on as if nothing had happened . . . and was marvellous. But, unfortunately, during that season she started to crumble completely. She was found dead shortly afterwards.

Garland was a Hollywood legend, and my club attracted the great movie stars from all over the world. Every night it was a case of 'spot the faces'. Gregory Peck, Peter Ustinov and Curt Jurgens were big fans and popped in from time to time; Yul Brynner had fantastic magnetism, but I was surprised at how small he was in real life. I'd seen him so many times in movies that I expected a giant. Natalie Wood came along in plaster after breaking a foot, while Phyllis Diller was just as zany offstage as she was on. She was so taken with me that she almost pleaded with me to go to America to work. 'You'll be so sensational,' she said. 'A huge, huge star.'

There were many others – Ginger Rogers was divine, Shirley Mac-Laine and Ann-Margret were both enchanting. Sammy Davis Junior would come in and buy everyone a bottle of Dom Perignom champagne, which certainly wasn't cheap. He came backstage afterwards, and chatted the night away. He loved to be amongst pros. Debbie Reynolds came to the club many times. I liked her so much because, of all the many film stars I knew, she was a very practical worker, and a very good professional. She came from the same school as Judy Garland – the hard grafters, the Hollywood slog. You chatted away and then you realized exactly what they must have gone through for their art. It took great guts and dedication. On one occasion we had to turn Lee Marvin away because he came along to the club with a crowd of men. It wasn't that kind of club, but he was very gracious and understood. The following evening, he came back with a mixed party.

I remember Lena Horne turning up one night without booking, and we couldn't accommodate her because she had brought a party of six people with her. I felt so embarrassed, but she, too, took it in good faith and booked for the next night. Before she returned the following evening, two dozen red roses arrived from her with a note saying how pleased she was I was so successful. Throughout my career, I have found that the really talented people are so very nice. It's the also-rans whom I have found to be difficult.

I adored Vivien Leigh, she was one of Noël Coward's favourites. She was like a delicate piece of fine china. I sent her masses of flowers when she was ill and ironically received a special thank-you card from her on the very day her death was announced.

Hedda Hopper and Claudette Colbert both agreed I was like a modern-day Julian Eltinge, who was one of the greatest female impersonators of the century. He was another great original – a one-off. He appeared on Broadway for the first time in 1903 and three years later played a season in London at, of all places, the Palace Theatre. He later gave a command performance for King Edward VII at Windsor. For many years, he starred in his own shows which were specially written for his unique talent. In 1910, he had a theatre built and named after him in New York, which is something that appeals to me tremendously.

The zany Carol Channing, who became another one of the special ladies in my act, used to bring her own food and drink into the club. She would only eat food she had prepared herself. I believe she was on a macrobiotic diet, and only ever drank a special kind of mineral water. Carol was a stately lady who was lovable and fascinating. Often when I was in costume, many people thought we looked very similar. When she came to Drury Lane to star in her *Ten Stout-Hearted Men* revue, she was often stopped in the streets and mistaken for me. She took it in good heart.

In November 1972, I was lucky enough to be chosen to appear in the Royal Variety Performance at the London Palladium, and Carol was on the bill with me. She was waiting in the wings ready to go out on stage when Arthur Askey appeared from out of the shadows of the dimly-lit backstage area. He crept up behind her, and deliberately pinched her bum. 'Wotcha, mates,' he shouted, and beamed broadly. He thought it was *me*. Carol spun round quickly and simply said: 'You're a funny little fella.' Poor Arthur didn't know what to do with himself. He dined out on the story, however, for several years afterwards. So did Carol.

Bette Davis made me mad. She came into the club one evening and was very rude. She talked and made a terrible racket throughout the cabaret, although *not* when I was appearing on stage. Her behaviour was disgraceful for such a grand lady of the cinema. She was so outrageous that Peter Woodthorpe, a well-known British television actor, went up to her table afterwards and told her how disgusted he was with her as a professional. He had never seen behaviour like it. He had been a devoted, lifelong fan of hers, but no more. She was now off his list. I was fuming, too.

The next day, the phone rang in my dressing room, and Jimmy Hunt, my dresser, who was a devoted Bette Davis fan as well, took the call and when he realized it was her on the other end, he nearly fainted. He looked at me.

'It's Bette Davis, for you,' he said.

'Tell her I'm not in,' I fumed. 'I'm not taking any calls.'

'But . . . But . . . I can't say that to *her*,' he replied. 'It's *Bette Davis*.'

'I know,' I said. 'Then I *will*.'

I grabbed the phone: 'This is Danny La Rue speaking, Miss Davis. I'm not in.' I put down the receiver.

Lauren Bacall later told me Bette Davis thought she had upset me. 'Bloody right,' I said. 'I don't care what she thinks of me, but she was very rude to my company. When I am working, my company is my show and everyone of my colleagues gets the same respect I do. She is a star, she should know better.'

We made up later because I gave in and talked to her again, which was gentlemanly of me, but I don't think she realized that she had done anything wrong.

It was not only movie stars who came into the club. Robert Kennedy came in one evening and we met briefly, and so, too, did Ladybird Johnson. We had a large contingency of sportsmen as well. After England won the World Cup in 1966, several of the players came in to celebrate their famous victory.

Topolski, the world-famous artist came in one night. I was an enormous admirer of this brilliant man, so it was a great coup when he turned up at my club.

After the show, my *maître d'hôtel*, Mr Lovis, came up to me fuming. He was furious.

'That Mr Topolski has ruined two of our best tablecloths,' he said. I was puzzled. 'All through the show, he was drawing you on the tablecloth. And when he had finished, he asked for another one.'

It was a great honour, I thought. The man was such an erratic artist, and I was flattered and delighted to know that Topolski had been moved to draw me as I worked, in a moment of inspiration. I wondered excitedly how he had captured me, how he had seen me, and asked for the two tableclothes in question.

'He ruined them,' said the *maître d'hôtel*. 'So I sent them to the laundry.' I'll never know what he saw, it all went in the wash.

One of our regular customers was a very rich businessman from the north of England. I think he was a butcher. He seemed to come in virtually every other week and enjoyed himself immensely. He laughed so much at one sketch that he lost his false teeth. David Ellen and I were on stage trying to continue the sketch and all we could hear from the audience was, 'Eeeeee. I've lost me fuckin' teeth,' which he said at the top of his voice so that everyone in the club could hear it. In the meantime, he was on the floor and on his hands and knees searching for his dentures. The laughter went on for five minutes, and David and I couldn't continue because the audience was captivated by the man. He came back two weeks later, and the same thing happened again. But he wasn't the only one. Howard Marian-Crawford, the famous British actor, fell asleep one night and his teeth dropped out on to his plate.

Unlike Winston's and several other London clubs, we never had any trouble, everyone behaved themselves impeccably. People came in to see the show and to be entertained, and not to cause trouble. There were never any villains or gangland characters in the club. They stayed away, but sent their wives along instead.

However, we *were* raided one night. It was a terribly embarrassing experience. Without warning, the police descended upon the club after someone had tipped them off there might be drugs on the premises. They found nothing; there was nothing to find anyway. Everything we did was strictly legitimate and above board. It was all very inconvenient because everyone on the premises had to be searched and give their names and addresses to the police. After they had gone, and the show started, every policeman gag in the business came out, and got a huge laugh. I don't know to this day who set the raid up, but Jack believed it was a rival club owner, jealous of our enormous success.

Shortly after the incident, I arrived home at my flat in Maida Vale to find the police waiting for me. They had been tipped off again, and this time I was accused of harbouring one of the Great Train Robbers. The police were totally embarrassed about the whole affair, but told me they had to follow up reports. I got marvellous publicity the next morning when the story hit the newspapers.

Ronnie Corbett and I did a very funny parody on Margot Fonteyn and Rudolph Nureyev. It was a show-stopper, and people used to request we put the number in the show. It was that popular. I was Margot Bunting, Ronnie was Rudolph Nearenough. I had been a friend and fan of Dame Margot for a number of years, and she came to the club on a couple of occasions, once with her husband, Roberto Arias, and another time with Nureyev himself.

One day, she made a very special request. She wanted to hire Danny La Rue's to throw a party for the visiting Australian Ballet. It was something I was not very fond of doing, and rarely let the club for private functions. But Margot was different, and one Thursday evening we put on our cabaret parody for the great stars of the ballet. Rudolph Nureyev, who couldn't speak very good English, was one of the guests, and in honour of his presence, Doug Fisher, who spoke fluent Russian, introduced the show in Rudy's native tongue. It was the only time he laughed at the jokes in the right places. When the cabaret started, a little man would lean over to Rudolph Nureyev and translate all the jokes and parodies from the English into Russian just for him and he would laugh out loud, fifteen to twenty seconds after everyone else. It was a cabaret in itself just watching him. Rudolph Nureyev became a good friend and he once said he would have loved me to play the part of an Ugly Sister with him at Covent Garden.

Cabaret at Danny La Rue's was the high spot of the evening. Indeed, the shows became the best in town. We extended the revue tradition of Winston's and took the whole idea much further. The shows were slicker, funnier and certainly more glamorous and spectacular.

We staged four shows a year and, in each new show, I presented an even more glamorous line-up of lavish outfits, which were created for me, initially by Berman's, and later by a young designer called Mark Canter. On opening night of a new show at Danny La Rue's, there were queues in the street, with people almost fighting to get in. Afterwards, the audiences went potty, standing up, cheering, whistling. Barry Cryer once described the shows we presented at the club as 'filthy, but beautifully phrased'. It was all irresistible fun, in the true tradition of British music hall, bawdy vulgarity, littered with innuendo, double meanings and everything thrown in for good measure. But it was never smutty, or dirty, or snide. No one ever found it obscene. I knew my audience and played directly to them. I once told a very eminent man of the cloth: 'I don't sing hymns in nightclubs.'

Some of our parodies were totally over the top, but always very funny. Whatever came into fashion or vogue got the La Rue treatment: James Bond, Sonny and Cher – Ronnie Corbett was Sonny, I was Cher – the Avengers, Swinging London. We did ladies throughout history: I was Nell Gwynne, Lady Hamilton, Carmen, Madam Butterfly. And we tackled the classics, too, with Ronnie Corbett playing Napoleon to my Josephine, Othello to my Desdemona, and Caesar to my Cleopatra. We staged our own version of *Hamlet*, with me in the title role and Ronnie playing Ophelia, complete with Teddy Bear and bedroom slippers, and also *The Fall of the Roman Empire*:

POPITINEA: 'Will you buy a ticket for Nero's Ball?'

GLADYS: 'Sorry, I don't dance.'

POPITINEA: 'It's not a dance, it's a raffle.'

We used a lot of Lionel Bart's numbers for our parodies, mercilessly plundering his songbook to re-write his lyrics. But Lionel loved it, he thought some of our lyrics were better than his own.

I had quite a moving experience with Lionel Bart once when he was arrested on a drugs charge. I rang him up, it seemed the natural thing to do. 'It's strange,' said Lionel, 'we have never been close, but you are one of only two people who have telephoned to see if they can help me.'

When he had made his fortune, he was a very kind man to the profession, too kind possibly. As my mother used to say, he was a fool unto himself.

My 'ladies' were never forgotten. Indeed, they developed grandly and graciously, and flourished at my club. It was my own special showcase. Carmen Miranda was always one of my great characters with whom I could have lots of fun and go totally over the top. I never knew the lady, sadly, but I have had hours of pleasure with her over the years, in the nicest possible way. Although on one occasion, she became a disaster.

We were featuring a mardi gras, carnival-type Carmen Miranda number in one show and I had a superb costume for the song: a marvellous head-dress festooned with about three tons of fruit, a very tight pencil-slim skirt, and nine-inch high platform shoes. I'd captured the whole essence of Carmen Miranda to perfection. The entire illusion was fabulously bizarre, but the outfit was completely impractical.

As the music started up in its Latin American way, the chug-along rhythm and beat, I tried to get on to the stage, misjudged my step and came crashing down on to the floor flat on my face, in full view of the audience. I looked like an upturned greengrocer's barrow. The trouble was, with such an elaborate and tight costume, I couldn't get up again without help. Jenny Logan, Toni Palmer and David Ellen were on stage at the time, having hysterics as they saw this huge basket of fruit coming towards them on all fours, with Ronnie Corbett coming behind trying to help me up. It was hilarious. There was absolutely nothing that could be done except for me to go off stage, fruit first, and get help. But we carried on as if nothing had happened, crying with laughter. I'm sure the audience thought it was just part of the act. Ronnie's face was a picture.

The character of Lady Cynthia Grope was born at Danny La Rue's. She emerged as an aristocratic cross between Lady Dartmouth (now Lady Spencer) and her mother, Barbara Cartland. They were both good friends of mine, too, which helped. They were both political women in the background, so Bryan Blackburn and Barry Cryer thought it would be a good idea to have a fictitious woman – a Hory Tostess or Tory Hostess – who commented on the state of the country.

She gave us our political satire: 'Life's much better under the Tories and I should know. Harold Wilson's worried about the swing to the right. I told him to change his tailor immediately.'

She became a very popular character, slightly bluer than her own political persuasion.

CYNTHIA: 'I love Royal Ascot. Last time I shared a box with the Duke of Nuneaton.'

DAVID: 'Did he have a hot tip for you?'

CYNTHIA: 'No, it was a very cold day.'

DAVID: 'Is he a betting man?'

CYNTHIA: 'Yes, he likes a bit each way.'

When Margaret Thatcher came along, we had our own ready-made political character without having to invent one.

The climax to each night of cabaret was the finale, which took the form of a fabulous musical tribute to a star. We did the Beatles, Noël Coward, Lionel Bart, Judy Garland, and many others. At the end of each show, I always appeared on stage as myself, in a suit, or dinner jacket, or tails, out of make-up and my 'working clothes'. I still do. It is essential for the whole illusion I have created as a woman to work. I have only changed the rules once, when I appeared in *Hello, Dolly!*.

After one show I joined a party of elegant ladies, all ex-debs.

'Do you enjoy dressing up as a lady?' said one of them.

'No, dear,' I replied. 'Do you?' I think she had missed the whole point of the act.

When I was on stage, Jack, who looked after the club so well, would sit at a table in the corner of the room and watch the show. He used to have the habit of nodding off at odd moments. He just fell asleep. He did it regularly at dinner to a point where it was amusing, though, at one stage, I got quite worried, wondering if it was some kind of illness. At the club, however, he used to fall asleep usually halfway through my act. Sometimes you could never tell whether he was asleep because he had a way of propping up his glasses at the end of his nose, which gave the appearance he was wide awake, and concentrating intensely. But I could tell. Halfway through a sketch, I used to look up at the audience to see if the glasses were perched on Jack's nose. If they were, I'd bellow: 'Wake up, Jack.' It worked every time . . . Fond memories.

My mother loved the cabaret and visited the club often. I have one very happy memory which stands above all others – the night Pete Murray, Liberace and I waltzed with our mothers on the dance floor. It was a magic moment. Of course, Liberace was never out of the club when he was in London. We had so much in common: professionally, we both had the ability to laugh at ourselves and we always joked about it. We also worked together on several occasions, on late-night radio or television shows. After one such appearance, Lee insisted on taking me to see a house he was thinking of buying, somewhere in Knightsbridge. It was a strange building and had eerie murals painted on the ceiling, which I felt might be connected in some way with black magic. I was very uncomfortable and sensed evil. Four of us congregated at the house, with a few bottles of champagne and, after a few minutes, I left the main party to explore a rather ornate minstrels' gallery. I went upstairs, chatting to my friends down below, when somebody tugged violently at my jacket. I turned round, but there was no one there. All my friends were downstairs. It happened again. But still no one. I didn't like the place at all.

We left shortly afterwards and Liberace eventually decided not to go ahead and buy the property, which was a great relief to me. However, a few months later, I heard that Richard Harris had bought it. The next time he came into the club, I sought him out and told him that Liberace and I had looked at the place he had recently purchased. He looked me straight in the eye.

'I know what you're going to ask me,' he said. 'You want to know about the little bastards.'

Richard told me they had been a terrible nuisance to him when he first moved in. The tugging at my jacket was mild in comparison. They had almost driven him mad. So he decided to investigate the phenomenon and located a room where the feeling was at its strongest. Then he went out to a nearby shop and bought some toys which he threw into the empty room in question. 'Now play with these and leave me alone,' he shouted. They did! The Irish actor had found out that the house was built on the site of a children's home which had been destroyed by fire and many of the children had perished in the flames.

Danny La Rue's had only been open a few years, but it had become a roaring success. So much so that it allowed me the luxury of buying my first Rolls-Royce. I moved house, too, from Elgin Mansions to Prince Albert Road, overlooking Regent's Park, and later on to

Hampstead. I also bought a weekend home by the sea in Shoreham. But my partner, David Lowes, wasn't happy with the situation and called a meeting. He was a very honest man.

'I am taking money and I am not doing anything to earn it,' he said. 'Maybe it's time I left.'

We agreed on a suitable figure, and Jack and I bought out his share in the club. David retired graciously. It was now ours completely. David later took over a club himself, called United Hunts, which was a gentlemen's establishment catering for lunches. But Jack and I were very grateful to him for helping us to get the club off the ground. Without his help, it would certainly have been a different story.

The success of the club didn't deter me from pursuing other things in show business. Christmas wouldn't have been the same without my pantomimes, but I chose the locations very carefully within easy access of London to allow me the time to commute from theatre to club each night, so that I wouldn't miss a cabaret performance. No matter whatever else I did, I was committed to the club: it existed because of Danny La Rue. People came to see Danny La Rue and it was essential I was there at all times to play mine host and entertain. Its success was built on that philosophy. No one else could do it.

At the same time, though, I also felt a need to diversify my talent into other directions. I wanted to do everything. I have always taken on too many things at once, but it is part of my make-up. I have tremendous energy which needs to be channelled.

In 1964, Alan Haynes and I appeared together again in *Cinderella* at the New Theatre, Oxford, with Des O'Connor as Buttons. I had twenty-two changes of costume, twice-daily. I arrived at the theatre by Rolls-Royce and I had no trouble making my late-night appearances in town. The following year, we were booked on the doorstep, at the Golders Green Hippodrome. Dickie Henderson, who also starred as Buttons, was on a percentage of the overall box office take. I was second top, on a salary. For the first time, I had separate billing to Alan Haynes. He was marvellous about it. At the end of the run, Dickie presented me with a lovely clock, thanking me for his percentage, which was a most generous thing to do.

For nearly nine years, I lived a double existence, combining late-night cabaret appearances at my club with television and theatre engagements during the day, which culminated in 1970 with my own West End show at the Palace Theatre and gave me one of the biggest triumphs of my entire career. But it was so frantic. I didn't have a holiday for nine years, and many evenings I travelled back to London and the club from Brighton or Coventry, Birmingham or Margate. I rarely got to bed before five in the morning. Looking back, it was hard work, and I don't really know how I managed to do it at all. Yet, I'm proud to say, I never missed a single performance . . . though at times it was touch and go.

One night, I had been asked to appear at a charity function for the Grand Order of Water Rats in Solihull, just outside Birmingham. A splendid Austin Princess limousine had been laid on to take David Ellen and myself back to town in time for my club appearance. My dresser, Jimmy Hunt, followed behind us in another car, with the wigs and costumes. We didn't know it at the time, but the Austin Princess had only been used for funerals in the past. It certainly wasn't ready for charging down the M1 at an excessive speed.

Halfway into the journey I sensed David Ellen was agitated and asked him what was wrong. His eyes were watering, and there was a strange smell of burning coming from the back of the car. To our utter horror, we found that the bottom of the car had wooden floorboards because of the nature of its original business, and the exhaust pipe – unused to such speeds – had become so intensely hot, that the wood had started to burn. We discovered just in time. We stopped, put out the fire and then had to continue the journey back to London at a mere forty miles per hour to prevent it happening all over again.

That wasn't all . . . it was an eventful night. The car carrying Jimmy Hunt and the wigs and costumes, which was supposedly following us, broke down. So, desperate to get back to London, Jimmy decided to thumb a lift back into town. He stood by the side of the road, thumbing away, with a large suitcase in one hand, and a series of wigs on poles in the other, which, for convenience, he had stuck in the ground by the side of him. A beefcake man of a lorry driver pulled off the road for him.

'Been acting, mate?' he said.

'Yes,' replied Jimmy, 'and I've got Danny La Rue's wigs here.' The lorry driver was so impressed he took him straight to the club, even though he wasn't going in that direction at all.

And we both made it in time for the show . . . *just.*

At the beginning of 1972, however, things had become too much for me, and I was forced to take a fortnight's holiday in the south of

France, to unwind and re-charge my batteries, which were well run-down. It was here that I bought a magnificent twelve-bedroomed château called L'Hermitage St Jean, near Grasse, in the cypress-covered countryside between the mountains and the Mediterranean Sea, in the heart of the world's perfume-making centre. It was to be a holiday home, although I once toyed with the idea of converting it into a nightclub and restaurant. I knew so many people in the area that there was never a shortage of friends with whom to stay. But I really thought it would be a nice idea if I owned a house of my own there, and, with Bernard Delfont's help, I secured the splendid property, surrounded by the scent of flowers and pines, with a gorgeous backdrop of snow-capped alps, and a glittering sea at the foot of the slopes. It was idyllic. Yet, there was a major snag. I was always too busy at home ever to stay there. Elton John, who rented it from me on occasions, stayed there longer than I ever did. In the end, I fell out of love with France and sold the place.

Back in London, I was faced with a problem. Rather than close the club down completely, I handed the keys over to Larry Grayson, whom I predicted was going to be a big star. I first saw him at Stratford East and found him hilariously funny, and very original at that time. The audiences liked him, too, and he did a marvellous two weeks for me.

When he opened at Danny La Rue's my mother turned up on the first night to see him. She hadn't been very well. 'But,' she said, 'if that boy is taking over from my son, it is my duty to be there to see him.' Liberace also went to the club to see him, and came away raving. Larry was flattered, and he is the first person to acknowledge that I was instrumental in helping him to become a big star. After that season, his career really took off when Bryan Blackburn gave him his first television series. But I knew my club was in good hands right away. My company adored him.

But the era was rapidly coming to an end. When Jarvis Astair, who owned the building in which the club was sited, sold out to property developers, the future looked very bleak. They moved in quickly and wanted me out as fast as possible. It was a valuable piece of property for development, a prime West End site. I tried to keep it on for as long as I could, but I was always fighting a losing battle. The company in question had planning permission already, and time to them meant money. But I was lucky. I had a remaining lease with time to run, so I had to be bought out for a substantial fee. I wasn't giving in easily. The irony of it all was that permission for re-development for the site was later withdrawn, and it wasn't renewed until my original lease had long expired. By then, I'd been paid off. In the end there were only two of us left in the building, me and a little old Jewish tailor.

To be fair, the property developers did offer me premises in their new building for a new club, but I turned them down. I knew I couldn't create the same success again. When it was known that Danny La Rue's was closing, I had several major offers from West End night-club owners, all offering me partnerships in their clubs for *nothing*.

We shut down the club with a huge wake, and went out with a roar. I had a week of closing nights where tickets were as scarce as for an FA Cup Final. We ended with the same emotionalism and crowds as when we opened. We finished to capacity business, too.

The door finally closed on Saturday, 18 March 1972. The party was well and truly over and there would never be another one quite like it. As one newspaper put it: 'Danny La Rue's will certainly go down in history as one of the most famous clubs of the century.'

7

'Every inch a star, every other inch a lady'

Success can be frightening. A lot of people have been ripped apart, or destroyed completely, by success, particularly if it has come quickly or unexpectedly. They simply can't cope with it all.

I was very lucky. My own rise to stardom was solid, gradual. I was no overnight star made in the best traditions of Hollywood, earning a fiver one week and £10,000 the next. It took a long time. I have always been the most surprised at the way it all happened. I honestly never thought I would be a star. For that reason, I am never frightened of toppling off the pedestal. I climbed up a long staircase, and I learnt how to hold on to the banisters. It will take an awful lot to push me down.

I served an arduous and lengthy apprenticeship, learning my trade the hard way from the inside, packing in experience that couldn't be bought, but which has proved so valuable. Lord Olivier calls it 'paying your dues'. My background also helped me to keep my feet on the ground. My career was built on hard work, my own high standards and the utmost professionalism. I have retained a great love and respect for my profession and I have never taken anything for granted. My approach to my work has been positive and I have appreciated everything that has come my way.

Although I was in control of my own career, my manager, Jack Hanson, was always a vital controlling force.

Once my nightclub had established itself, I took stock of my career and determined that I should try to broaden out, to reach the widest possible audience I could, hopefully not just in London, but throughout the country. I also wanted to prove to myself as much as anyone that there was much more to Danny La Rue than a wig, a glamorous outfit and high heels.

My first West End stage appearance was chosen with great deliberation and set for early in 1965. Diana Dors and I teamed up to present an intimate stage revue, called appropriately enough, *The Two Ds*, which had all the makings of a hit show. It had a sensational opening with two blondes walking out on stage from either side, meeting in the middle and saying: '*Snap.*' Lights down – and the show was off and running.

Unfortunately, it wasn't. The show never materialized beyond rehearsals. The whole thing collapsed. Robert Stigwood, who was presenting the revue, went bankrupt and that was that. Di sued him; I put it down to experience.

Diana Dors was a remarkable woman. The word 'star' in show business has become an abused term. It is much misused and should be replaced. If someone appears on a television soap opera, they are automatically labelled 'a star', which is nonsense. They are performers, not stars. You have to *earn* that title, you have to grow to become a star. And I dismiss such words as super-star, mega-star and hyper-star as complete and utter rubbish. They don't mean a thing.

Diana Dors *was* a star. She had her ups and downs, but she always acted like a star, she always conducted herself like a star, and always looked like a star, even when she went shopping.

One of the most moving and heartfelt moments in my entire life came in May 1984, while I was appearing on the *Queen Elizabeth II*, and news of Diana's death was announced. It touched everyone on board. An eerie quietness fell upon the whole liner and it became like a ghost ship. She endeared herself to millions. Diana Dors was of the people.

She was a good friend. I admired her tremendously and she epitomized honest vulgarity, that wonderful brazen attack. She was also a versatile actress. No one will ever replace her. I don't think something as marvellous as friendship ever dies. It is what keeps us going. I pray each night before I go on stage. I have long heart-to-heart talks with my departed friends and say: 'This is for you. I'll do my best.' I put Diana with the women I dearly love. They watch over me.

With the failure of *The Two Ds* to get off the ground, I began to wonder if my West End theatre aspirations might be stifled at birth. Perhaps it was meant that I would never make the step up from late-night cabaret, where I reigned supreme and had become a major box office attraction, on to the legitimate stage. I wasn't unduly worried: if it wasn't to be, then it must have been ordained, and I would accept it, no questions. I still had my club and my pantomimes, which had both elevated me into star status and given me a substantial income and a very good life. Noël Coward had once told me that any artiste should know his limitations. 'He should stick to what he knows and what he does best.' Well, I thought, maybe this is what I know and what I do best, and I should be happy with my lot.

However, I didn't have to wait long for a second chance at the theatre. Within a matter of months, my agent, Sonny Zahl, approached me with the script for a new and original comedy musical called *Come Spy With Me*. It was written by my old friend, Bryan Blackburn, and had been presented on a small scale in fringe theatre, but with little success. Impresario Peter Bridge had designs on bringing the show into the West End after an initial try-out in the provinces and agreed to re-write the original script and graft me on to the plot. It was a very funny show and a clever idea, revolving around the misfortunes of an incompetent MI5 secret agent called Danny Rhodes, played by me. But the role also gave me ample opportunity to emerge as an array of glamorous women during the course of the plot, and I played, amongst others, a Chinese waitress, a seductive temptress, a nightclub singer and an Irish nurse. We also found a spot for Lady Cynthia Grope, who was a big success.

The show featured a very talented cast and I worked with such super people as Barbara Windsor, Richard Wattis and Gary Miller. Ned Sherrin was the director.

We opened in Oxford on 28 April 1966, and spent the next three weeks putting the show together, ironing out the little problems, tightening up, cutting, adding new lines and generally knocking it into shape.

Richard Wattis was amazed at my stamina. He couldn't believe that I could leave the stage at the New Theatre in Oxford at ten thirty and drive back to London to be on stage at my nightclub three hours later; then to make the return journey to Oxford straightaway, arriving around five in the morning and *still* appear as bright as a button at rehearsals the following afternoon for a two thirty start. It didn't worry me, I was having too much fun.

From Oxford, we played a week in Brighton, where a most memorable incident occurred. After the show, I was in my dressing room, putting on some of the make-up I needed to wear for my nightclub performance. Most evenings I travelled back to town already made-up. It saved time at the other end. I had been in the dressing room for quite a while since the final curtain had fallen, and when I finally emerged outside I felt a presence and told Jack I thought I could see someone lurking in the shadows. It was all rather mysterious. Then I heard laughter, booming laughter, from out of the darkness. It was Paul Scofield, who had been waiting ages to see me. He was such a gentleman and so quiet. He hadn't let anyone know he was there. He just waited.

The Brighton newspapers had not been over-enthusiastic about my performance in the show, and Paul had stayed behind to offer his encouragement and to tell me how marvellous he thought I was.

'Of course, you do realize you are a very good actor,' he said. 'And don't listen to anybody. You don't just dress up.' He was not the first great actor to say it to me.

At Golders Green Hippodrome, our final try-out point before the West End, tragedy struck when dear Gary Miller was taken ill with a heart attack only nine days before we were due to open at the Whitehall Theatre. Unfortunately, he never fully recovered and died shortly afterwards – another tragic loss, and so young. We opened finally with Craig Hunter playing Gary's part of Secret Agent VO3 while Bryan Blackburn himself took over Craig's role.

We put on a special dress rehearsal of the musical for charity on the Sunday before our Tuesday opening night to which Rudolph Nureyev and Noël Coward came and were most impressed. However, I didn't exactly 'kill' the audience with my performance that night. For some reason, I felt ill at ease. Afterwards, Jack took me to one side. 'Well, mate,' he said, 'tonight was what you can do with direction. On Tuesday night you will do what has made you a star.'

Two days later, on Tuesday, 31 May 1966, *Come Spy With Me* opened at the Whitehall Theatre. It was the first play to be presented there after so many years of Brian Rix farces and to follow such a West End comedy institution was in itself a nerve-racking experience. I had been thrown in at the deep end, but the fright had gone. I altered my performance only slightly from the dress rehearsal, as Jack had advised. The first night audience, *and* the critics, went wild. I opened to a tremendous press reception.

Harold Hobson, one of the legendary British critics, said I 'was Monroe, Raquel Welch and Mae West all rolled into one'. He was a great admirer of mine and likened me to Max Miller 'with sequins'. He also called me, 'every inch a star, every other inch a lady', and urged the Royal Shakespeare Company to use me.

Come Spy With Me played to outstanding audiences for over eighteen months: 468 performances in all. It would, and should, have run far longer, but it was proving an expensive operation to present a show of this kind in such a small theatre, despite its success at the box office. Throughout its run, so I was told, it made no money, and barely broke even.

One of the most exciting scenes in the entire show came right at the very end when I had to sing a duet with Craig Hunter. I started the number as a woman, in costume, in a wonderful gown. Halfway through the song, I moved behind a large screen at the back of the stage, which acted like a shadowgraph for the audience to see me in silhouette changing, and emerged moments later as a man, to finish the duet. It was a very clever sequence. When Wee Georgie Wood came in to see one of the previews, he sent backstage one of my favourite compliments: 'Danny, you are like a magician,' it read. 'Don't give your tricks away.'

Later, we altered the scene totally. Instead of changing behind the screen in full view of the audience, I left the stage and changed in the wings, reappearing mere seconds later.

Barbara Windsor still talks in glowing terms about the quick-change routine today, and admits it was one of the most dynamic things she has ever seen on stage – 'pure theatrical magic', as she put it. I virtually walked off stage as a beautiful woman and, in an instant, I was back again as a man, *without* make-up, nail polish or any single trace of the glamorous character I had been seconds before. It was breathtaking, and bewildered many in the audience every night. I could hear people whispering to each other: 'Who's that bloke?' 'Where did that geezer come from?' 'Where did the girl go?' Judi Dench, who saw the show, told me later that when I walked off stage it really did look as if I came straight back again without pausing, that's how quickly it had been achieved. An illusion. Wee Georgie Wood had been right again; the new scene created an incredible impact and became a talking-point in the West End.

In 1977, *Come Spy With Me* became a big hit all over again when we recorded a special television version of the musical for peak-evening viewing on London Weekend Television.

I lost a stone in weight during those fifteen months. It was such hard work, but I loved every minute of the experience, and found no difficulty making the transition into the West End from my other work in cabaret and pantomimes. Far from it, I revelled in it all. When I am performing, it doesn't make any difference to me whether I am in Shaftesbury Avenue, or in a pub in Accrington. I have a job to do and I do it to the best of my ability. What misguides some artistes is that they condition themselves into thinking London must be better. But I don't believe it is, it's just a different type of audience.

During the course of the run of *Come Spy With Me*, Luise Rainer, who was one of my great Hollywood idols following her fabulous performance in the movie *The Good Earth*, came to see me and I did something I have only rarely agreed to do. I had my photograph taken with her, with me in make-up. I had only done it once before, for Coward and Nureyev, but she was a rather special lady.

In 1967, I was to top the bill in pantomime for the first time when I starred in *The Sleeping Beauty*, which became the very last show to play Golders Green Hippodrome. It was a new pantomime, too, written by Bryan Blackburn. *Cinderella* has always been my favourite. It was, and still is, the personification of what pantomime represents – a strong storyline, good characters, fantasy, romance, pathos, comedy and plenty of glamour. Yet, topping the bill in *Cinderella* would have caused problems. What part could I have played? I could not have appeared as an Ugly Sister because, as Tom Arnold said: 'The star must never be booed.'

One of the great pleasures of appearing in pantomime is that it allows me the rare opportunity of working with children. They are so unpredictable and yet I don't ever feel frightened of them. I always look forward to the audience participation spot at the end of each performance, where I can bring children out of their seats and on to the stage with me for a chat, a laugh and a singalong. It is quite rightly one of the great traditions of British pantomime.

One of the tricks to learn very quickly is that children are frightened of grotesque make-up, and some pantomime dames do go over the top with theirs, drawing in heavy ageing lines on their faces, and often wearing distorted false noses and funny eyebrows. It can terrify a small child. I would hate it to happen. I believe that to a child I appear like a large walkie-talkie doll and that's the way I have always played it.

The secret of success with children on stage is to treat them seriously as young people. I never try to put anything over on them, and I can usually gain their confidence by asking them to help me out. It is no use trying to be funny with children. If they have screwed up their courage to make that daunting journey from somewhere in the darkness of the auditorium and from the security of their families on to the stage, it is because, in some way, they have become part of the show.

For *The Sleeping Beauty*, I decided to have a glamorous Tyrolean outfit created for me to wear for the participation spot. Julie Andrews in *The Sound of Music* was all the rage at the time. The movie was a smash hit and had run in the West End for many months. So I tried to create a little of the charm, and a little of the flavour, of the film by asking the kids on stage to sing 'Do, ray, me' from the musical.

At the dress rehearsal, performed cold without an audience of any kind except for the production team and a few stage technicians, I just marked the number and the spot for timing and walked through it. Tom Arnold was watching. Afterwards we chatted over drinks, and he said he had seen the best comics in show business die with the children routine. 'I'd like you to cut it out, I can't see it working.' I was horrified and refused.

On opening night, it went down so well and proved to be one of the high spots of the pantomime. It was a huge talking-point and afterwards I was inundated with letters.

Two incidents directly related to that pantomime happened to me many years later. In the autumn of 1986, just before I was due to appear in the pantomime, *Mother Goose*, at the Theatre Royal, Bath, I received a letter from a lovely lady: 'I am now living in Bristol and the biggest thrill of my life will be your pantomime in Bath at Christmas. I will be able to bring my little girl along to see the show and she will be able to come up on stage with you, just like I did at Golders Green.'

A few months later, in March 1987, some of my fellow Water Rats and I went along to the Star and Garter Hospital on Richmond Hill to bring a little cheer and some entertainment into the lives of the patients and staff. We spent a very pleasant evening chatting with the inmates, some of whom had sustained terrifying injuries fighting for their country in the Falklands. They seemed like Britain's forgotten people: they had given so much and in return they appeared to have been ignored.

I was particularly touched by one young man who wasn't very old but who had tremendous courage in coping with an appalling injury. He could hardly walk, and it took a very great effort on his behalf to walk up to me, which he insisted on doing. He smiled when we met and shook hands together, and he told me the last time we met was when he came up on stage at the Golders Green Hippodrome, and I had given him some sweets. He was so proud, his eyes lit up the ward. It was a happy memory for us both.

I used that *The Sound of Music* routine in many of my subsequent pantomimes. It never dated, and had the same impact each time.

Julie Andrews used to come and see me at Winston's and later at my own club, but we lost touch with each other for a while until 1982 when Paddy Stone, the choreographer, asked me to design a make-up chart for Julie's role in the movie, *Victor, Victoria*, in which she played the part of a man. It is a very warming testament to one's talents to be respected in the profession in this way.

When Dustin Hoffman was making *Tootsie*, I was extremely flattered to hear that he had been influenced by my work and he thought I did it the way it should be done. He's a great actor, and he spent months preparing for that role but, as far as I was concerned, it was always obvious that here was a man dressed up as a woman. I'm not saying I could have played the part better, but I certainly could have looked more like a woman. Dustin later admitted to me that his female role in *Tootsie* was the one which taught him most about life. His wife said afterwards he was a much nicer man for playing it.

The Sleeping Beauty became such a substantial hit at Golders Green that I had to change my telephone number at the theatre to avoid being inundated with calls from people in the business asking for tickets. Noël Coward came along early in the New Year, and wrote in his diary after the performance: 'On Thursday evening we all trailed off to Golders Green to see Danny La Rue in *The Sleeping Beauty* in which he played the Queen Mother with his usual style and elegance. He is a remarkable performer, incapable of bad taste.'

It was the beginning of a wonderful year for me. Everything I had carefully planned, all the hard work, began to come together. One of my great strengths and possibly a pointer to my success in show business has been that my career wasn't built or created by television. These days that is quite rare. Television has become all-powerful and can make, or break, artistes overnight. I can remember a girl singing a song on the television soap opera, *Crossroads*, and within days the record had been released and was in the charts. That's prime-time power.

I established myself and made my name as a live performer in theatre and cabaret where I shared a very intimate relationship with my audience. It was public demand, pure and simple. The joy in what I was doing came over in the realization that the audience and I were as one. I reached across the footlights and they responded. We worked together to make a marvellous atmosphere. It was something that was utterly impossible to do on television because there is no direct contact with people. If someone wanted to see me, I just wasn't readily available at the turn of a switch. I wasn't instant. They had physically to go out to a theatre, or to my club, to see my work and, for that reason, they enjoyed it all the more *and* spread the word. In that way I built up my following.

However, to be realistic, no entertainer trying to establish himself can do without television exposure, and I was no exception. But I chose my appearances with the utmost care and attention to detail, and made them work to my advantage to cause maximum impact. I fought shy of the variety spectacles and chat shows. I used the medium as the briefest shop window to showcase my talents to a wider audience because I wanted to protect what I had achieved already and not destroy it all for the sake of a few minutes air time.

I made one exception, *The Good Old Days*. I loved the show. It was like a holiday and pure British – a complete expression of good old-time music hall and everything it stood for. The audiences were wonderful and loved to dress up. The first time I appeared on the show, I spent the whole of my fee on a grand party for everyone concerned. The show ran from 1951 until 1983 and I appeared no less than sixteen times over the years. I was very honoured, too, to be asked to take part in the very last programme of all time.

In May 1968, I was fortunate enough to be chosen to appear before Her Majesty The Queen in *The Royal Television Show*, which was seen by an audience of millions. As a result of my success there, London Weekend Television gave me an hour-long television spectacular in the autumn, *An Evening With Danny La Rue*. It was the perfect vehicle for me. I had complete control and I made sure the show was not only written to my specifications, but also contained all the glamour and sparkle of my live performances. I wanted to create a unique illusion for the viewers and to leave them wanting more. It was something Noël Coward had often said: 'Danny La Rue always goes off leaving you wishing for more.'

I had already broken new ground in my career a few months earlier when I was offered my first summer season, *Let's Get Swinging*, at the Winter Gardens, Margate. The show was written as usual by Bryan Blackburn, and staged by Freddie Carpenter, the Australian director/producer, who had recently worked with Tommy Steele, Jimmy Tarbuck and Stanley Baxter.

When I was first offered the summer show, both Jack and my agent, Sonny Zahl, tried to talk me out of signing the contract. They thought me far too sophisticated. Margate, they said, was cockles and whelks and brown ale, while I was champagne and oysters. The two couldn't possibly mix. Yet, they underestimated me. What Jack and Sonny didn't realize was that my audience came predominantly from the working classes, and I was one of them, despite my success. I believed I was made for the Kent coast resort.

However, before I finally settled the issue and committed myself, I sought the advice of my old friend and mentor, Ted Gatty, who lived in the area, and had for many summers appeared in old-time music hall in Margate. He only confirmed what I already knew. 'Danny,' he said, 'you can't go wrong. This place is screaming out for a glamorous show like yours. You'll be marvellous.' He knew what he was talking about.

I did the show, and took Ronnie Corbett and David Ellen with me from the Hanover Square club. Between us, we shattered the theatre box office records to such an extent, and took so much money in the process, that the local council actually reduced the rates for the following year on the strength of the revenue!

Shortly afterwards, I was asked to make a record of another kind when Page One Records approached me to record my first single. I was a novelty with the public, and they wanted to cash in on my success. Although I never thought I could sing, I could hold a tune and had quite a pleasant voice. But was it good enough to make a record? I wasn't convinced. Still, the people at the record company were insistent, and it was another string to the bow, so I agreed.

'I'll do it on one condition,' I said, knowing I had nothing to lose. 'I will only record, "On Mother Kelly's Doorstep".' They thought I was mental.

'On Mother Kelly's Doorstep' was an old music hall number which had become the signature tune of Randolph Sutton, of whom I had been a fan since childhood. My mother had taken me to see him on several occasions. Yet Randolph had never recorded the song himself. My version was released in November 1968, and by Christmas had reached the Top 30 in the British Hit Parade. I was a pop star at the ripe old age of forty-one, which in those days was ancient. The record company had underestimated me. The song went on to become my very own signature tune and remains so today, although I read later that Randolph Sutton was none too pleased when he found out, and thought I'd pinched his song.

It was during the run of *The Sleeping Beauty* at Golders Green at the beginning of that year that Tom Arnold brought Bernard Delfont and Richard Mills, who were then the biggest and the best theatrical producers in British show business, along to see the show and to witness for themselves the enormous success people had been raving about. They, too, were very shrewd and realized it had potential for the West End, and talked about a possible transfer. Bernard Delfont, however, refused to bring the show straight into London, much to my disappointment. I had already savoured the delights of the West End stage and couldn't wait to get back. But the timing was all wrong. Bernard Delfont could see no point in opening a new pantomime in London halfway through the season. He preferred to have the show refurbished and tarted up to West End standards for a Christmas opening at the end of the year. Bernie was right, but then he knew his business. He and I have been friends ever since and our professional association, too, has flourished.

Queen Passionella and the Sleeping Beauty, as the show was retitled, opened at the Saville Theatre in Shaftesbury Avenue on 21 December 1968 and ran for six months, twice as long as originally intended. It could have run for a year, Christmas to Christmas, but I was committed to other things and had to decline. It went on to become the longest-running pantomime in history. It broke every known record for a pantomime in the West End, taking over £250,000 at the box office. And I became public property.

A few weeks after *Queen Passionella* had opened, Betty Grable arrived in town to star in a new cowboy musical, *Belle Starr*, at the Palace Theatre. It opened in April 1969 but was an unqualified disaster. The press totally destroyed her. They really should have remembered what good she had done in the war and been gracious towards her. Instead, they were terrible and criticized her performance in the show mercilessly.

'All I want to do is please the public,' she said. 'I am a professional and I always set out to do the best I can.'

One afternoon, she rang me. She was distressed. 'You seem like a nice man,' she said, 'can I come round and talk to you?' I was completely taken aback. Here was my great American dream girl, whom I had worshipped from afar, wanting to talk to me and asking for my help and advice. I couldn't believe it.

Betty needed someone to reassure her after the awful mauling she had received from the critics and I was touched she turned to me in her hour of need. I only hope I was able to help her. I filled her dressing room with flowers.

We corresponded right up to her death. She used to come to my home and, of course, on to the club, and spent her Sundays with me, telling me wonderful tales of movie stars and Hollywood. She never stopped for a moment trying to persuade me to work in Las Vegas. But apart from my refusal to fly, I was always slightly apprehensive of American audiences.

'If you came to Las Vegas, Danny,' she said, 'England would lose you for ever. The Americans would never let you go.'

It was ironic. On the day Betty Grable died on 2 July 1973, at the age of fifty-seven, I received a letter from her thanking me for the flowers I had sent. It was the second time such a coincidence had happened. Betty later became one of my special 'ladies'. I chose a typical pose, and did a rock 'n' roll number to her in tribute.

Betty Grable was one of many American stars and friends who tried to persuade me to go to the States to work, including Lauren Bacall, Ginger Rogers, Carol Channing and, of course, Liberace. But I refused them all.

If I was asked if there was any dramatic mistake I think I have made in my career, it came at that time, in 1969. After one matinée perform-ance, I came off stage at the interval and Jack asked me if I had seen David Merrick in the audience. Merrick was revered as one of the biggest American impresarios in show business. I went back on stage and noticed the seat in which he had been sitting was now empty. 'He didn't enjoy the show, he couldn't wait to leave,' I remarked almost viciously to Jack afterwards and felt quite distraught that such an important man should walk out on me halfway through my show. But, at the next matinée, Merrick came in and watched only the second half.

The following morning, Sonny Zahl telephoned to say David Mer-rick wanted to see me, and a meeting had been arranged at the Globe Theatre. I'll always remember, it had the smallest lift I've ever seen. It held only one person. I had an audience with this great entrepreneur, who had been responsible for staging *Hello, Dolly!* on Broadway since its opening in June 1964. The current American production was a unique one, starring Pearl Bailey and Cab Calloway in an all-black version, which was proving a big success.

David Merrick told me he had been very impressed with me and added he had never seen anybody work so hard at a matinée. A lot of American stars won't even do matinées and send on their understudies instead. Then he came to the point of his visit to London and outlined his plans for the future. He wanted to stage a new production of *Hello, Dolly!* on Broadway when Pearl Bailey left the show, and offered me nearly a million dollars to take over from her and play the part of Dolly Levi. He added I would be sensational in the role and the show would make history. I was flabbergasted. You had to be a bit special for David Merrick to take an interest. Calm as anything at such a tremendous offer from such a distinguished and internationally renowned producer, I told him I had to think about it and left.

We met on two further occasions and discussed the offer again. Knowing of the success of my nightclub, Merrick even offered for me to appear in a similar cabaret situation in New York. But at our third meeting, I turned him down. There was simply too much going on for me in England. I know now I made a big mistake. I have always maintained that my timing, theatrically, has been impeccable, but on that one occasion I got it wrong. Looking back with hindsight, it would have given me my best entrée into America and everything might well have been different. It is probably far too late for me to go there now.

Queen Passionella closed on 21 June 1969 in the saddest of circumstances. On the final night, the theatre was packed to capacity, except for two solitary seats I was holding for Judy Garland. She had been in good spirits following her marriage to her fifth husband, Mickey Deans, and the couple had set up home together temporarily in London. Judy had promised me she would come to my last performance. I trusted her, she had never let me down in the past. So I wasn't worried when she didn't show up and told the stage manager to hold the curtain to await her arrival, until it was obvious that something might have happened. She never appeared. The seats remained empty.

The next morning, I discovered Judy Garland had died in the night from a drugs overdose. I am certain it was the result of a terrible accident and she never intended to take her own life, which was speculated at the time. Judy had been in great form after her recent trip to New York and seemed to be enjoying her life again. But she had been destroyed by the Hollywood system that created her. As a child, she was given pills to wake her up, to put her to sleep, to calm her down and to pick her up again. It was no way to grow up. She moved from one tablet to the next without ever knowing any difference. She relied too heavily on narcotics after a lifetime of use had left her vulnerable, and it became a habit which was abused and overdone. A lot of people think she drank heavily. She didn't. The combined effect of tablets and alcohol screwed up her life completely. She was forty-seven when she died. It was a waste of a life and a remarkable talent of which we will never see the likes again. I was shattered and felt physically ill.

I heard the news of dear Judy's death on my way to Oxford the following Sunday morning, where I was set to start filming a new television adaptation of the Brandon Thomas evergreen farce, *Charley's Aunt*. The production was the brainchild of Peter O'Toole and Jack Hawkins, both old mates and regulars at my nightclub, who had persuaded me to play the leading role of Lord Fancourt Babberley in a spectacular international television production. Peter and Jack owned a film company, Keep Films Ltd, in partnership with the American Jules Buck, and they produced the programme in association with the BBC for screening all over the world. When it was first shown in Britain on BBC1 in their *Play for Today* series, it broke all current records for a single BBC drama presentation, with an audience of almost fourteen million. It was repeated within three months and opened up a totally new kind of audience for me.

When the play, about the antics of Oxford University undergraduates, was first produced in 1892, it was a very original idea. But as time passed, the basic theme of a university student dressing up as a woman to fool the father of the women he loves was wearing a little thin. It was implausible, particularly as most interpretations of the leading role had become a gross caricature of a man in a black dress, smoking a cigar and looking like anything but a woman. It was completely unbelievable. I maintained that someone would have to be deranged *not* to know that the person in the dress was a man. And so the whole idea fell down.

I added another dimension to the character of Charley's aunt by becoming totally believable as a woman. I loved the part and it became a great triumph for me – one that was to play an important part in my career.

John Gorry was a brilliant director who helped me immensely. Most of the people I worked with were either television actors or film stars:

Coral Browne, Cheryl Kennedy, Dinsdale Landen, Ronnie Barker and John Standing were all experienced professionals, who were completely at ease with camera and recording techniques. I wasn't. No matter how hard I tried, I needed the contact of a live audience to spark me off and give me the necessary feedback to start the adrenelin flowing. I seemed to be getting nowhere. I couldn't time anything. I was agitated with myself and annoyed that I might be letting the entire cast down. Then John Gorry gave me a piece of advice: 'Make your fellow actors your audience,' he said. It was simple direction, but brilliant and worked so well. When I was speaking my lines, I would look into the eyes of the person with whom I was acting. If I could see a twinkle, I knew I was on the right tracks and amusing them. I timed the whole play like that. It was an utter joy to work with such a talented and understanding company of accomplished actors. I admire them all.

After *Charley's Aunt*, playing the part of Lady Godiva in the 1969 Coventry Birthday Show at the Coventry Theatre was a doddle. Each night I rode around the stage on the back of a white horse, wearing nothing but a flesh-coloured leotard and masses of long flowing hair. The audience went wild. Fortunately, the horse didn't! The show, which was called *A Tribute to Coventry*, was another record-breaker and played to full houses. For the two months I was there, Coventry was just like a holiday city. I couldn't believe my luck or the show's outstanding success. Three years later, I starred in a similar show at the theatre, and the box office was sold-out nine weeks before I even opened!

For the entire eight weeks of the Birthday Show run, I drove back to London nightly to appear at my nightclub. It was a long journey and, inevitably, on one evening the car broke down. As was my habit, to save time I was already made-up in the car ready for my club performance later that night. I must have looked like an exotic ballet dancer when the police arrived on the scene to find out what had happened. A constable stuck his head through the open car window and stared at the apparition staring back at him. I stayed calm, but he was calmer. 'Evening, Danny,' he said. 'Been working?'

It is always flattering and so satisfying to be given awards in show business and to gain recognition for your work. We all strive for excellence. I still believe the finest of all honours, with all due respect, is when your colleagues personally thank you. You know then you have done your best for the profession. It is mutual respect; there can be nothing higher. However, one of the *most* rewarding honours came in 1974 when I was chosen as one of 'The Men of the Year', and attended a luncheon at the Savoy Hotel. I was in the company of such other distinguished recipients as Lord Shinwell, Professor H. J. Glanville, Sir James Stuart-Monteith and Norman St John-Stevas. Not bad for a man dressed as a tart.

In 1969, I received two of the highest accolades the business can bestow upon an artiste. I treasure them both. In November I was chosen to appear in my first Royal Variety Performance at the London Palladium in the presence of Her Majesty The Queen. I was petrified. My mouth went completely dry and I bit my lip so hard through sheer tension that the next morning I had sores all round my mouth. But it was worth it. I featured several of my 'ladies' in my performance and stopped the show. I never actually left the stage, making a series of lightning changes behind a screen. My caricature of Vikki Carr was well-received, but my Sandie Shaw brought the house down, and me with it, after I slipped on the stage in my stockinged feet. The audience thought it was part of the act, and laughed even louder.

After the show when I was presented to the Queen, Her Majesty was glorious and told me she was quite worried when I fell over. She had started to walk away to be presented to the other artistes taking part in the show when she came straight back to me again to tell me how clever I had been with my quick changes. 'I do a lot of quick changes myself,' she said. 'Perhaps you can give me some tips.'

Yet the undoubted highlight of such a memorable evening was to see my mother looking radiant with an ecstatic look on her beautiful face. It is a sight I have long cherished. Someone said to me, 'We've never seen anyone so proud as your mother.'

I have become an old hand at royal shows since then, having appeared in over twenty, including Royal Variety Performances in 1972 and 1978. They are all nerve-racking experiences and filled with an excitement that is very stimulating, very emotional and packed with tension. My most thrilling came in 1976 when I was invited to appear before no less than twenty-one members of Europe's royal families and King Hussein of Jordan at a gala charity show, *Once Upon a Century*, to celebrate the centenary of the St John Ambulance Brigade. The show was held at the Talk of the Town where maximum security was in evidence. Tickets for the event cost £500.

We met the royals before the show and I'm sure that night there were more of them in the line-up than performers on stage. I have never bowed so much in all my life. Besides the Queen and Duke of Edinburgh, and several members of the British royal family, we entertained kings and queens, princes and princesses, from Greece, Yugoslavia, Prussia, Sweden, and Monaco. It was a glittering occasion, and if someone had thrown a bomb into the nightclub half of the world's monarchs could have been wiped out in one fell swoop.

In 1983, I was presented to Prince Charles on three different occasions, at three separate charity functions. Within a few weeks, we met at the re-opening celebrations for the Palace Theatre in Manchester, at the Grand Theatre in Blackpool, and at a special Falklands Gala. On the third occasion, His Royal Highness looked me straight in the eyes and said: 'Danny, we can't go on meeting like this, people will talk.'

My second honour of 1969 came from the Variety Club of Great Britain when they generously voted me Showbusiness Personality of the Year. I was so excited, I leapt over a table when my name was announced. It was a great distinction to hold such a title.

It was at that awards ceremony that I met Laurence Olivier, another Variety Club winner, for the first time. In my home, I now prize a photograph of Larry signed, 'To Danny, in admiration'. He wanted me to play the part of Fool in *King Lear* but, owing to other commitments, I had to decline. However, it was a great honour to be asked by such a revered actor.

The following year, in 1970, I returned to the West End stage and achieved a long-held ambition when Bernard Delfont presented me in my very own show at the Palace Theatre I had always loved. It was like a homecoming for me, having lived a mere stone's throw away in Earlham Street for many years. As a young man I had often looked out at the grandiose old theatre across Cambridge Circus and dreamed I might one day appear there myself, never imagining I would headline my own show. It was Bernard Delfont's own suggestion, too, that I should return to the West End after my recent success with *Come Spy With Me* and *Queen Passionella* to present a sparkling intimate revue, the kind on offer in my nightclub, only on a much grander scale. I had recently signed a three-year contract with Delfont to appear in two major London shows. He was confident of my success.

Danny La Rue at the Palace became one of the greatest triumphs of my career. It was fun, it was fast-moving, it was glamorous, gorgeous and glittering, and, above all else, it was fashionable and caught the public's imagination immediately. People who couldn't see me at my club in Hanover Square, for various reasons, flocked to see the show, and word of mouth did the rest. It was written by a special team of writers, Barry Cryer, Dick Vosburgh, Bill Solly and Bryan Blackburn, and directed by Freddie Carpenter. Lionel Blair was the choreographer, while Toni Palmer, Jackie Sands and David Ellen – stalwarts from the nightclub – appeared with me along with Roy Hudd, making his West End musical début.

I was contracted originally for a year-long run when we opened with a special charity performance on 8 April 1970 in the presence of Princess Margaret and Lord Snowdon. The evening raised over £3,000 for the Invalid Children's Aid Assocation. The final curtain fell two years later on 15 April 1972, by which time over 1,250,000 people had seen the show, grossing nearly £1,500,000. It cost £80,000 to stage with an allocation of £10,000 for my costumes. The insurance premiums alone were £260 a week, the highest ever known, and I felt like a car with a no-bumps, no-claims bonus after two years.

Theatre critic Clive Barnes, often dubbed 'the butcher of Broadway', travelled specially from America to see the show and review it for *The New York Times*. He called me 'a wonderful performer . . . an exotic plant', and added: 'I wonder if this rare blossom will survive.' He advised all the American visitors to London to see it, 'if you can get seats'.

We tried the show out in Birmingham before bringing it into the West End. But, while we were out of town, Paul Raymond tried to steal a march on us by opening his own all-male show, *Birds of a Feather*, at the Royalty Theatre in Kingsway. It cost a fortune to stage and the advertising billed the production as including 'international drag acts'. I presume the thought behind the exercise was that the show would open before I did at the Palace and take away my audience. But what they failed to realize was that the great British public have never looked upon Danny La Rue as a 'drag' act. I have always gone beyond that.

Ziegfeld put it better. When someone said to him it must have cost hundreds of thousands of dollars to stage one of his shows with all the glamorous costumes, he replied: 'That's only the immediate thing. It's the talent and the brain that must then take over. There isn't a frock or costume in the world that can hold an audience all night.' C. B.

Cochran was just as realistic: 'You can give the audience three minutes of spectacle and then you've got to start to entertain them.'

Birds of a Feather opened to not very good reviews and, once I was in residence at the Palace, the ruse backfired and the show closed very quickly.

It really was a wonderful two years for me, with a new challenge at every performance and over 1,500 people each night to entertain. I enjoyed every minute. Someone once asked me if I ever get bored when I am involved with a long theatre run, doing the same things every night, the same routines, the same gags. But how could I when I am doing what I love best of all? I am never bored. I love the theatre, it fascinates me. Making people laugh is the greatest thrill in the world.

No two nights at the Palace were ever the same, no two audiences, either. And yet the show might never have opened in London. We very nearly met with total disaster during rehearsals. There was one absolutely spectacular scene which saw me making my entrance down a staircase of twenty steps. I was extravagantly dressed in one of Mark Canter's designs in beaded pink lace and tulle, with a twenty-foot train made entirely from ostrich feathers. The illusion was created as I walked delicately down the stairs because the train followed me in such a way that when I reached the bottom rung the end of the train was still on the top rung with the rest of the exotic garment spread out and draped over the entire staircase behind me. It was a magnificent effect, and ingenious in its execution. I reached the top of the staircase to make my descent to the stage by means of a special hand-cranked hydraulic lift at the back and out of sight of the audience. It worked very well indeed. It was very safe and secure.

We had rehearsed the scene several times in the past, although never in the costume itself. It had worked as well as could have been expected in the circumstances, but on the day the outfit was introduced, we were breaking new ground. We were all a little apprehensive of the outcome at this late stage. It was such a visual illusion, it *had* to work perfectly each time. Still, we could foresee no undue problems and nothing had been left to the slightest chance. Everything had been tested thoroughly and worked extremely well.

The lift carried me slowly up to the top of the staircase where I prepared to make my entrance on cue and to pick my way gingerly down to the bottom in full costume, when Freddie Carpenter called a halt. Something was wrong.

'The timing is not quite right,' he called out. 'Can we do it again, please?'

'No problem,' I replied, 'I'll just get set.' I stepped back on to the lift to prepare my entrance once more. Someone had forgotten to put the brake on to secure the elevator at the top and as I stepped back, it plummeted down to the ground, twenty feet below. I could have been killed, or certainly seriously injured in such a fall. Luckily, I was actually saved by the elaborate costume itself and the heaviness of the train which restricted my movements to such an extent that none of my weight was placed on the lift. I am also very agile. As I stumbled backwards, I managed to jump up and scramble clear of the rapidly descending platform. It was all over in a terrifying instant. Jack Hanson was watching rehearsals from the stalls when it happened. I had never seen him move so fast. He was a big man and not the most athletic of people, but I am told he leapt out of his seat and physically vaulted over the orchestra pit, which was quite a feat, in his rush to get to the stage to help me. Fortunately, I was unhurt, just a little shaken at what I realized might have been, and the show opened on schedule. That one scene, and its fabulous costume, received an ovation every single night.

I nearly had another nasty accident later in the run. At one point, I came on to the stage alone and had to position myself in the dark. On one night, there was a tremendous whirring noise and a fearful crash, and I thought here we go again! I tried to move and I found that I couldn't. I was stuck rigid to the stage and in the blackness I didn't know what had happened. It was unnerving. An iron bar had fallen across the train of my costume and missed my head by perhaps two inches. But I was completely restricted in my movements and it needed six men to lift it off.

A funny thing happened when we came to photograph that outfit for the show's production pictures and front of house display material. At the time of the photo-session, the dress and train were finished, but the headdress wasn't. The photographer, Tom Hustler, decided to stick just a few feathers into my wig to give me some sort of head covering, and started snapping away with his camera. The finished pictures were also featured in the souvenir brochure for the show, which was on sale at the theatre. I am very superstitious about lions, being a Leo, and when I saw the photograph in question, I had to look twice. I just couldn't believe it. Once it was turned upside down, the features in my makeshift headdress and feathers in my wig gave the uncanny illusion of a lion's head and mane. I considered it a lucky omen.

We played to a great audience every night, very receptive. One of the usherettes confided in Toni Palmer that some members of the audience laughed so much they peed themselves and soaked their seats. Apparently, it was a regular occurrence, and I suppose it was an inverted form of flattery really. Another time, the entire company was on stage doing a very complex tap-dance routine when I came on and joined them, dressed in a suitably wonderful creation. From out of the audience, I heard a little whisper to a friend: 'Now that's what I call a nice pair of shoes.' Someone else said: 'I bet they're not his *real* legs.'

Danny La Rue at the Palace attracted tremendous coach-party trade and, on many occasions, there were mix-ups over tickets with people being double-booked or given the wrong seats. One night there was a major problem. We had opened the show in the usual way only to find the first few rows of seats in the stalls were in uproar. There had been some trouble over seating arrangements, tickets didn't tie up with seat numbers, and people were having great difficulty finding their places in the darkened auditorium. Someone, somewhere had made a few mistakes. It was impossible for us to start under such conditions so I stopped the show and called for the house lights to be raised so we could see what was happening.

'Now, what's going on?' I called from the stage. 'What's the problem?' There was one lady who looked very distressed. 'Can't you find your seat, love?' I said to her, and she burst into tears. She had obviously never been to a West End theatre before and was so bemused and confused by the whole procedure. She was crying because she wanted to sit next to her friend, who in all the ticket confusion had become separated. Now she didn't know where to sit, or what to do.

'We'll soon have it all sorted out,' I said, and went down into the audience to lend a hand. In a few minutes, I had re-organized the first three rows completely, moving people around to allow this dear, distraught lady to find her friend and sit next to her. It was easy, really. It only took an ability to organize. The people just listened to me and moved accordingly. They trusted me to help them out. I do believe the audience loved all the extra banter and rushing around and it became an added part of the show. When it was all over and they had settled down sufficiently to re-start the show, we got a tremendous round of applause for our efforts. But it was just a question of knowing my audience. I have always prided myself in that.

The show had been running only a few months when I achieved another ambition. During the week I celebrated my forty-third birthday, I invested over £100,000 to purchase the Swan Inn, a delightful 28-bedroomed, eighteenth century hotel on the banks of the River Thames at Streatley, Berkshire, situated in the Goring Gap. Included in the purchase was Hegmore Island. I had always dreamed of running a good old English country hotel. Now I had the chance. Later, I put on cabaret there and Ted Gatty often provided the entertainment for me.

Within twelve months, I bought another Thames-side property at Mill Lane, Henley, which was to be my own country home. I was a next-door neighbour of Lady Peel, better known as Noël Coward's leading lady Beatrice Lillie, for whom he wrote the song, 'Marvellous Party'. It was a number I was delighted to perform myself when I was invited to be one of the guests taking part in a splendid Noël Coward celebration show on television to honour the master's seventieth birthday in 1969.

Noël, unfortunately, was unable to come and see my show at the Palace, which was most disappointing because I valued his honest and forthright opinions. Instead, he rang me from Switzerland to say he was sending along some friends in his place – the Lunts. Lynn Fontanne and Alfred Lunt were the most formidable acting partnership in the American theatre, equivalent to our own Laurence Olivier and Vivien Leigh. He was eighty-one, she was seventy-nine. Noël knew I admired them both tremendously. I had seen them on stage together in London in *The Visit* which played the Royalty Theatre, where they were sensational, so I was highly delighted when they came in to see my show. It was Noël Coward's way of saying he hadn't forgotten me.

A few months later, when Noël was back in London, we met again at the first night of a new musical production of *Gone With the Wind*, which opened at the Theatre Royal, Drury Lane, in April 1972. I was sitting behind him and I could see he was restless and fidgety. He wasn't enjoying the show, I could tell.

Two incidents happened which caused a stir. In the most dramatic scene of the musical, the burning of Atlanta, Scarlett O'Hara's horse crapped all over the stage in the excitement. The audience went hysterical. June Ritchie, playing Scarlett, was unbelievably professional about the whole thing and stood her ground. I really don't know how she did it.

Then, in the second half of the show, the child who was supposed to bring love between Scarlett and Rhett Butler appeared on stage, kicking her legs in the air.

'Hi,' she said in a tweaky voice, 'my name's Bonnie Butler.' She was a little monster.

At the first-night reception afterwards, Harold Fielding, who was presenting the show, cornered Noël and asked him what he thought of it.

'Well,' he said, 'if they had stuffed that awful child up the horse's arse, they would have solved two problems.'

The little girl in question was a six-year-old Bonnie Langford, who has since blossomed into a highly talented professional.

Danny La Rue at the Palace played to 95 per cent capacity business throughout its two-year run, and for months you couldn't get near the place. Tickets changed hands on the black market for fortunes. It was in fact one of the first shows to have blackboards erected at the box office, advertising odd seats available for purchase. The theatre management later claimed it could have run for another five years. In recognition of my success, the Gallery First Nighters named me as their Theatre Personality of the Year.

On 22 June 1972, the television version of *Danny La Rue at the Palace* was screened by Thames TV and went on to top the Jictar tele-ratings for the *most-watched* ITV programme of that week, beating *Coronation Street* into fourth place. My success was complete and I was very proud that I seemed to be liked by the public. I had conquered cabaret, pantomime, the West End stage, and now television . . . only films remained.

right I achieved a long-held ambition in 1970, when I invested in a delightful country hotel, the Swan Inn at Streatley, on the River Thames in Berkshire. I also purchased a nearby farm with the intention of growing most of the produce to serve the hotel's needs. I enjoyed my all too brief visits to the farm – and, being a country boy a heart, what better way to get about than on horseback? (*Sunday People*. Photo: Brendan Monks)

below Outside the stately O'Keefe Centre in Toronto, Canada – where I made my *international* show-business debut in 1976 – with Jack Hanson and my company manager, Gerry Phillips.

top In 1972 I took a two-week holiday in the South of France and ended up buying this magnificent twelve-bedroomed *château* called L'Hermitage St-Jean, near Grasse, between the snow-capped mountains and the Mediterranean Sea, in the heart of the world's perfume-making centre. It was idyllic.

bottom A breathtaking aerial panorama of Walton Hall in all its splendour. I fell in love with the building when I first saw it in 1974 and bought it 1976.

above A quiet drink and a chance to swap stories with Hughie Green (*centre*) and David Ellen in the Clown Bar at Walton Hall. Each of the life-sized, hand-painted pictures and murals depicted clowns through the ages and were the work of Gerry Binns, a dancer in my company until we discovered his outstanding talent for painting and design. (*Reveille*. Photo: John Curtis)

left Descending the spectacular sweeping staircase in the entrance hall at Walton Hall with an old mate, Liberace. Lee adored the place and called it 'Danny La Rue's castle'.

top I always regarded Gracie Fields (*left*) as the greatest of all the variety artistes. It was my great pleasure and privilege to appear with her in the 1978 Royal Variety Show at the London Palladium, in the presence of Her Majesty Queen Elizabeth The Queen Mother. Also in the picture are Lord Delfont (*right*) and Frankie Howerd. (Doug Mckenzie, Professional Photographic Services) *opposite page, bottom* Of all the members of the Royal Family I have had the honour to meet, I have a great fondness and affection for Princess Margaret, seen here with me in the company of Jack Hanson (*left*) and Wayne King at a special gala evening. I first met Her Royal Highness at a charity ball at the Savoy Hotel, and we became good friends. She came to my club in Hanover Square on many occasions. (Doug McKenzie, Professional Photographic Services)

right Elizabeth Taylor has been one of my special ladies since my days at Winston's. She paid me the great honour of personally inviting me to attend her fiftieth birthday celebrations in 1982, when she was in London appearing in *The Little Foxes* at the Victoria Palace. I travelled down from Birmingham for the occasion and presented the marvellous Hollywood star with a lilac hippo as a present. (Doug McKenzie, Professional Photographic Services)

In 1975 I arranged a special charity gala at the Prince of Wales to raise money for the terrible Darwin cyclone disaster that devastated the Australian city. It was a great delight when Her Royal Highness Princess Anne graced us with her presence. After the show she met the artistes, who had all given their services free to such a worthy cause, including Australians Freddie Carpenter (*left*), Anona Winn and actor Ray Barrett. (J. A. Ballard Photography)

right Hello, Shirley! After one performance of *Hello, Dolly!* Shirley Bassey joined me and my co-star, Lionel Jeffries, backstage at the Prince of Wales. Shirley is one of my dearest friends, and she always goes hysterical when she sees me as 'Bassey' on stage. She is a wonderful example of a shining British star, and I love her deeply. (Featureflash)

below One of the great pleasures of appearing in pantomine is that it allows me the rare opportunity of working with children. I always look forward to the audience-participation spot, when I can bring them on to the stage with me for a chat, a laugh and a sing-along. For many years I used to get all the kids singing the 'Doe Ray Me' song from *The Sound of Music*, and it proved a great success, particularly in *Aladdin* at the London Palladium, where this picture was taken in 1978. (W. D. & H. O. Wills Photographic Dept)

left The *Two* Musketeers: crossing swords with Harry Secombe. Harry and I have been friends since we appeared together on tour in *Forces Showboat* back in 1949. He and his wife Myra actually tried to make me give up show business during that first tour. They were convinced I wasn't cut out for it. 'Take my advice,' said Harry, 'get a real job.' We have laughed about the incident on many occasions since.

below Two of the many people who appeared with me on *This Is Your Life* in 1984 were the delightful Australian actress Googie Withers and her husband, John McCallum. They tried for many years to make me change my mind about touring Australia before I finally made the trip to the Antipodes in 1979. (Thames Television)

right The highest and most revered accolade that can be bestowed in show business is to become King Rat of the Grand Order of Water Rats, the distinguished charity organization. It is a position that has been held in the past by such legendary figures as Dan Leno, Little Tich, Will Hay, Bud Flanagan and Ted Ray. It was my great privilege to join such a noted company in 1986, when I was elected by my brother Water Rats to wear the gold emblem of office. It was a great thrill.

below I was very lucky in 1979 when the Variety Club of Great Britain paid me the highest of compliments by holding a very special luncheon in my honour at the Savoy Hotel to celebrate my twenty-fifth anniversary in show business. It was a glittering occasion, with tributes from my mates in the profession, including John Inman (*centre*), who had the other guests in fits of laughter. (Doug McKenzie, Professional Photographic Services)

8
'Danny would have been terrific in the *Carry On* films'

Within the space of twenty-eight days in the spring of 1972, when my club in Hanover Square closed due to re-development and my West End stage success, *Danny La Rue at the Palace*, finished its long run, I was technically out of work. I had always been the eternal workaholic, taking on anything and everything that came my way, but now, for the first time since I opened at Churchill's in 1954, I didn't have to prepare myself to go out and entertain on stage at one fifteen in the morning. It took some getting used to.

I am a very positive person. Once something has come to an end, it is finished for ever. There can be no going back. I always look forward to the future with excitement and move on to the next project with hope. It is far better to enjoy memories than to try and relive them, and create the same thing all over again. Quite honestly, it can *never* be the same. So as one phase of my career came to an end, I looked forward to opening up another. I'm a great believer in tomorrow, never yesterday.

Whenever an artiste becomes successful, he takes a tremendous amount for himself out of the business. But I have always tried to share my success with others. It is the only way I know how. By the time the club closed, I had built up a huge wardrobe of clothes which I didn't need any more. So I sold them off to the Bernard Delfont Organization, and used the money to buy two Sunshine Coaches for the Variety Club of Great Britain. At a special Variety Club luncheon in May, attended by His Royal Highness Prince Philip, the coaches were presented to two Berkshire hospitals, the Wayland Hospital in Bradfield and the Borocourt Hospital in Peppard.

My days of 'resting' came to an abrupt end in June, when I started work on my first feature film, *Our Miss Fred*, for Anglo E M I, on location in Norfolk. Before finally agreeing to appear in the movie, I must have turned down at least twenty-five other offers because they were almost all stories about female impersonations, which wasn't for me. I think I was a little apprehensive about making films. I was very definitely a live performer, and I had reservations about transferring to the large screen. After all, I didn't much care for television and I couldn't really see how the glamorous illusion I created on stage could come across to cinema audiences. I wasn't convinced at all.

At one time, there had been talk about my becoming a member of the *Carry On* crew, but nothing ever materialized and I'm glad it didn't. I'm sure I would have hated working as just a member of a team. Barbara Windsor was lovely, she said I would have been terrific in the films.

Our Miss Fred was Lord Ted Willis's idea. He took me to lunch at the House of Lords and talked me into making the film. It was an interesting idea, a wartime comedy thriller, which never dates. It gave me the scope, not only for wearing glamorous outfits, but also the opportunity to prove myself as a serious actor as well, which I grabbed with both hands. It was a complete break away from my normal work. I even did my own stunts, such as they were.

In the film, I played the part of Fred Wimbush, an end-of-pier seaside entertainer, called up for national service at the outbreak of war and posted for active service in France. Here, he becomes the star of concert party, playing all the female roles and, during the course of the movie, he is mistaken for a very glamorous woman by everyone he comes in contact with, including the Germans. The mainstay of the plot revolves around Fred Wimbush – disguised as a woman – rescuing a party of stranded English schoolgirls and their teachers from the clutches of the Germans, to lead them to safety and back to England. I looked upon the role as a twentieth century Scarlet Pimpernel. Most of the time I was seen in female attire, but I was also called upon to play a German SS officer, a regular soldier and a flying officer. What appealed to me was that my part could have been taken by almost any actor, and it wasn't necessarily a 'drag' role.

I found filming an incredible waste of time. We were on location for ten and a half weeks in Cromer, Norwich, Melton Constable, Panshanger, in Hertfordshire, and at Elstree Studios. I did all my own make-up. I was up at four each morning to be ready for filming at seven, and sometimes we would work well into the night. It used to frustrate me no end that the film people would be quite happy to get three minutes of actual film in the can each day after all the long hours and hard work. I hated the fact that we did an awful lot of work each day and got very little from it in the end. I used to feel filming was an exercise on how to *waste* time and money. But it was at least another experience and I thoroughly enjoyed working with my marvellous co-stars, Lally Bowers, Frances de la Tour, Lance Percival and Alfred Marks.

Alfred played the part of a German, General Brincker, and together we appeared in a memorable eating scene in which Fred Wimbush, suitably disguised as a glamorous temptress, tries to vamp Brincker over dinner. The General, in turn, tries to get the lady tipsy on cham-pagne. It was a tremendous scene worthy of Noël Coward's high comedy and it lasted for a good ten minutes. We filmed it straight through in a single take. When the director called, 'Cut,' the entire crew of technicians stood and applauded our efforts. Then some bright spark discovered a fly in the camera gate and all our good work ended up on the proverbial cutting-room floor and we had to shoot it all over again. It was so annoying. Yet in the end it was worth all the time and effort we put in. Several of the critics later commented that it was the best scene in the entire movie.

There were lighter moments, too. Many of the external scenes were shot in parts of Norwich, where its cobbled backstreets and compact buildings looked very much like the French town we were trying to create in the film. In one sequence, Lance Percival and I, dressed in Gestapo uniforms, literally stopped the traffic. We were filming outside a very grand building in the city which was bedecked in swastikas and banners to give the impression of Gestapo Headquarters, and props had done a very realistic job. The building in question was situated on the side of a hill. Over the hill, out of sight of the activity below, all traffic had been stopped to allow filming to take place. No one apart from technicians and crew knew there was a movie being made only a few yards away.

At the end of the scene, director Bob Kellett gave instructions for the traffic to be allowed through while the next shot was set up. Lance and I unwound by the side of the road, preparing for the next piece of action, as the traffic came streaming past. It was instant recognition, despite our uniforms.

'Hello, Danny.'

'Hello, Lance.'

The drivers called to us and waved as they drove off.

'Making a film?'

'When is it coming out?'

The very last car through was a left-hand drive Volkswagen with a German numberplate and German driver. He shot down the hill, took one look at Lance and me, and the building covered in banners and swastikas, and thought the war had started all over again. He swerved his car in panic and drove off at speed in a cloud of smoke, hardly daring to believe what he had just witnessed. The look on his face was sheer terror. It was such a great reaction. We all broke up.

Our Miss Fred had its premier on 14 December 1972. I was very pleased with the reaction. It was a new challenge for me and I felt at that time the best thing I had ever attempted. Several leading film critics agreed with me and were kind and complimentary. I was delighted when Margaret Hinxman, writing in the *Sunday Telegraph*, called me, 'a very adroit comedy actor'. It made all the hard work and hanging around on the film set worthwhile. Other critics slated the picture. But I'm glad I made the film, although I certainly have no great desire to make another.

Shortly after we finished filming, I appeared before the biggest live audience of my career when huge crowds, estimated in excess of ten thousand, turned out in Blackpool on 8 September 1972 to watch me perform the switching-on ceremony for the illuminations. It was the sixtieth anniversary of the world's greatest free light show, and I felt privileged to have been invited. I shared the celebrity duties with Concorde, that great lady of the sky, which flew over the Lancashire seaside resort in tribute to sixty glorious years, and we were able to effect a live radio link to talk to the pilot in flight. Later, I felt humbled when the vast crowd of people in Talbot Square joined me to sing 'On Mother Kelly's Doorstep', and ten thousand voices were raised as one. It proved an exciting and memorable prelude to my great season at the Blackpool Opera House the following year. It was only my second summer show, but nevertheless broke box office and attendance records at the theatre.

Within six days of my switching on the Blackpool lights, I experienced a bitter blow. The house I had bought in Henley, which my brother, Dick, was painstakingly renovating and refurbishing, was ravaged by fire. The blaze started in the swimming pool in the basement, when some electrical pumping equipment exploded, and soon spread throughout the house, damaging or destroying carpets, furniture and paintings. Only weeks before I had filled the place with my priceless antiques in anticipation of moving in myself to live there permanently.

I was rehearsing a new show in the bar of the Prince of Wales Theatre when Richard Mills came down to break the news. He looked drawn and anxious and I knew instantly something was wrong. I feared the worst. Funnily enough, I can remember his exact words: 'Danny,' he said, 'we've had a telephone call. Your house is on fire.'

When my brother arrived to inspect the damage after the fire had been extinguished, he broke down and cried with sheer emotion. He had worked for nearly a whole year on the house with loving care and had just completed the finishing touches when it happened. All his delicate work had been for nothing. Ironically, I was already planning to hold a house-warming party the following weekend – house-warming was appropriate! I lost a lot of the treasures I had spent many years collecting. Much of my silverware was in storage in the basement and it melted very quickly in the intense heat. Fortunately, the quick action of the fire brigade meant that we managed to save a considerable amount of valuables, but the water from the fire hoses and the acrid smell of smoke lingered in every room for weeks afterwards. The whole house had to be totally re-decorated again. Had I been living in the property at the time of the fire, I think I would have left immediately and walked away, never to return. Strangely enough, only a week before the accident occurred, I had opened a fête for the local fire brigade.

At the end of 1972, I returned to the pantomime stage for the first time in nearly four years when I starred in *The Queen of Hearts* at the Manchester Palace. It was another new pantomime, specially written for me, and it reunited me with an old friend, Ted Gatty, who was invited to play my mother. I had last appeared at the Palace fourteen years before in *Cinderella* with Bob Monkhouse. Now I returned as a star. It was a good feeling.

The pantomime ran for seventeen weeks and had already been extended by a further month, due to public demand, even before we opened. It was good to be back. But, just as we came to the end of a spectacular run, I learned of the death of my great inspiration, Noël Coward, who passed away on his beloved island of Jamaica on 26 March 1973. He was a dear, dear friend and such a major influence on my life. With his death passed a whole era of British show-business traditions. He was a marvellous institution and part of our heritage. Like Novello before him, Noël was utterly irreplaceable. And yet, he has left us such a wonderful legacy through his work.

Once my club closed its doors, I at last had the freedom to travel

FROM DRAGS TO RICHES

much further afield for my work, instead of having to limit my engagements to areas within easy distance of London so that I could get back easily for late-night cabaret appearances. Now I had no restrictions.

At that time, an increasingly large number of provincial cabaret clubs started to establish themselves all over the country, many of them away from the large cities, in such unlikely settings as Batley, Farnworth, Eccles. They were an extension of the great northern tradition of working men's clubs and socials, only on a much bigger and grander scale. Batley Variety Club had emerged as one of the most formidable nightspots of its kind in the whole of Europe, attracting all the topline American stars to its stage for appearances. No money was spared in the quest to bring the very best to West Yorkshire, and vast sums were paid over the counter. It seemed totally incongruous: the London Palladium could not afford to play them, Batley Variety Club *could*. Louis Armstrong was just one. He appeared there for a fortnight engagement in 1971 and was paid £20,000 a week for his troubles, an astronomical sum even then. Club owner, Jimmy Corrigan, had been trying for over five years to lure me away from London, when he finally succeeded.

In November 1973, I became the first artiste of my kind to take a spectacular West End revue into the northern clubs when I starred for three weeks at the Batley Variety Club. I was paid £40,000, and for three weeks the two thousand seats of the custom-built theatre club were jam-packed full. According to one newspaper survey, the bars sold over 110,000 pints of beer during that time. But the audiences had seen nothing like it before. I knew exactly what I was doing. Nearly twenty years experience of late-night cabaret had taught me that if I could conquer any nightclub audience, I could conquer anything. Here was an audience of the people, utterly British, unlike London which was such a cosmopolitan city that it attracted a mixed patronage from all over the world. I reached them immediately. It was a sensational season. When I finished, Jimmy Corrigan and his assistant, Derek Smith, threw a lavish party to celebrate its success, and presented me with an antique French fob watch as a token of their respect and gratitude.

Two years laters, I did a British tour made up entirely of cabaret dates, and sold out every one. Steve Bartle, owner of Wakefield Theatre Club, gave me a solid gold identity bracelet with my initials, D. L. R., picked out in diamonds, to say *thank you* for such phenomenal business.

I found this new breed of nightclubs to be far less sophisticated than those in London, yet much more human and endearing places to play. They were my kind of audiences, and during the seventies they were all outstandingly popular throughout Britain. It was a lucrative business, until the bottom fell out of the market almost overnight, and clubs started to close almost as quickly as they had opened their doors. It became self-destructive in the end: club owners priced themselves out of existence in an effort to buy success. They were paying incredible amounts of money to attact artistes from all over the world, trying to outbid their rivals. It was suicidal, the money had to run out. Artistes, too, became greedy at the sight of such money being banded about and, as the cost of living increased and things became more expensive, clubs could no longer afford to compete with each other. There was also a great lack of entertainers who could be guaranteed to bring in the big audiences the clubs needed to keep running seven nights a week. Television put paid to that and people, quite rightly, stayed away. It all became prohibitively expensive and the clubs were forced out of business. However, they had a good innings for a dozen years or more, and gave a lot of people a great deal of pleasure. Several clubs did survive, run by people who really knew their business: supreme showmen like Bob Potter at the Lakeside Country Club, Frimley Green; Pat Cowan at Blazer's, Windsor, and the guv'nor of them all, George Savva, at Savva's, Usk. These clubs are still going strong and I love playing them.

Everything in entertainment has its day. I do regret the passing of the clubs as a major circuit because it has taken away another earning outlet for performers and I am terribly saddened by anything that takes away a person's livelihood. But there is another, far greater, reason to mourn their demise: the profession has been robbed of a vital training-ground for young talent to evolve and grow. These days, up-and-coming artistes have nowhere they can go to learn their trade and get valuable experience; nowhere where they can go and be downright *bad* and find out how to entertain an audience; nowhere where they can serve their apprenticeship in show business, which is so essential. The clubs certainly helped to nurture and develop new talent, to sort out the good from the bad and separate the potential from the pretentious. Today, it is no good creating potential stars through television talent shows if there is nowhere for them to appear.

Nothing will ever replace the clubs. They have gone for ever like vaudeville, burlesque, and music hall. Entertainment must progress and move on, and something different always comes along to send it off in another direction.

Immediately after completing my season at Batley, I returned to London where it was announced I was going back into the West End to star in a spectacular £150,000 production of *The Danny La Rue Show* at the Prince of Wales. At the same time, the newspapers picked up on something I said at the reception to launch the show which intimated I was 'going to hang up my boobs for good' at the end of the run, and do other things. The story made every paper; in the popular press, it was front-page news. I didn't realize I was so popular and warranted such treatment. The story, however, was a complete misunderstanding. What I actually said was that I would very much like to hang up my boobs for *a change* and play a straight role. I told the reporters I had appeared in the West End for so long I had forgotten my roots. I wanted to tour more and generally do other things in the business like directing or producing. I was misquoted, and the story was blown up out of all proportions. One newspaper even said I was retiring from the stage altogether, which was ridiculous. I was only forty-six and still looked forward to a long theatrical future. Within days of the story hitting the streets, I was bombarded with letters from the public telling me that *they* would decide when it was time for me to hang up my boobs. It was a touching show of loyalty from my fans. I have never forgotten it.

The new show was resident at the Prince of Wales theatre from 15 December 1973 until 22 March 1975, and was later taken on a long and comprehensive national tour. In its fifteen-month run in London, it grossed over one million pounds at the box office. Nevertheless, the show hit trouble almost as soon as it opened.

A winter of discontent plunged Britain into the throes of industrial action. As the miners challenged the authority of the government, the country was set on course for the introduction of a three-day working week in a desperate effort to save energy. Lengthy power-cuts occurred everywhere. Cities went on a rota system – three hours with power, three hours without. Once again the lights of London's theatreland were temporarily extinguished to save electricity. It was something only Hitler had managed to do in the past.

We were lucky. We were only affected on a couple of occasions throughout the dispute, which seemed to go on for ages and eventually *did* topple the government. At that time, the Prince of Wales theatre had no generator to keep us going in case of a power failure. So, when the lights went out, it was down to torch power – we had no intention of stopping the show. Gerry Phillips, my company manager, came up with an ingenious solution. We were always warned beforehand when to expect a power-cut. If one was imminent, Gerry would sit in one of the boxes at the side of the theatre, while a member of the Prince of Wales theatre staff perched in an identical box on the other side. When the lights went out, they each shone two large car headlights, powered by twelve-volt batteries, down on to the stage, to give us some kind of illumination. It was crude, but effective in the circumstances. It was like being back in the Blitz, and the audiences loved it and completely entered into the spirit of the evening. That's the marvellous thing about British audiences, they never kick you when you are in trouble. I think they are superb.

We had other problems with electricity in that show. For one of our big production numbers, we staged a gorgeous tribute to the *Folies Bergère*. Each night, I arrived on stage in a glittering cage, which was lowered down from the theatre flies. One night it stuck halfway down, just as the bottom half of my body came into the audience's vision. All they could see was a pair of legs, covered in feathers. My head and upper body were still covered by the fly curtains above, and the cage stuck fast. While one of the stagehands slowly and meticulously hand-winched me down to the stage, I knelt down on the floor of the cage, peered under the fly curtain at the audience, and spent the next ten minutes ad libbing my way through comedy patter with David Ellen, which was all I could do in the circumstances. It was hilarious.

Experience has taught me never to panic. Nowadays, I can get myself out of most situations that occur on stage. Nothing throws me. You learn as you grow in this profession. I was on stage at the Golders Green Hippodrome once when I thought the grill above my head was going to come crashing down on top of me. I could feel dust and plaster falling from the theatre ceiling and I didn't want to take any chances in case anything did happen. I calmly walked forward and started to sing: 'There'll be bluebirds over, the white cliffs of Dover . . .'

The audience could see what was happening and, like me, they were anticipating the entire ceiling collapsing at any minute. I looked as if a bomb had dropped on me, covered in dust. When I finished singing, I received a standing ovation.

I met Wayne King, who has become a major inspiration in my life and a great friend and support ever since, during the second year of our run at the Prince of Wales. I heard him by accident, rehearsing in a bar in the theatre. Jack and I were making our way from my dressing room to the front of house, where a cocktail party had been arranged by the theatre management in my honour, when I heard this superb piano music filling the foyer. It was absolutely beautiful, and stopped me in my tracks. It was Wayne playing, and I was so impressed by his talent. He had such great attack and so much style. A showman in the Liberace mould.

When we were introduced, I found out he was part of a double act with a singer called Terry Turner. They were quite well known in Australia and were now trying to establish themselves in Britain. It was a strange coincidence because Wayne had been discovered in Sydney, and brought to Britain, by Harry Secombe with whom I appeared in my very first professional engagement. It was ordained, our meeting was destiny.

Within weeks, I introduced Wayne on the television talent show *Opportunity Knocks*, where his flamboyant style and brilliant talent received a rapturous reception. He won the show on five consecutive occasions. It became quite obvious that Wayne King was a star in his own right and didn't need to be part of any double act. But it was a whole year before they decided to split the act up, and for Wayne to go it alone. He has worked with me regularly since 1976, the date of his first Royal Variety Performance. He divides his time between England and Australia, where he tours in his own show and, incidentally, receives a standing ovation at almost every performance. What baffles me, with such incredible talent, is that he isn't a much bigger star all over the world.

Liberace had a great warmth and feeling for Wayne's work, which he endorsed and acknowledged when he wrote the sleeve notes to one of Wayne's albums. He realized that if anyone could take over his own dynamic mantle, it was Wayne. Lee was stunned by his sheer knowledge of music.

Since we met, Wayne King has had a tremendous influence on me because he has taught me to appreciate music. We often go to classical music concerts together and share many mutual friends, especially the brilliant Shura Cherkassky, who, next to Vladimir Horowitz, is, in my opinion, the world's leading classical pianist. What amazes me about

Shura Cherkassky is that, like several people whom I have met in my career, he has become an admirer of mine and a great fan. I asked him about it once. I was intrigued to know why.

'With respect, Shura,' I said, 'you are one of the great classical pianists and here I am with my feathers.'

His answer surprised me. 'Talented people,' he replied, 'always love talented people.'

We had a very pleasant run at the Prince of Wales despite all the initial problems, although for me the season was tinged with great sadness when my sister, Joan, died. By then, she was living in my house at Shoreham in Sussex. One evening, she rushed downstairs in order to catch one of my rare programmes on television and tripped and fell. She never recovered. I loved her dearly. It took all my courage and sheer determination to go out on stage and entertain an audience – *and make them laugh* – on the day we buried Joan. It was one of the hardest things I have ever had to do in my entire show-business career.

Joan was a kind and loving girl who would do almost anything for anyone. She was very much like my mother, although not as resilient. She lived a sad and tragic existence in many ways, and I often felt she was terribly lonely, but she said nothing. She was very influenced by the Catholic church. Sadly, the man she hoped to marry was already married, and I don't think she ever recovered from the blow. It was never to be and she lived most of her later life alone. She was just fifty-six when she died, and one of my most vivid memories of my mother is seeing the pain and suffering on her face when Joan died. It is a terrible thing for a mother to see a child die before she does.

A few years later, after my dear mother passed away, I donated two statues to St Patrick's Church in Soho, dedicated to the memory of Mary Ann Carroll and Joan Carroll, depicting St Thomas Moore and St John Fisher. The priest told me the originals had been destroyed by a young boy, probably high on drugs, who just wandered in through the church's ever-open doors one evening and smashed them to pieces for no apparant reason. I promised to replace them. It wasn't being grand, I just thought my mother would like it. Both she and Joan served their church and their community so well during their lives.

The Danny La Rue Show completed its London run in March 1975, and I was set to return to the West End the following Christmas in another new pantomime by Bryan Blackburn, *The Exciting Adventures of Queen Daniella*, at the London Casino. Yet before I could take on such a new and exciting project, I had a small personal problem to attend to. A few years earlier, whilst I was appearing at the Palace, I sustained a very slight hernia during a particularly vigorous stage routine which ended up with me doing the splits. It was very painful, but, I told myself, an essential part of the show, so I suffered in silence. However, as soon as I had sufficient time available, I went into the hospital of St John and St Elizabeth, in St John's Wood, to have it fixed. The *Daily Mirror* discovered the story after they had been tipped off by a 'reliable source', and claimed that I was admitted to hospital to undergo major cosmetic surgery, which was completely untrue. When I explained the real situation to the editor and invited him to come along to take photographs of my operation scars, he declined.

The Exciting Adventures of Queen Daniella ran for fourteen weeks in the West End during the Christmas season of 1975/76 and proved so successful that we reprised the pantomime the following year at the Coventry Theatre, where it emulated the London run. I couldn't under- stand my good fortune. I was on a high and running on overdrive. Earlier in the year, I'd established new box office records with my first summer season in Great Yarmouth.

And yet, 1976 became a bitter-sweet year for me. Two years before, I had been taken to see an absolutely magnificent stately home near Stratford-upon-Avon, called Walton Hall. It had been developed un- successfully into an hotel and, at that time, it was slowly decaying. Still, it looked an interesting property and I was very much impressed. I could see all manner of possibilities for the beautiful old building and warmed to the idea of buying it if it ever came up for sale on the open market. I could always hope. When it finally did come up for sale in 1976, the property needed extensive re-development and renovation, but I was carried away with a romantic notion and looked upon it as my pension, to help me through my old age. So, for nearly half a million pounds, I invested in my future.

When the news of the purchase was announced in the local paper, I was bubbling over with excitement.

'All the money going into Walton Hall, and it will be about £750,000 by the time I have finished, is my own,' I told reporters. 'No one else is involved. If it goes under, I go under.' I didn't realize at the time just how prophetic that statement was to become.

It was at Walton Hall, on 15 September 1976, that my mother, Mary Ann, died. Several years before, while appearing in *Queen Pas-*

sionella and the Sleeping Beauty at the Saville Theatre, Gerry Binns, who was a dancer in the company, brought a clairvoyant to see me. She was an enchanting lady.

'You love your mother very much,' she said. 'I just want to tell you she will die very quietly in bed, with no illness, no suffering.'

She was right. Mary Ann died of natural causes. She was seventy-nine and was buried next to Joan in London, and I will be buried with them both.

I was on my way to France on holiday and was told the news when I arrived. I returned immediately. We had been so close. After each new show, I gave her a present – a piece of jewellery or something like that. I gave her her last present just eight hours before she died. It was a beautiful cameo and I now keep it with me at all times. It was the last thing she held. She passed away in her sleep.

Mary Ann was a great lady, and a great friend. Some people I know don't even talk to their mothers. I can't understand it and tell them so: 'A mother is so important, for God's sake, you'll be sorry.' I miss my mother terribly, but I know she is with me all the time, watching over me. Great love like that doesn't end with the grave. Only the body dies; the spirit lives on. I am utterly prepared for death. I am never afraid because I know I am not going far and that helps me. I also know I will be reunited with so many dear people who have gone before me. I don't believe you can die and just finish. There has to be more. I believe in re-incarnation; people do come back and I have tremendous faith in the idea that a child with no limbs in one life is a concert pianist or a ballerina in the next.

My mother helps me, and I talk to her for guidance. I feel there is a sort of motivation of good feelings and vibrations. On my opening night of my very first engagement in Australia, at the Regent Theatre, Sydney, in 1979, I spoke to Mary Ann in my dressing room before I was due on stage. I asked her for encouragement, to guide me through my biggest challenge.

After the show was over, the theatre callboy came to me and apologized.

'I am sorry, Mr La Rue,' he said. 'When I gave you the five-minute call, I would have come into your dressing room, but I could hear you had company.'

'No, I didn't,' I replied. 'I was talking to my mother.'

He looked at me strangely. 'But your mother is dead.'

'Yes, I know, but I *was* talking to her,' I repeated.

Tragically, she died just a few weeks before I was honoured by the Variety Club of Great Britain, and fêted with a luncheon at the Savoy Hotel to celebrate my twenty-five years in show business. It was a glittering occasion with tributes from my mates – John Inman, Fenella Fielding and Arthur Askey. Mary Ann would have been very proud of me and I was sad that I was unable to share every moment with her: she loved the big occasions. But she was with me in spirit.

9
'It's the first time I have ever seen a heart working'

Hughie Green was the first person to put me *on* the air in 1958 when he gave me my very first television engagement for Rediffusion. A decade later, he became the first man to put me *in* the air and started me flying. It opened up a whole new world. Before then, I had no desire whatsoever to fly. I had a terrible phobia that was so bad I wouldn't even go to meet anybody at an airport. I had a very strong feeling that it wasn't intended for me to fly at that particular time. It wasn't ordained. Maybe at some time in the future, but certainly *not* then. My senses told me to shy away.

Once I had established myself as one of the biggest box office attractions in Britain, and a major West End star, I received numerous offers to appear all over the world, particularly from managements and impresarios in Australia, who were falling over themselves to gain my signature on a contract. I turned them all down.

They had been trying to make me change my mind for ten years, and I had been offered incredible money for my services. However, nothing in the world would have made me go because it would have meant I had to fly. There was certainly no other way. If I went by boat, it would have taken me six weeks to get there, and six weeks to get back, which meant I wouldn't have been working for three months. So that was completely prohibitive. Money couldn't make me do anything I didn't want to.

In 1981, I was offered £500,000 to top the bill in a glittering extravaganza being staged in the Southern Sun Hotel complex in Sun City in Bophuthatswana. I was flown out to Johannesburg, all first-class expenses paid, to discuss the project, but I rejected it out of hand. I felt oppressed in South Africa, under pressure all the time. I was uncomfortable. I react to my vibes – my intuition has served me very well – and I didn't like what I saw.

People are my life and I find an offence to a human being very degrading. I can't understand brutality. I can't understand why life appears to be so cheap. I refused to play South Africa because, as a

Christian, my beliefs and feelings for my fellow man wouldn't allow me to take the money and go where there is so much discrimination. I abhor apartheid and everything it stands for. It is a complete affront to humanity, although I would never try to influence people. Many British performers have appeared in South Africa and that is their own choice. It wouldn't work for me. I never see colour. I see only good people and bad people.

Australia, however, was a different proposition, and several of my antipodean mates had tried to persuade me to make the journey. Googie Withers and John McCallum were always tempting me. So, too, were Freddie Carpenter, Maggie Fitzgibbon, from my days at Winston's and Rod McLennan from Hanover Square. But my mind was made up. I was staying at home, for the time being at least.

I actually felt a very strong affinity with Australia and, in 1975, I arranged a special charity show at the Prince of Wales theatre to raise money for the dreadful disaster in Darwin the previous Christmas when a cyclone devastated the city causing death and destruction. We had an Australian choir, and featured such Aussie artistes as Bill Kerr, Jim Smilie and Dick Bentley. Princess Anne graced us with her presence.

The thought of extending my talents by appearing on an international stage away from Britain was very attractive. It was another new challenge and appealed to my romantic attitude to life. But it had to be an English-speaking country, although I wasn't too sure about America. I would never have been so stupid as to even attempt to appear in a non-English-speaking territory. Wit and sense of humour differ considerably around the world and it would have been useless to try and do my act in pidgin English with a few well-chosen sentences from an ethnic phrasebook thrown in for good measure. Yet, I had received several very lucrative offers from Spain, Italy and France where *The Good Old Days* had been shown for many years on television. My brother-in-law, Johnny Vecchio, my sister Nancy's second husband, actually received a letter telling him that my movie, *Our Miss Fred*, had been seen in Rome, such is the power of celluloid.

For several years, a London Palladium show had been presented annually, and with great success, in Toronto and Ottawa. Morecambe and Wise, Harry Secombe, Des O'Connor and Tommy Steele had all topped the bill there, and I had received offers. I warmed to the idea because I knew Canadians were very close to Americans in attitude. I realized that if I went down well in Canada, America could be next. I was looking for confidence. I was already known in North America through my domestic television specials and Royal Variety Performances, which were shown all round the world, so it was worth taking the gamble.

In 1976, Bernard Delfont arranged a fortnight's season for me at the O'Keefe Centre in Toronto, where we took the complete *Danny La Rue Show* straight out of the Prince of Wales theatre, including scenery, props and a company of thirty. It was a costly exercise.

Because at this time I wouldn't fly, I travelled to New York on board the *Queen Elizabeth II* and from there drove up across New York State to Toronto. It was a long and arduous journey, but gave me an opportunity to discover and get to know a beautiful part of America, albeit through the window of a car. The entire trip took me nine full days.

Niagara Falls was breathtaking and spectacular and all that I always thought it would be. I took the kids from the show on a second visit with me shortly after arriving in Canada, and we all wore our funny plastic macs and looked like a chorus-line of nuns from *The Sound of Music*.

Toni Palmer, David Ellen, Wayne King and my musical director, Derek New, joined me on the *Queen Elizabeth II* and we presented two nights of cabaret on board to entertain our fellow passengers. When I was first asked if I would consider appearing in cabaret on board ship, I refused immediately. I hadn't performed on a boat since my concert party days in the Royal Navy which were long gone, and I definitely *wasn't* going to start all over again, or so I thought. When I discovered we were to be given luxury first-class passage for free in return for those two shows, I was shrewd enough to review the situation – and agreed! In the end, I enjoyed it greatly and I have returned to this form of 'busman's holiday' on several occasions since, but I hasten to add, only on the *Queen Elizabeth II*.

We made the crossing to New York, in a Force 10 gale, the worst weather they had experienced for quite some time. It was so bad we had to cancel our first performance because nothing would stay upright on the stage, including the piano, the ship was rolling too much in the giant waves. The following evening, however, the liner altered course to find calmer waters, which allowed us the opportunity of putting on our show. It went ahead without a hitch. There was a large contingency of Americans on board with us, and they seemed to enjoy the show immensely judging from their reactions. It was an encouraging sign for what lay ahead.

However, only minutes after we came off stage, the ship changed course once more and ploughed headfirst back into the maelstrom. A mighty wave hit the side of the liner, buckling one of the decks and flooding the second-class dining-room. The piano, which literally moments before we had been using, was thrown across the stage and slammed into a little girl breaking her arm, and every single plate in the restaurant was smashed to pieces. It must have cost Cunard thousands of pounds in damage. The sea was quite horrendous for the entire voyage, but I have always been a good sailor, a legacy from my days aboard HMS *Loch Ruthven* during the war, and I took it all in my stride. Poor David Ellen had a permanent appointment in the medical bay, receiving daily injections to combat his sea-sickness. It was an eventful journey. As soon as we docked in New York, I had my passport stolen, and I thought the whole episode was doomed to failure. I was very pleased to be proved wrong.

I thought I was going to dislike New York. I loved it, mainly because the people were so nice to me. I was invited to see Tessie O'Shea in a nightclub there, and she was fabulous. The audience gave her a standing ovation which surprised me as I had not thought they would love her so much. But she was very clever; she did what she knew she could do, but Americanized her act, and the audience appreciated it so much.

It gave me great confidence, yet I was still nervous and apprehensive when I eventually arrived in Toronto. I had never appeared outside Britain before, and although I was an invited artiste to another country, with a good track record behind me, I had never been seen live in Canada. I was thoughtful – what would the audiences expect of me? Would they *even* come to see me? I hoped they wouldn't be disappointed. I kept asking myself the same question: had I made a mistake in coming so far? The show opened in Toronto on 19 October 1976 to a packed house. My fears seemed groundless.

The O'Keefe Centre is a massive theatre, holding well over four thousand people. It is a very long and narrow building and from the stage gives a false impression, as if there are 24,000 people packed inside. When Mary Martin appeared there in *Hello, Dolly!*, she was extremely worried about the vastness of the auditorium, and whether or not she would be seen from the stage in such a cavernous venue, being so tiny herself. So she asked her maid to go out front and take a look at the show from the very back of the building. Mary went on stage for one particular scene in the musical dressed in a full-length evening dress in gold, which complimented her bright red hair to perfection. She looked stunning.

After the show, she confronted her maid.

'Well, what did I look like?' said Mary, eager for a reply. 'Could you see me? Could you hear me?'

'Honey,' said the maid. 'You looked like a *lipstick*.'

I really didn't have any such problems myself. Part of my success has happened because I look very tall and lean. I am a very good clothes horse. Some people who are small can't wear fabulous outfits, but I can wear the most outrageous clothes and get away with it through being so tall. I'm good for large theatres. I am not only physically big, I work big as a performer, projecting myself.

Toronto has a large Irish population and there were many ex-patriates in the first-night audience, which helped me enormously. I felt very much at home. The audience also appreciated the fact that I had done my homework, too, before I appeared. I didn't present the same act I performed back home. I had gone out of my way to have some new material written for a Canadian public. I localized a lot of the humour and made the patter and jokes far more parochial to appeal to North American tastes. I thought it was essential for me to treat my new audience with utter respect. I wouldn't have dreamed of offending them. By tailoring my show to their likes, I was paying Canada and its people a supreme compliment. It worked well. The warmth of my reception was outstanding. I received a standing ovation, which became a nightly occurrence.

We had an exciting and tearful opening and, afterwards, Dom Deluise came backstage to see me. He was crying, not from laughter, but from emotion. He hugged me.

'Danny,' he said, 'it is the first time I have ever seen a heart working. You are wonderful, full of warmth.' I was thrilled.

The following morning, the press were very kind to me, too. We received some very good reviews, apart from the *Toronto Globe and Mail*. Their reviewer, David Sauve, destroyed me and called the show 'tasteless, witless and mindless'. He also delighted in telling his readers he had actually walked out in disgust because he could take no more.

Fortunately, I have enough conceit to know that if everyone disliked me when I first appeared, I certainly would not want to appear again. But there can never be an artiste, anywhere in the world, that everyone will like 100 per cent. It's not possible, and if they did, it would be very boring. Thank goodness we all have different tastes and opinions. I am delighted when people don't like me and go to great pains to say so. I admire and respect their honesty. I wouldn't want anyone to be half-hearted and say, 'Well, he's not too bad.' I much prefer people to come out into the open and be blunt. After all, I often go to the theatre myself and dislike some of the performers. Then, the next day, I'll read the reviews to find out how brilliant someone else thought they were. *You can't win*. That is the whole beauty of our profession. I have never been deterred by a bad notice. My only critic is my audience.

Despite one critic, we played to capacity business for a fortnight, although, when we first arrived in Toronto, the show was anything *but* sold out. Once we had opened, once the people could see what the show was all about, word of mouth did the rest. I was so thankful that my first overseas engagement should have been so well received.

The Danny La Rue Show was a huge artistic success but a financial failure. We made very little money because of the cost of travelling with such a vast production and company. Yet, it certainly succeeded in establishing the name of *Danny La Rue* in another continent, and made me think twice about my future. I went back to Toronto in 1983, to appear in cabaret at the Royal York Hotel, which was then the biggest hotel in the world, and the audiences flocked to see me again. It was a lovely three-week season. I wasn't forgotten. I would dearly like to go there again in the future and stage a traditional British pantomime. I think it would be sensational.

I came back to Britain brimming over with confidence and excitement. I had done what few British entertainers had ever done before me, travelled overseas and returned in triumph. I was stimulated at the prospect of extending myself even further. Now Australia looked very tempting, but there was still the same old barrier in my way. *Flying*.

Back home, I completed pantomime in Coventry and set off on a hectic tour of the country, which included a round of concert and cabaret engagements. But, gradually, I began to realize that I couldn't keep on going back to the same places every twelve months, and in some cases twice a year, even though I was continuing to break box-office records wherever I appeared. I had always prided myself that my success had been based on the careful selection of television appearances to avoid over-exposure. I did just enough to keep my name prominent. But now I was in danger of doing just what I feared most, over-exposing myself, in the medium I loved best, live theatre and cabaret. I needed to broaden my horizons once more to give me new challenges. Hughie Green provided the solution.

Apart from his marvellous work on television, with such shows as *The Sky's the Limit*, *Double Your Money* and *Opportunity Knocks*, Hughie Green was a former RAF pilot with a distinguished war record. He was employed at that time by British Airways in an advisory capacity. It was his job to undertake personal appearances and give lectures, and generally make suggestions to the company to help them improve the service and promote the name.

Hughie was in the Beverly Hills Hotel in America one Sunday morning when he discovered a unique idea, which he believed British Airways should introduce immediately. Reading through the Sunday newspaper, Hughie came across a story about a former Pan-Am pilot who was now running a scheme to help people to overcome their fear of flying, and went into great details of the methods used. The course cost 150 dollars and the success rate was quite astounding. What was more important, he discovered that a staggering 60 per cent of those people who had conquered their fear of flying later flew with Pan-Am. It was too good to be true.

Hughie told British Airways about it and asked if something might be set up in Britain. The airline agreed to organize a similar venture on a lesser scale, and in turn asked Hughie if he could find a show-business personality, who had never flown, to spearhead the project. It had to be someone well-known and popular with every strata of society in Britain.

'I know just the person,' he said. 'This man is acceptable to the Queen Mother right down to the lady in the fish and chip shop on the corner: *Danny La Rue*. I have been present when Danny has told me of the many offers he has had of employment in Australia, but can never go because he can't afford the time to travel there and back by ship.'

British Airways grabbed at the idea. I was appearing at the Wakefield Theatre Club when Hughie telephoned and asked if he could come up and see me. He said he had something very important to discuss with me, but couldn't tell me on the phone what it was all about. I knew exactly what it was. If he saw me face to face, he determined, he had a chance of changing my mind. On the phone I could just refuse and that was that. Hughie wanted to play with better odds.

We had been friends for a long time, so I agreed to a meeting at the Queen's Hotel in Leeds for the following day, and as soon as he walked through the door, I told *him* why he had come to see me.

'You want to talk to me about flying,' I said.

He was completely surprised. 'Yes, but how on earth did you know?'

'Instinct,' I replied. 'I had a feeling.'

'I hear you have turned down Australia again,' said Hughie, and proceeded to put forward his proposition. Hughie told me he would take me step by step through all the basic rudiments of flying, and added that, at any time I wanted to, I could pull out. It seemed fair.

'The only time you can't stop is when you go for your first ride in an aircraft and they have closed the doors,' said Hughie. 'Then you've got to go as far as Paris. But I'll arrange for a Rolls-Royce to be on standby on the runway in Paris when we arrive and, if you are scared, and don't want to go through with it any more, you can get off the plane and into the car, and we'll have you back in London for your show that night.'

It was very difficult for Hughie to grasp why people like me had a phobia about flying. He had been flying since he was seventeen, and had over 150 Atlantic crossings to his credit as pilot. But he was very sympathetic. I asked him all the stupid questions one does. How is it planes don't collide in mid-air when they are in cloud? What would happen if the engines stopped? I wanted to find out as much as I possibly could before I even attempted to get on a plane for myself. I told Hughie that I was scared the plane might crash, although I knew there were far more accidents on the roads in Britain than in the air. But when a plane went down, it was always a huge disaster and front-page news, and that stuck in my mind. Hughie helped to alleviate the fear by telling me something I had overlooked, and never really thought about before.

'The pilot of the plane is a very skilled and highly trained man,' said Hughie. 'But he is also human and wants to get home to see his wife and family each night just like everyone else. He certainly doesn't want to end up in the side of a mountain.'

After he showed me how much care was taken of the aircraft, how much they were looked after and maintained by quality engineers, I agreed to go along with the scheme. But I had to be certain in my own mind. To be honest, I had been thinking so much about Australia, I had even considered going to a hypnotist to help cure my aversion. Hughie Green's timely intervention was uncanny. Destiny?

Shortly after we had talked, I was taken to Heathrow airport and put in a flight simulator. For the next half-hour, I underwent a simulated flight from London to Johannesburg in tricky conditions, which experienced engine failure and a few other hair-raising goodies to keep us all on our toes. I was fascinated by it all, and utterly calm throughout. I listened and watched and saw the three members of the cabin crew on the flight deck, working very carefully and closely together as a superbly trained team. I saw all the lights flashing in the cockpit and took it all in. It was a totally new feeling for me, and I loved it, and felt completely safe. By then, I was driving myself around a lot more and I realized afterwards I felt more scared driving a car. When I came out of the simulator, Hughie was waiting, anxious.

'Will you fly?' he asked excitedly.

I nodded . . . and beamed. Hughie was absolutely elated, he looked as if a great weight had been lifted from his shoulders.

He had arranged for me to fly to Paris the following morning and, after all I had been through, I was really looking forward to the trip: it was a great romantic adventure. But that night, there was a dramatic new development: the weather. A heavy fog set in, and an announcement was made that all morning flights had been grounded until further notice. So it was off. Paris had to wait. I thought that was it. Providence telling me something: I wasn't meant to fly. I'd known all along really. I believe Hughie was convinced I would change my mind as well and back down. He phoned me late the following evening, and said that everything was now set for Paris in the morning, *if* I was still prepared to go through with it all. I had come this far, I told him, I might as well see it through.

The next day, I was very tense and tentative about what was going to happen as I boarded the plane.

What was I letting myself in for? I hoped I wouldn't panic if I didn't like the experience, and things started to go wrong. Then, before I could even ponder on the questions again, the plane doors were closed behind me, tight. There could be no turning back now.

I sat next to Hughie and swallowed hard. My hands were sweating profusely. Beads of perspiration trickled slowly down my face; my mouth dried. I was trying to make conversation to take my mind off what was happening to me, but try as I might, my brain was racing. A thousand questions jumbled themselves up in my head and fought to be asked. I was trying not to let anyone know I was apprehensive. I joked nervously for confidence. There was a lot of noise as the engines roared briefly. I took a deep breath and gulped a mouthful of hope as well.

'When are we going to take off?' I half-whispered to Hughie.

'We already have, Danny. We're in the air,' came the reply. I had been totally unaware of what was going on around me. *I was flying*. After all these years, *I was flying*. A tremendous sense of relief welled up inside me, the sticky palms had gone. In the elation at my discovery, I had completely forgotten about being nervous. I looked out of the window and saw London and the home counties stretched out before me like an endless model village. It was a beautiful clear day and I was spellbound by it all. I had never seen anything like it before in my life. I was so delighted with myself and my achievement, I kept bobbing up and down to look out of the window. When the stewardesses served champagne, we drank a toast to my achievement. Hughie Green was so proud of me. I was so grateful to him.

Although the weather had turned nasty by the time the plane landed in Paris, I was already on another plain and no longer cared. As I stepped out on to the airport runway, I turned to Hughie and shook him by the hand.

'I'm a flyer,' I said. 'I'm a flyer. You have made it all possible.' I was enormously flattered that he and British Airways had gone to so much trouble on my behalf, but it happened exactly when my destiny said it would. The timing was right.

We had the full VIP treatment in France yet I couldn't wait to get back on the plane for the flight home. It was like a big bus with drinks – a wonderful experience. I had made one of the most important decisions of my life, which was to change my life completely. I owed it all to Hughie Green. Once I had conquered my fear of flying, the last great barrier that for so many years had stood in the way of an international show-business career had been swept away. Now I was able to take up the many offers which had come my way over the last dozen or so years.

The problem now was that I was at the peak of my success in Britain and booked up for months in advance through the sheer weight of public demand to see my shows. It was a nice position to be in, but frustrating because I was turning down so many other projects I wanted to do like restoration comedy and straight plays.

In the space of eighteen months since my summer season at the Blackpool Opera House in 1977, I had completed two major club tours and starred in another money-making summer show at the Futurist Theatre in Scarborough. I had recently signed a contract with Louis Benjamin, head of Moss Empires, to star as the Merry Widow Twankey in the pantomime, *Aladdin*, for the 1978 Christmas season at the London Palladium. It was every entertainer's ambition to work at the London Palladium, and I was no exception. I had appeared at the theatre before in royal shows and galas, but to top the bill at the Palladium was a dream come true. There was something magical about playing the world's most famous theatre. I found it so romantic to think of all the fabulous stars who had trod those famous boards before me: Gracie Fields, Danny Kaye, the Crazy Gang, Bing Crosby, Flanagan and Allen, Jessie Matthews. I was proud to be in such a fine company. Once I'd signed the contract, I made arrangements that as soon as my pantomime season had completed its fourteen-week run, I would at last go to Australia to tour. I was fairly well-known in the antipodes, but I didn't want to take any chances. This time everything *had* to be right, I had waited too long to go and I couldn't fail now. I appreciated the value of billing me as 'Danny La Rue – Direct from the London Palladium'; it was a stroke of genius.

Aladdin at the London Palladium was one of the most enjoyable seasons I have ever experienced. I loved playing the theatre. I just found it so warm and intimate, everything a theatre should be. The pantomime cost £300,000 to stage and was worth every penny. The sets were magnificent, and my costumes, for which £30,000 had been set aside, were dazzling. One outfit alone, a mirror-studded train, cost £7,000. We opened five days before Christmas, and the newspaper reviews reflected the quality of the show. The *Daily Mirror* called it: 'A Christmas Cracker'. The *Financial Times* labelled me 'impeccable'. The audiences loved it, too, and over a quarter of a million people came through the doors during our limited season.

West End success like that has never gone to my head. I am a very practical performer in a hard business. I am too busy trying to make it a success to think about what it all means. I work very hard, but I am very lucky, I have lots of energy. I treasure the respect of my profession and cherish the friendships I have made at all the theatres I have played, not just from my companies, but from the entire theatre staff as well. Whenever I go back to the Palace, Prince of Wales or the Palladium, they are always very nice to me. 'Hello, Danny. Lovely to see you again.' They look upon me as a friend, which is so rewarding.

The success of *Aladdin* was later echoed in the provinces. We took the Palladium production to Bristol in 1980 and to Birmingham the following year for Christmas seasons. On both occasions the pantomime opened to advance booking figures in excess of £500,000, which at that time was the highest advance in show-business history for any theatre outside London. The Bristol production broke every record for a pantomime outside the West End, and *Aladdin* established itself as the most successful pantomime ever staged in the provinces. My pantos always became an occasion.

Throughout my Palladium season, however, I prepared myself thoroughly for the new and exciting adventure that lay ahead in Australia and the forthcoming six-month tour that impresarios Hugh and Leonard Sadleir had set up. They were both good friends and had tried for many years to persuade me to tour their country. Since then we have remained close mates and business associates. I faced that first visit with trepidation. I had been nervous about appearing in Canada, but this was different. Wayne King was very helpful. He gave me tremendous encouragement and calmed any doubts I had about going to his native country. He assured me I would be a success. 'The audiences are waiting for you,' he kept telling me, and added that I would be given a fabulous welcome. 'They'll love you.'

Wayne did a superb job to put my mind at rest. He talked to me about the vastness and beauty of Australia and put me in touch with all kinds of people to give me a feeling and a flavour of the country itself. To understand Australia, I had first to understand Australians. I had learnt from my season in Canada how essential it was to do my homework. If *I* didn't make the effort, how could I expect the audiences to? It was a great consolation to be forearmed.

I spent a lot of time learning about the continent, researching into its people, its customs and politics. I found out information about the towns and cities which I was to be playing, and Wayne helped me find local writers to help me put the finishing touches to my act. They looked at it very carefully and gave me guidelines. I replaced all references to British politicians with their Australian counterparts. It was only common sense. You have to change certain things, and your attitude to your work, according to the audience. It's simply not good enough to adopt a holier than thou approach and expect people to like everything you do.

I suppose my biggest worry was how the Australian audiences would react to what I did. We prepared the way carefully, and I did masses of advance publicity before I arrived. But, even with my track record of success and triumph in England, there was no guarantee that every society in the world would accept a man who dresses up as a woman, no matter how tastefully. I was certain, though, that once the Australians realized I was an entertainer who created fabulous characters in shimmering outfits I'd be home and dry. However, I was slightly intimidated by the country's macho image and expected to be entertaining people who were all six feet six inches tall with shoulders to match, who carried surfboards wherever they went.

There was a very famous and long-established drag club in Sydney called Les Girls, which had become a great landmark in the city in the same way that the Windmill Theatre had endeared itself to London. Les Girls presented a spectacular show, featuring glamorous artistes who mimed to records for a specialized audience. But, it was totally different to the kind of performance for which I am famous, and the Australians' view of 'drag' entertainment was very limited.

Barry Humphries, whom I had known since the days when he did a five-minute spot for Joan Littlewood at Stratford East, had managed to reach a much wider audience with Dame Edna Everage. Of course, comparisons were made immediately between the two of us, which again were utterly wrong. What people failed to accept is that Edna is a character that is played. A 24-hour a day caricature who is presented in an aggressive, destructive, and slightly grotesque manner on an intellectual level, yet remains always brilliantly funny. I am not like that at all. I create glamorous illusions of women, which are warm, enchanting and pure music hall. I needed to get that across to the Australian public. I was not a commentator on world affairs. There were no messages, no underlying meanings or deep comment, it was all just a giggle – and entertainment, nothing more.

When Barry Humphries first started to become famous in England with Dame Edna, the British press tried remorselessly to get the two of us together in frocks for interviews and pictures. I refused. One of my rules has always been that I am *never* interviewed in costume. If I ever allow that to happen, I will destroy the whole illusion forever. Costumes are for performance only, and I think the public respect me for it. The press, too, have a sneaking admiration.

As soon as *Aladdin* completed its Palladium season, I left London for Sydney, taking with me over one hundred gorgeous outfits with which to appear in a splendid new production of *The Danny La Rue Show*, featuring a truly international line-up of my 'ladies' to appeal to any audience – Mae West, Shirley Temple, Liz Taylor, Betty Grable, Marlene Dietrich and Margaret Thatcher. For a recent convert to air travel, I took the 24-hour flight half-way around the world in my stride. I loved it and thought it amazing I had never done it before.

I arrived ten days before my opening night to allow me time to acclimatize and get to know this new country. But it was as if I had been there a million times. It was like walking across the road, not travelling 13,000 miles, and I felt instantly at home. There was also a vast amount of promotion and publicity to do.

In Sydney, I was introduced to the local press at a special reception in the Hilton Hotel, and I hit it off immediately with the hard-bitten, news-hungry reporters and cameramen. If they had been expecting to see a fella in a frock, they were disappointed. I slayed them instead. When I appeared on *The Mike Walsh Show*, the country's most successful daytime television show, shortly afterwards, the Australian people got a glimpse of the real Danny La Rue and they warmed to me, too.

I made my Australian début on 19 April 1979, at the start of a four-week season at the Regent Theatre in Sydney, prior to touring. I was so nervous, Jack Hanson asked me to take a drink to calm me down. It was something I had never done in the past. Then just before I was due on stage, I was politely informed there were over four hundred of my fellow professionals from all branches of the business in the packed audience, as well as civic dignitaries, film and television personalities and Sydney socialites, all eager to see Danny La Rue's first night in Australia. It was awe-inspiring. They are going to destroy me, I thought. I so desperately wanted to succeed and do well.

I went out on stage and gave one of the best performances of my career. I like to think that every performance I give is the best ever, but this one was very special, and completely captivated my audience. I left to a standing ovation and cheers. Wayne King had been right. Australia *was* waiting for me. It was the scene of one of the outstanding

FROM DRAGS TO RICHES

highlights of my life, and if I had written the reviews myself, I couldn't have done a better job: 'Danny Hits the Top' said one newspaper; 'The Diamond that is La Rue' echoed another; 'Danny's Glitter All Gold', said a third. Danny La Rue had done it again.

Sydney was the start of a landslide. By the time I had completed my month at the Regent Theatre, the numerous appearances I had made on television and radio – everyone vied with each other to interview me – guaranteed excellent business wherever I went. It didn't take me long to find out, either, that radio has a tremendous influence in Australia; it has become a way of life for many people. I appeared on it as often as I could. Barry Ferber, managing director of the 4GG radio station on the Gold Coast, and his beautiful wife, Judith, were very supportive towards me and helped to establish my name. They continue to be a great encouragement, not only to me but to all the British acts that appear in Australia.

The tour took in all the major cities: Adelaide, Melbourne, Newcastle. In Canberra, the High Commissioner gave me a huge party at the Consulate to celebrate my arrival in town, while Dr Ella Stark, the premier of Darwin, flew over especially to present me with a plaque and thank me personally for all my efforts in raising money for the North Australian city, following its terrible cyclone disaster in 1974.

After I'd opened at the Canberra Theatre, I was invited to attend a special literary luncheon, to which tickets were sold and the money raised donated to charity. The people at the function were very kind to me and I thanked them for making me so welcome. Once we had finished eating, the president of the society introduced me to several of the dignitaries in attendance, including the local chief rabbi and his wife whom I found very gracious. He told me how much he had enjoyed my show, but made a rather provoking comment. 'Tell me,' he said, 'I wonder what Jesus Christ would have thought of you?'

My reply was instant. 'He would have thought, sir, that I might have made a very good second to Mary Magdalene.'

Although I love most Australian cities, and absolutely adore Queensland and its unbelievable beauty, I found Canberra a little too bland. It was built especially as the capital of Australia to end the friendly rivalry between Sydney and Melbourne, and the city was inaugurated into its exalted position in 1927, the year of my birth, by the Duke of

York. But when I was asked by one Australian journalist for my honest opinion of the capital city, I didn't mince my words. 'If I were a Russian ballet dancer, I would defect.'

I liked Brisbane. I did three weeks at Her Majesty's Theatre there and, when I first arrived at the magnificent theatre, I saw several large posters on display advertising a concert for Dame Edna Everage, next to a solitary one of mine. There was a lengthy queue at the box office which I thought was for her, a national Australian institution. But, it was for me, a stranger in a new city, and I was so thrilled. Shortly afterwards, I appeared on Channel 9 television and bumped into a lovely, unassuming man at the studios as I was waiting to go on air.

'Good morning,' I said and smiled.

'And good morning to my Queensland,' came the reply, and he asked me if I had ever been to the city before.

'No, it's my first time,' I volunteered the information. 'But it looks beautiful.'

'Well, thank you,' he said, shook my hand and walked away.

I didn't know who he was, until someone told me it was Sir Joh Bjelke-Peterson, premier of Queensland. You would never have known, he was so down to earth and genuinely in love with Queensland. I found him charming and not like a politician at all.

In 1987 the Queensland government paid me the supreme compliment of making me the Honorary Ambassador for Expo '88. I was personally asked by the Hon. Sir Llewellyn Edwards, the chairman of World Expo, and the Hon. Sir Edward Williams, KCMG, KBE, the Commissionaire General.

After Brisbane, the tour moved on to New Zealand, with equal success and acclaim, returning to Melbourne for a final six-week season at the Princess Theatre. But it had become such an outstanding success and since demand for tickets had far exceeded anyone's expectations, and the feedback was so overwhelming, it was decided to extend the tour by a further six months. I had been taken to Australia's heart and accepted as one of its own. I was ecstatic.

The six-month extension allowed us to take the show out to the people and into some of the tiny country towns, where the reception was unwavering. The Australians love their theatre, and some of the civic centres are truly magnificent places. They are very supportive, too. At Mackay, which is like a cowboy town stuck in the middle of the desert, the theatre had one of the best pianos I have ever seen in my life, a nine-foot Steinway, and they regularly presented concerts and recitals. It was incredible.

We later appeared in one theatre that left a lot to be desired and I nearly fried in the process. We were booked into a tiny town to the north of Brisbane, and presented at a theatre made entirely of corrugated tin, with slats on the side, and no air-conditioning. The only form of relief from the incessant sun came from fifteen large electric fans, strategically placed on the roof. When the fans were turned on to full capacity, no one could hear a thing above the din they made, not even with the sophisticated sound system. If the fans were left off to allow us all to be heard, the temperature of 120 degrees outside was soon intensified to 240 degrees inside, as the sun beat down on to the corrugated iron roof. It was a vicious circle. But I'll always remember the sight of a crowd of Aborigines outside the theatre, peering through the slats at the sight of this fella in a frock romping about on the stage and sweltering under the costumes, the wigs and the make-up.

That first tour was the start of the long and lasting love affair I have had with Australia, which continues and flourishes today. Since 1979, I have toured the continent each year. It has become a vital part of my annual work schedule, and today I am as well known 'down under', through my television appearances and live performances, as I am in Britain. I have been spoilt. In 1985, I was lucky enough to star in ten one-hour television spectaculars for Australian Television. Each one was a sizeable success in the ratings. My career had really taken off. The TV shows were produced by an ex-patriate, Paul Sharrat, for whom I have great respect. Each year he also presents traditional British music-hall along the Gold Coast, with his wife Sue.

I am very lucky to be successful on both sides of the world, and I can work my year just in the two countries if I want to. I have always been invited back; I think the Australians realize now that I am quite a nice bloke and I don't really walk around in a frock.

Before my first tour, my vision of a typical Australian was as a fat-bellied, beer-swilling chauvinist with corks swinging from his sun hat. Nothing could be further from the truth. They are really very similar to the British in make-up, which is not surprising when you consider how many ex-patriates there are living out there. I appeared for a whole month in Perth and 75 per cent of my audience throughout the entire run were ex-patriate English.

Many Australians are Cockneys with suntans, who have a bawdy sense of humour and are very forthright in their attitudes; they call a spade a spade in no uncertain terms. And yet, I find them warm and sensitive people, wonderfully generous and hospitable; and they admire anyone who does something well.

I have made many marvellous friends, particularly amongst Wayne King's family. Robert Finikiotis, who brilliantly handles all my affairs in Australia, has become a very great buddy of mine, and I can't thank him enough for everything he has done for me since my first visit. We are very close. Johnny Lockwood and Peter Colville, both fellow Water Rats and old buddies from England, have been living in Australia for many years now. They have an organization akin to the Grand Order of Water Rats over there called Echidnas and raise a tremendous amount of money for charity. An echidna is an animal much like a porcupine, and I was delighted and honoured to be made a member of these Australian show business brethren in 1986.

For all their marvellous qualities, however, Australians do tend to take things far too seriously and almost go into mourning when they lose at cricket. But they have an enthusiasm we used to possess many years ago, which now, sadly, we sorely lack. Despite what people say to the contrary, the country has an enormous culture – wonderful writers, designers and painters – and is blessed in the arts, especially in the direction of the ballet, opera and cinema, competing on an international level with the best of them.

Noël Coward never disguised the fact that he hated Australia and made several unfortunate remarks to that effect. The feeling was completely mutual! It was his great loss. Noël did tend to get pompous at times; Australians tend to be outspoken.

To me, Australia is the world's best-kept secret and I adore the place and its people. It has become my second home, and I am only glad the country is so far away from anywhere because otherwise it would have been invaded and totally spoilt by now.

One of the funniest sights I have ever seen came one Christmas on the beach at Sydney. The sun was beating down, the temperature soaring, and yet there, standing ankle-deep in sand was a Father Christmas character, resplendent in full regalia, including a white bushy beard. Sweat was pouring down his face. Next to him stood a bewildered little boy, totally naked. Christmas takes on a different complexion at 100 degrees in the shade, where cotton wool is stuck to window panes as makeshift snow.

In the spring of 1981, I returned to undertake my first cabaret tour, which was presented by a superb entrepreneur, Lionel Abrahams, for whom I have worked in Australia on many occasions since. I was expecting the clubs to be similar to those in Britain, at Lakeside, Batley or Wakefield. There was no comparison. These were vast entertainment complexes, catering for every taste, every preference. Beautiful clubs, tastefully designed and built with outstanding facilities. The club room is only a small part of the buildings, which might also have a 100-foot swimming pool, gymnasium, restaurants, squash and tennis courts. Gambling is allowed as well, so they can afford to pay out incredible amounts of money to attract international entertainers because they are subsidized by the one-armed bandits. The St George's League Club in Sydney is revered as Australia's London Palladium. I was rather proud of my achievement because I became the first person to take a glamorous West End show into the Australian clubs. The audiences went wild, and history was repeating itself over ten thousand miles away from home.

A couple of years later, I was appearing at Twin Towns, a spectacular club overlooking the Pacific Ocean, when several of my friends from the profession, who were also working locally, asked me if it might be possible to arrange an extra show. They hadn't been able to see me on this trip because we were all working at the same time. Australian schedules are similar to American ones: clubs open Tuesdays to Sundays, with Mondays as rest days, and a Sunday show which usually starts mid-afternoon. All my friends working the same hours as me had no chance of seeing my show, so I took my problem to the manager and proposed staging an early-evening performance one Sunday if he would be obliged to lay on the facilities. He agreed without hesitation, but added sceptically that 'nobody else will be there. We've never had an early-evening show on a Sunday.'

When my friends arrived for the hastily arranged Sunday show, they couldn't believe it. The place was filled to the rafters, and my mates had great difficulty getting in themselves, which had been the whole point of the exercise in the first place. It had never been known before because nobody ever went to a Sunday-evening show in Twin Towns. I had set a precedent once more.

And Hughie Green didn't realize what he had started.

10
'I didn't know a fella in a frock could make so much money'

I fell in love with Walton Hall as soon as I saw it and wanted to buy it immediately. That was in 1974. It took two years before it came on the market.

Show business had been very good to me. I had emerged as one of the most successful and highest-paid performers in Britain, and I certainly had no intention of taking my money out of the country and running away to become a tax exile. That wasn't my style. I had never forgotten the kindness and hospitality of the British people when we first arrived in London as strangers, Irish immigrants alone in a new country. So I wanted to invest my money in Britain and not take it abroad.

Quite truthfully, I had never thought about money. I stopped worrying about it when I stopped running to the bank with the next cheque. That was the only difference it made. However, I had earned a sizeable sum from the business over the years and I needed to use it wisely to secure my future in such a precarious industry as show business. I had seen money go straight to the heads of some of my colleagues in the profession too many times. Instead of seeking financial advice and putting money away for a future, they had been content to fritter it away too readily and, before long, found themselves in all kinds of trouble. I was a bit shrewder. I certainly didn't want it to happen to me. I had always been careful with my money, too much hard work and hard graft and sweat had gone into making it for me to throw it all away.

My mother was very much in favour of my investing in property. 'Put your money in bricks and mortar,' she would often say, and I had taken her advice on a number of occasions with the purchase of the Swan Inn at Streatley, my château in France, and my home in Henley. *Bricks and mortar*. I had never bought a share in my life, although I was very partial to investing money in antiques of all kinds with which I filled my home. I have a superb collection, going back to the sixteenth century. When I was much younger, the first time I had any money of

my own, I went out and splurged fifty quid on antiques. My mates
thought I was mad. I have never stopped. I love beautiful things. My
mother was a great encouragement. She used to say, 'The pound isn't
worth anything any more.' And she was right. She was the first person
who made me buy a diamond ring.

When you are born ordinary, you want to achieve something special
during your life and that was one of the reasons why I eventually
decided to buy Walton Hall for £500,000. I wanted to show my mother
that the lad had made it on his own.

England had been very good to me, too. I wanted to give something
back. Restoring this particular piece of its heritage was my way of
doing it. I was proud of my achievements, coming from my Irish
background, I had now bought a stately home and a stake in England's
history. It was ideally situated, too, for the Midlands and for my work.
The Midlands had always been good to me in my theatre career. I had
a great affection for the whole area.

Yet, there was a lot of hard work ahead. Walton Hall was in a
battered state of genteel decay and was virtually falling down when I
first saw it. I was astounded that anyone could ever let such a magnificent building fall into such a pitiful condition. Had I not stepped in
and bought it, there was a very real possibility it would have become
derelict. It would take time to renovate the house, but that was what I
intended to do, to bring it back to its former glories. Even in such an
appalling state, I could see the potential. It would make a marvellous
hotel again with all manner of possibilities for the future. It was happening all over the world, hotels with their own cabaret rooms, restaurants and bars, and leisure facilities in the grounds. That was my
ambition for the place and I wanted to make it work for me. Eventually,
I saw myself as a kind of mine host having the best of both worlds. I
could work when I wanted to, entertain in my own restaurants, or
simply pull pints behind the bar. I wasn't fussy. I saw Walton Hall
very much as my future, and I was excited at the prospect. It was my
Pandora's box and I wanted to lift the lid.

It was a wonderful setting: situated in seventy acres of parkland,
near to the village of Wellesbourne in Warwickshire. It had its own
church and graveyard, and had once had its very own village, which
was now separate, although the villagers came to use the chapel, which
had a Norman font and a hand-operated organ. The whole place had
an aura. It was right in the middle of nowhere, almost cut off from

everything. But it also had the air of elegance, belonging to another time. You might have been in the eighteenth or nineteenth century. It was uncanny.

Walton Hall had a chequered history, dating back to Norman times. It was for centuries the home of the Mordaunt family, whose ancestry went back to William the Conquerer, although the present building had been constructed by Sir Gilbert Scott in the early nineteenth century. He put in the spectacular sweeping staircase in the entrance hall, with magnificent marble pillars and tiers of stained-glass windows, depicting the Mordaunt family history. It was a breathtaking sight and one to behold as soon as you walked in. Sir Gilbert was a brilliantly gifted man, whose works included designing St Pancras station in London.

There was plenty of scandal surrounding the tenth and last baronet, Sir Charles Mordaunt, who was MP for South Warwickshire from 1859 to 1868. He was involved in a bitter and notorious divorce case in 1875 after discovering his wife, Harriet, had been having an affair with the Prince of Wales, later to become Edward VII. The acrimonious divorce severely damaged the Mordaunt good name and standing in the area and shook the foundations of London society. Sir Charles was never the same man again.

Three years later, he married Mary Louisa Cholmondeley, who bore him five daughters and a son. The heir to the family title, however, was certified incurably insane, so the direct male line ended with Sir Charles's death in 1897, leaving Mary Louisa to preside over the fading family fortunes for another fifty years.

During the Second World War, the Army moved in to Walton Hall, which became a training centre for the Czechoslovakian SAS suicide squads, before reverting to a normal barracks for cadets. On Mary Louisa's death, in 1947, the building housed a girls' boarding school for several years, until financial pressure forced its closure. Occasionally, we were visited by former pupils of the school, wanting to see their old dormitory or where the refectory used to be. They were all grown women by then. It later became a hotel which failed, too.

The house and grounds were reputed to be haunted and I often felt a mysterious presence myself. I would arrive home very early in the morning and feel as if I was in a cottage. It was an eerie sensation and I am sure I saw the ghost on one occasion, but the mind plays funny tricks. According to legend, a young girl was given two horses by her lover, who then shot them. She died shortly afterwards, and is supposed to be seen riding in the grounds at night on her horses. They were buried in the grounds.

Strangely enough, when Sir Charles Mordaunt arrived home unexpectedly from Parliament one day, he found two pedigree Welsh ponies in the Walton stables. When he discovered they had been a very recent gift from the Prince of Wales, he took a gun and shot dead both animals in a mad frenzy.

I always think it is romantic for old homes to have a ghost, providing the spirits are friendly, and not evil.

Once I had completed the purchase, and set about renovating the building, the local council were very unhelpful towards me. They wrongly assumed I would turn Walton Hall into Las Vegas and fill it with one-armed bandits, and didn't credit me with any taste or common sense. I wanted to make it beautiful, not vulgar, and the local residents loved the idea. I think they revelled in the fact that a celebrity had taken over the estate and warmed to the whole idea. They were very possessive towards me, too, and accepted me as one of their own as soon as I arrived. They realized I wasn't going to harm the place. I was going to take nothing away from it. I was only going to add to its beauty which I wanted to share with everyone. The villagers were very loyal. Once a year, I allowed the grounds to be used for the neighbourhood fête. I also let it out to the local police force to use the lawns as a football pitch. Each Saturday morning, local residents would ride over on horseback for drinks and they also used the facilities in all the bars and restaurants. We had a regular clientele from our villagers who gave us tremendous support. The local hunt also held its annual ball and banquet at the Hall.

One of the first things I did get rid of in the grounds of Walton Hall were the peacocks. I hate peacocks. Sadly, a fox took one of them before I could send the others off to a bird sanctuary.

Over the next half-dozen years, I invested everything I earned in Walton Hall to turn my dreams into reality and transform a fading Victorian sandstone building into an elegant luxury hotel. I wanted my guests to feel as if they were staying in a home – my home. With the help of my brother, we renovated and refurbished all seventy-six bedrooms, many with antique four-poster beds that proved a great attraction with American visitors who stayed there. Dick also delicately restored the hand-painted nineteenth century ceilings and brought them back to their original splendour. He did a brilliant craftsman's job.

When I first took over the building, the entrance hall had been covered from wall-to-wall in a hideous carpet, which was ripped up to reveal underneath the most exquisite hand-painted tiles I had ever seen, dating back a hundred years and more. They deserved far better than to be hidden under the shag pile. To complement the designs, I installed four magnificent cut-glass crystal chandeliers.

At one end of the building, we established a piano bar, decorated in black velvet and gold. Liberace, who was a regular visitor to the hotel, adored it and spent many happy hours tinkering on the piano. One of the highlights of our evenings was to gather around the piano and sing to Lee's accompaniment. He called Walton Hall my castle and whenever he was in England, and was asked where he was staying, he would reply: 'At Danny La Rue's castle. Where else?' He loved the whole place. The first time he stayed, he couldn't wait to get back to America to tell the folks back home in California all about it. In 1978, I paid £3,200 for an antique Edwardian Bechstein grand piano to complete the room. It set it off to perfection and looked magnificent.

I tried to give each of the bars its own individuality. The Hunters Bar was rustic, while the Victorian Bar was immaculately furnished in red and gold with brown luxurious leather furniture. The Clown Bar was very special to me. Since I was a small boy, I have had a strange affinity towards clowns. When I was a child, I found them degraded, and hated to see them persecuted in the name of comedy, by others. If someone poured water down their trousers, I cried. My mother couldn't understand my reaction.

Today, I collect clowns from all over the world. To me they represent the ultimate sadness, and yet they are so beautiful because sadness is like utter happiness. There is only a thin dividing line between the two emotions. We can laugh one minute and cry the next, and clowns explain this state perfectly. They are the ultimate paradox. Clowns are always degraded and yet they are no fools. I dislike all that symbolism, but they have helped me enormously to understand that from a quality of sadness you can only build. They remind me that life is beautiful – and there is an amazing beauty in sadness.

The bar itself reflected that expression with some marvellous life-sized, hand-painted pictures and murals depicting clowns through the ages, from the fabulous Italian *Commedia dell'arte* in their exotic make-up, to the modern clown. It took four months to be painted, and was the work of Gerry Binns, a dancer in my company until we discovered his outstanding talents at painting and design. He once sent me some hand-painted place mats as a birthday present and I was astounded when he told me he had painted them himself. He went on to establish himself as a major theatrical designer, working with some of the premier opera companies.

My own apartment, tucked away in one of the wings, was a testament to my love of fine antiques. Chinese rice paintings from the seventeenth century, in mint condition, hung on the tan and gold striped Regency-style wallpaper. I had Dresden vases, Meissen porcelain, and elegant gilt mirrors, and a superb collection of tables. My favourite piece was a bronze statue of David, which represented the ultimate triumph of the weak overcoming the strong. It was important to me when Jack and I bought a house or flat to buy little things as mementoes, not necessarily antiques, but pieces of china, bronzes, memorabilia. They can be taken anywhere with me and remind me of my life and each one carries with it its own memory.

The suite had green leather sofas, velvet curtains and thick pile carpets with masses of green plants everywhere, which I found cosy and relaxing. I love to live with green plants, I talk to them and thank them for being so beautiful. It's true, they are.

In my loo, one of seventy throughout the building, I had a set of Vernet drawings offset on the gold, black and brown wallpaper. I designed the suite myself and I do believe that if I had not gone into show business I would have dearly loved to pursue a career as a designer or interior decorator. I have many friends in that business, whom I admire greatly. One particular mate agreed to do up Dame Edith Evans's apartment for nothing. I think he felt sorry for the darling lady, and her flat was so dark and needed re-decorating. While they were tidying up the place, a Van Gogh drawing was discovered hanging under the stairs. There was a general shriek and commotion at the find. 'Edith this is so valuable,' cried my designer friend. 'What made you hang it in there?'

'Well, dear boy,' she said, 'there was a hook.'

It had always been my intention to present entertainment at Walton Hall and to appear in cabaret there myself as often as I was able. I also wanted to develop the conservatory and turn it into a Victorian music hall, and relished the idea of performing there with a few show-business mates and the famous Players' Theatre. The idea had a great appeal. I warmed to that era of entertainment. It was a romantic time and I had met many stars from the music hall now in the twilight of their years, who regaled me with wonderful stories of a bygone age.

I also visualized staging Shakespeare on the lawns, being so close to Stratford-upon-Avon, and opera in the open air had a great attraction for me. There was no shortage of ideas, but we had to build gradually. I had already re-opened the swimming pool and tennis courts and wanted to develop the grounds even further.

Many of my show-business friends came down for weekends and provided a late-night Saturday cabaret for me. Dustin Gee was a regular and great favourite. I wanted to build up to a situation where I was presenting some kind of entertainment for the public on every night of the week, instead of the three we started off with. We held some wonderfully colourful masquerades at the hotel. Walton Hall with its long, sweeping staircase lent itself to masked balls with everyone dressing up so elegantly. We could have been transported back to another era.

At Christmas and on New Year's Eve, I performed in both restaurants. On one occasion, I had just finished my first appearance when I stepped out into the corridor in a lovely chiffon gown. An elderly gentleman saw this grand lady coming towards him, and opened the door for her. His face went white when I said, 'Thanks mate,' in my normal voice.

Being a professional, I had the utmost confidence in the people who ran Walton Hall for me. I was happy to leave the catering side to the professionals. I wouldn't have expected them to start telling me how to do my act. I left well alone, apart from keeping a watchful eye on what was going on. We soon built up a reputation for fine cuisine which pleased me no end. Michael Oxford, who managed the Swan at Streatley, and who had worked with me in my club at Hanover Square, helped me establish the hotel, and later, my brother-in-law, Johnny Vecchio, took over, while my sister, Nancy, represented me when I wasn't there.

Unfortunately, I had to sell my hotel at Streatley to help me finance the development of Walton Hall. I couldn't keep the two hotels running together. It was far too costly. Walton Hall, I thought, had more potential. The Swan had to go. Walton Hall, however, had to become a working hotel – and a going concern that made a profit – and not just Danny La Rue's folly. As such we attracted a lot of customers. Our excellent conference facilities, too, were well used and several major international companies held seminars in the building. It also became commonplace for film stars and show-business personalities to drop in by helicopter. The Norwegian ambassador arrived this way to attend one conference. Just like show business, reputations counted for everything.

Shortly after I opened the hotel, my career started to take off internationally, and the demands for appearances increased tremendously. Being a compulsive workaholic, I wanted to accommodate everyone who wanted to see me perform, so I turned down very little in the way of engagements. It wasn't in my nature anyway. But time was precious and I found I was spending less and less of it at the hotel. The pressure intensified in 1979 with my first visit to Australia, and my subsequent success there only exacerbated the problem. I simply couldn't be in two places at the same time no matter how hard I tried. *And I tried.* If it had come down to my making a choice between my professional career and my hotel, it would have been an extremely hard decision for me to make, almost impossible. I wanted the best of both worlds.

Part of the outstanding success of my club in Hanover Square lay in the fact that I was always there, every single night. Danny La Rue's existed and flourished because of Danny La Rue. The public went there to see me and, being on the premises at all times, I was in total control of my destiny. For that reason, I should have spent more time at Walton Hall. I realize now that people in show business should never run that kind of business unless they can be there all the time, particularly if they have an established name and reputation. At Walton Hall, potential customers would ring up to find out when I would be in residence and then book their accommodation accordingly. It was Danny La Rue's hotel, and they wanted to see Danny La Rue, it was as simple as that. If I wasn't there, they stayed away. Things started to change. I was the figurehead, but my name alone wasn't enough to attract business, my presence was needed instead. But I was a working professional and, such was my make-up, I went wherever my work took me. Unfortunately, I had to leave the running of the hotel to others. It was a mistake, not because *they* couldn't cope, on the contrary, everyone who worked there did a magnificent job and things ran smoothly. *I* couldn't cope.

By the early eighties, it was becoming an impossible situation for me.

I had settled down to a comfortable niche in the business and my year was well-planned in advance. At Christmas I starred in pantomime, before leaving for engagements in Australia. Back home for summer season in Eastbourne (1980), or Great Yarmouth (1981) or Paignton (1982), before embarking on a comprehensive club or theatre tour in the autumn. Then it started all over again. There was no time for Walton Hall. I was trying to cut myself into little pieces in an effort to make time. It was impossible to do.

It was Jack's idea to put the hotel on the market for sale. He could see the situation could never right itself and something had to go. I agonized over the decision for a long time. The hotel was just starting to come together as I wanted it. All the plans I had made at the beginning were coming to fruition. But there was no other choice. Jack was right. There was no way I was going to give up a show-business career I had spent years establishing. I didn't want to anyway. So, reluctantly, I agreed to sell. It was in the best interests of Walton Hall and Danny La Rue. At the beginning of 1983, the hotel went up for sale.

And then something happened to make me change my mind.

In March, I was approached by two Canadian businessmen – Gary Salter and Howard Wax – who called themselves entrepreneurs. They wanted to buy the hotel from me. They had been introduced to me by a very reputable firm of Warwickshire estate agents, who acted in good faith as go-between. Before long, they made me an offer, which Martell Securities, my own company controlling Walton Hall, accepted. They were utterly charming people, though a little too gushing for my liking. Yet, shortly afterwards, when we met to negotiate the finer points of the agreement, they were both extremely positive in their attitude and made me a very attractive new offer.

In return for my remaining as the hotel's figurehead, I would receive a directorship and become a major shareholder in the property, into which the Canadians wanted to invest up to three million pounds on a face-lift and new expansion scheme. We discussed the offer at length over the coming weeks, and later they showed me a beautiful coloured brochure that had been specially printed and manufactured to sell their ideas to would-be investors, depicting their plans for the hotel. These included a sports complex in the grounds, and an Elizabethan village to present Shakespeare, everything I had wanted to do myself. They also told me that they had secured a contract with a top American airline to fly guests into Britain to fill the hotel rooms throughout the year. It was an ideal location, so close to Stratford-upon-Avon. The financial running of the hotel had been guaranteed, or so they reassured me. When they told me the re-launch would create up to five hundred jobs in the local area over the coming years, I was naturally very interested in joining them in such a scheme. It looked tremendous. They had certainly done their homework. Of course, I wasn't stupid enough to rush headlong into the situation without covering myself, and making scrupulous checks to safeguard myself. I even found out that Howard Wax was a justice of the peace. And, when I had satisfied myself that everything was in order, I agreed to go ahead. I wouldn't be losing my beloved Walton Hall after all. They both assured me I could go off safely on my tours and leave the business to them. I trusted them.

We launched the new scheme in May with a glittering show-business party at the hotel to announce our future plans for Walton Hall. We had exhibition stands in the grounds and extensive diagrams, showing exactly what was going to happen in the future. Everyone who attended the party and saw them was impressed and wished us all luck for a successful venture. I couldn't wait to get started and had promised my Canadian partners that I, too, would invest more into the project.

Looking back with hindsight, I should never have accepted the offer to become the hotel's figurehead. That was my biggest mistake. But what Wax and Salter did was very clever. As soon as our agreement was signed, the two Canadians moved in and started living in the stately home, from where they controlled their business operations and managed the hotel at the same time. I had been paid nothing. They were both very grand and gave the impression they were big-time businessmen with fast cars, and secretaries following them around everywhere. They flew in and out of the country like I go to Brighton, but still everything had an aura of elegance about it. The image was perfect.

I have been about a bit and I thought I was shrewd, but I don't mind admitting, I was fooled, completely taken in by them. I suppose I should have sensed something was wrong when they offered to buy my hotel from me, and then asked me to leave my money invested in the property while I became the company's figurehead. But we investigated their backgrounds and checked them out thoroughly, and their credentials were fine. I was wrongly advised. I fell for a five-card con trick. However, I am convinced that if things hadn't started to go wrong for them, if they had been allowed to continue trading, they were both so stylish I think their ideas might well have taken off. There are plenty of crooks in the world, but their intentions for Walton Hall were admirable, as I found out later.

I was in the middle of a hectic British tour with *Danny's Dazzling Roadshow* when the story broke in the newspapers on 22 July 1983, revealing that my two Canadian business partners had been arrested by police investigating a million-dollars airline and travel ticket fraud in Britain and Canada. It was also reported that massive debts had accumulated at the hotel, cheques had bounced and creditors were moving in to recover their money. It was like a bolt out of the blue. I was dumbfounded. I knew nothing about it, but my name was con-nected with the Canadians, I was involved by implication. Fortunately, the police issued a statement clearing me: 'This is part of a long-running inquiry involving many people,' it said. 'But it in no way involves Danny La Rue.'

The following day, bailiffs acting on behalf of the Customs and Excise, moved into the hotel in an effort to seize furniture and assets worth £30,000 in payment of an outstanding VAT debt. Solicitors acting on behalf of Walton Hall took out a court injunction to prevent them. But something crooked was going on. Local tradesmen, who had been my friends for seven years, claimed they hadn't been paid for several weeks, others had received cheques which had subsequently bounced. No one involved with the organization of the launch party in May had received a penny for their services. We found out that all the items for which the creditors were demanding money had been ordered by other people since the new management arrived.

Wax and Salter had carried out their own business operations using my name to pay for it all. Everything had been ordered through the hotel accounts on *my* reputation and good name which at that time in the area was impeccable. They had hired large cars, bought expensive champagne and flashy equipment, the lot. Everything to keep up the pretence and nurture the image of extravagance. Nobody involved had bothered to ask questions and had simply adopted the same atti-tude. 'It's okay, it's for Danny La Rue,' and that solved all the problems. It was a straightforward case of fraud, embezzlement.

Luckily, money that had been owed to the local suppliers before the new regime took over *had* been paid in full and none of the people now pressing to be paid in the wake of the débâcle blamed me directly for what had gone on. But I felt responsible. My name had been used, albeit in vain; my impeccable reputation had been seriously tarnished and was now on the line.

I took legal and financial advice immediately, but it was too late and far too expensive to launch a rescue operation simply to save face. On 27 July 1983, a day after my fifty-sixth birthday, Martell Securities, my company in charge of Walton Hall went into voluntary liquidation. As no one could be sure exactly what the debts were, it was the only course of action to take. It was some birthday present. The hotel had never officially changed hands. It was all down to me.

I had fallen for one of the oldest tricks in the business and, in the space of five days, I had lost over one million pounds. I had invested every penny I earned in my life into the project and I had lost what I laughingly called my pension and my nest egg for when I finally retired from show business. It really was my life's work. But I vowed I would do everything in my power to make sure everyone involved was paid. In the end, I was forced to sell my beautiful house at Henley to pay off the bank.

The following day, the hotel closed. It was terribly sad that so many good people lost their jobs and were affected by it all. It was a great tragedy which I never wanted to happen.

When I found out how much I lost over Walton Hall, no one was more amazed than me. I never thought I could make that kind of money. I was strangely proud because as I said at the time: 'I didn't know a fella in a frock could make so much money.' But it was like having a death in the family, I cared about it so much.

On the very day the crash occurred, a magazine astrologer chose me as his subject, and predicted: 'Apart from his talent as a performer, he's a shrewd businessman . . . he can look forward to a lively and successful next twelve months.'

Two things kept me going through it all. My religion was an enormous help. I have always maintained I am just an instrument and that is why I am able to accept failure and success together. I believe everything is intended and I have never used the expression, 'Why *me*?' That made it much easier for me to accept what would have shattered most people in business. I had been content to accept my success in the past, now I had to live with failure. I counted myself lucky; I was strong and I still had my career. Some people lose everything.

The reaction of the British public was also a marvellous tonic. I was having to go out on stage every night in very difficult circumstances following days of revelations and counter-revelations in the newspapers where no one was actually sure if I was responsible for any of the actions or not. Yet, despite all the controversy, my audiences never distrusted me and certainly never abandoned me. There was a tremendous bond between us. People used to stand up and cheer when I went out on stage because in their eyes someone had wronged Danny. I have never been so flattered in my life. Taxi drivers refused to accept payment from me, and that's pretty rare. Also I received two beautiful antique vases dating back to the eighteenth century. They arrived in a box with a note, saying: 'We don't want a reply. We are very elderly and we want you to have them. They are all we have, but we know you will love them. Thank you for everything.'

On the day the papers carried the news of the arrest of the two Canadians, I was appearing in Margate. As I was preparing to go on stage, at the start of the second house show, the chain which hoisted the safety curtain up and away from the stage, broke, making it impossible to shift the vast fireproof barrier and for us to start the show. I thought it was providence kicking me in the teeth when I was down. I had never missed a performance in my life and now an immovable safety curtain was putting that record in jeopardy. There was nothing for it but to wait while a crew of stagehands and technicians slowly winched the curtain up by hand, inch by inch. David Ellen, however, was very quick-thinking.

'Whatever happens, Danny,' he said, 'you must go out there now and entertain the audience. If you don't, the press will think you are running away and can't face a packed house because of the stories today. They will believe that the safety curtain fault is a ruse to let you off the hook.'

He was right. So I went out on the apron of the stage, while the stagehands beavered away with the curtain behind me, and ad libbed my way through forty-five minutes. David Ellen and Shades, the group appearing in the show with me, joined us in an impromptu entertainment, and not once did we use any of the material from the show. Eventually, the curtain was hoisted back into position and we started all over again.

The Walton Hall incident also showed me who my true friends were. Colleagues were very supportive, though some of my rich friends probably thought I would want to borrow money from them, and didn't ring me for a while. But the business as a whole was saddened by the events. Ronnie and Anne Corbett telephoned immediately to see if they could help. Larry Grayson came over to see me at Northampton. He was charming as usual. 'Danny, if all your friends could be with you tonight,' he said, 'they would be. We have been friends for thirty years, and we all know what has gone wrong has nothing to do with you.' I was also very touched at the generosity of Lionel Abrahams, who within twenty-four hours rang me from Sydney to offer me enormous financial help. It was a magnificent gesture, but one I declined.

Walton Hall was later taken over by the Spanish villa company, El Capistrano, and has been developed into a vast leisure complex, housing forty time-share apartments. But I would never go back to see it, or even drive past the place. It would only remind me with sadness of too many wonderful moments. As far as I am concerned, it doesn't exist any more. And I will never go into business again in my life.

With the collapse of Walton Hall, I threw myself into my work. I was shattered for a long time afterwards, but work was the best antidote to it all, the best remedy for my ills. I still had my life and a pair of very broad shoulders. I worked harder than ever, with a compulsive drive and desire to carry me through. My *Danny's Dazzling Roadshow* tour played a mammoth thirty-nine venues in just fourteen weeks all over the country. At the end of it all I felt completely drained and exhausted. But I wanted to work. I had to keep on working; I knew nothing else.

I faced another new challenge in the autumn as I prepared to start rehearsals for one of the most ambitious projects in the theatre, and the biggest gamble of my career: the part of Dolly Levi in the hit musical *Hello, Dolly!*. It was the first time in theatrical history that the part of Dolly had been played by a man. More than that, it was the first time that a man had played a major female role in a musical. Fourteen years before, David Merrick had offered me a million dollars to follow Pearl Bailey and play the same role on Broadway and I had refused. One of the reasons I had turned down the role, apart from my commitments to my nightclub, was the fact that I was far too young. I looked about thirty then, and Dolly had to be at least forty-five. Now I felt ready. I had gained valuable experience since then, in living, as well as performing, and it would all be put to the ultimate test as I strove to bring my own credibility to a part that had been played by some wonderful actresses and some dear friends – Carol Channing,

Ginger Rogers, Betty Grable, Mary Martin, Ethel Merman and Barbra Streisand. I had to play it straight, too. I could never burlesque burlesque. I couldn't play the role for laughs in my usual style. Any laughs I could get would have to come from the written role and my interpretation, not from Danny La Rue. Yet, I saw Dolly as a larger than life character and simply an extension of my other 'ladies', in the mould of Mae West, Marlene Dietrich, and Shirley Bassey. There was one other problem, however. At the end of my stage act, I had always appeared as myself, *Dan*, so that my identity was never lost on my audience. To be accepted as Dolly Levi, I had to remain in character throughout. It would be a true test of my skills as an actor to carry it off. I knew I could do it.

Starring opposite me in the role of Horace Vandergelder was Lionel Jeffries, who had been a patron of my nightclub in the sixties. The first time we met was in 1963 when I was appearing in pantomime at the Bournemouth Pavilion. He brought his daughters backstage to see me. I can remember it vividly. The girls were so polite, they curtsied when we were introduced. Lionel had asked to meet me because he said I was absolutely sensational. In 1985 I gave him his first pantomime role when he joined me in *Mother Goose* at the Alexandra Theatre, Birmingham. He was very good, indeed.

Lionel allayed any doubts I might have had about my own acting ability after *Hello, Dolly!* had been running for a few weeks. 'Each night I meet Danny La Rue coming into the theatre,' he said. 'On stage, I am performing with Dolly Levi, a very glamorous and sensitive woman, and I only meet Danny La Rue again after the show is over. When he is in costume, he is giving a marvellous performance. It doesn't matter to me that I have to waltz with a fella, and propose each night to a man. I am playing a scene with a character called Dolly Levi, never mind who is under the wig. That is what I call professionalism. I have enormous respect for Danny. I have always thought what a fantastic actor the guy is.'

Hello, Dolly! opened for a season at the Birmingham Repertory Theatre in November 1983. It played to capacity business throughout its short run and, if I had had any fears about taking on such a barnstorming role, the audiences soon dispelled them. The local press were kind to me. The *Birmingham Mail* headlined: 'Danny Says Hello to a Hit'. It was a good production, directed by Peter Coe, and it gave me the opportunity of being reunited with a friend and colleague from way back, David Toguri, who had been one of my dancers at Hanover Square, and who choreographed the musical brilliantly. Time had only improved his immense talents.

It had been the original intention for *Hello, Dolly!* to be staged on a lengthy British theatre tour during 1984, culminating in a West End season in the spring, until local party politics intervened. When we opened in Birmingham, we were set for a nine-week run to take us into the New Year, before going on the road. However, one member of the Birmingham City Council was outraged at such a suggestion. At a council meeting shortly afterwards, she demanded to know why the theatre's long-standing policy of presenting a pantomime or Christmas show had been changed to accommodate *Hello, Dolly!*. The Arts and Entertainment Committee had no answer and, in the end, common sense gave way to tradition. Diplomatically, the season, which would have ended up breaking box office records, was cut by a month, and replaced by *Toad of Toad Hall*. It killed off any chance of a provincial tour as dates were hastily re-arranged. Instead we went straight into London, and opened at the Prince of Wales Theatre on 3 January 1984, after previewing over Christmas. It was exactly the *wrong* time to open a major musical production of this kind in the West End. It was suicidal and, after such an astronomical success in Birmingham, a great shame.

On opening night, there was only one other name above the title in the West End beside me, and that was Penelope Keith. I felt that was an achievement in itself.

Playing the part of Dolly Levi was a revelation for me and taught me so much. I wouldn't have missed it for the world. I loved it. She was an exciting woman, witty, generous and slightly eccentric, and I found there was a lot of my own personality in the character. But it was a very demanding role, the self-discipline was intense. When I appeared in my own shows, or revue, I was able to drop in and out of whichever character I was playing at the time. Now I had to sustain *one* part throughout, it took me over completely and enveloped me. I cried every night as Dolly when she spoke to her departed husband, Ephraim.

Unfortunately, the critics didn't share my enthusiasm. The show was mauled by the press. I didn't read a single review, Jack wouldn't let me, but he told me delicately what they had said. One wrote I was brilliant; others thought I was dreadful; only a few were indifferent. That pleased me, I would have hated to have been called 'mediocre'.

One journalist said: 'Seeing the show was like watching a champion jockey without a horse.' which I suppose was an inverted compliment. But their reviews had virtually killed off any hopes we might have had for a long West End run.

Critics are a strange breed. They criticize you for doing the same things over and over again, and invite you to do something different with your career. When you do it, they tell you to stick to what you were doing before. Bad reviews have never worried me, though, because I only go by the reaction of my audiences, and for *Hello, Dolly!* it was very good indeed.

Rod Steiger came to one performance and we met backstage. He was very complimentary. 'Today,' he said, 'the extraordinary became commonplace. If you open tonight in New York, tomorrow Broadway will be at your feet.'

I think *Hello, Dolly!* was one of the best things I have ever done and I could live with the part of Dolly Levi for a long time.

When the musical ended its all too brief run in March, the show was playing to respectable houses, after a stuttering start throughout winter. Business had started to pick up and looked very healthy indeed. If the management company had kept faith with us, I think it could have become a sizeable hit. But they had lost a lot of money. We had been due to transfer theatres in March, anyway, as the Prince of Wales had been booked to house *Little Me*, but there were no other suitable theatres available to take us. So it was the end of a happy road. It had been pure joy appearing with Lionel Jeffries and the rest of a fine company.

Before we finished our run, there was a surprise in store for me when we reached our one hundredth performance. I was taking the final curtain call at the end of the show when Lionel stepped forward for no reason at all. I looked puzzled wondering what it was all about.

'No, Danny, I haven't gone stark staring mad,' he said. 'Tonight is a very special night because, as you know, it is our one hundredth performance of *Hello, Dolly!* in the West End. And, as a great tribute to you, we have a special bouquet.'

On cue, on to the stage emerged an enormous display of silk flowers. It was beautiful. Lurking behind the man-sized flowers was Eamonn Andrews with his large red book. My face dropped. I knew what was going to happen, but I was absolutely stunned.

'Oh, no, Eamonn,' I babbled. 'Not after all these years.'

He thrust the leather bound book in front of me.

'I don't have to tell you it's not *Hello, Dolly!*, but "Hello, Danny",' he said. 'Tonight, Danny La Rue, star of this show and many, many others . . . this is your life.'

I had been well and truly caught. A feeling of horror went through my body. I went cold. Hot. And cold again. I was mortified, dumbstruck. I didn't know what to do. I didn't know what to say.

Apparently, the people at Thames Television had spoken to Jack and the family on several occasions to try and organize a programme. Each time, they always decided against it. This was the fifth time of asking. In the past, I had maintained that, if I was ever approached by Eamonn Andrews and the book, I would walk out immediately. Yet I knew if Jack had given his agreement for the programme to go ahead, he must have had a very good reason for it, and I respected the man too much. I knew I had to go through with it. Jack had always said he would only agree for *This Is Your Life* to go ahead if they presented an hour-long show instead of the usual thirty minutes, which was very rare. Thames had agreed.

I had been taken completely by surprise. I knew absolutely *nothing* about it. And yet, thinking back, there had been several incidents which should have made me suspicious. So that was why Richard, my hairdresser, had insisted on cutting my hair at that particular time. That was why Lionel Jeffries had insisted he take me out for dinner for no apparent reason after that particular show, and he made sure I wore a suit to the show instead of my usual jeans and casual gear. It all made sense.

I didn't panic, I was going to give a performance.

I was actually in a daze for the entire hour-long show as people from my past popped up to pay the most marvellous tributes to me and my work. It was like a conveyor belt of nostalgia and memories. My family and friends from Devon: Winnie Ratcliffe, Ted Gatty, Mrs Hutton, who had all influenced my life. My wonderful colleagues from the Grand Order of Water Rats. It was all very emotional. There were some marvellous comments, too. Margot Fonteyn was glowing, Jimmy Tarbuck was hilarious, and Liberace, on film from America, didn't miss a single opportunity to get a plug in for his restaurant in Las Vegas, as only he knew how.

However, I was saddened when my best friend, Ronnie Corbett, couldn't be there in person, as Eamonn Andrews said, 'through other commitments'. He was under contract to the BBC and had to ask for their permission to appear on the ITV show. He was turned down. I was very much offended by that kind of stupid attitude and pettiness on the part of the BBC. Ron's wife, Anne, came on with the children, while Ronnie had to stay in the audience. He was desolate. But it didn't spoil a marvellous night. We had a smashing party and reunion afterwards and talked long into the next morning, and reminisced about old times. It was a great honour for me, but I didn't recover from the shock for a whole week.

Sadly, since then, I have lost several of the dear friends who came to pay tribute to me on that show: Dame Anna Neagle, Noele Gordon, Winnie Ratcliffe and Liberace. But I treasure their memories.

After all the problems of the previous twelve months, it was a relief to return to Australia and New Zealand in the autumn. The antipodes had a calming, revitalizing effect on me. I always came back to Britain inspired and ready to start again. My work benefited tremendously from the time I spent there. The experience gave me a new edge and a different approach to entertaining audiences at home; a new attack and renewed zest. It was refreshing.

It was good to be back amongst friends. Nothing had changed since my last visit. The Australian part of the schedule had been a great success once more. Our new show had been well-received and I had now included a twenty-minute musical extract from *Hello, Dolly!*, which brought the house down and started me thinking that there could be merit in touring Australia with a new production in the future. It was a thought worth pursuing. So it was with great elation that we moved on to complete the tour in New Zealand at the end of November.

Then, totally unexpected, tragedy struck. Jack and I had spent a very pleasant evening in Rotorua with some delightful friends. We had just returned from seeing a splendid Maori concert and renewing old acquaintances from our visit in 1979. It had been a very entertaining night, and the friends had come back for a drink with us at our hotel. Jack was feeling tired and had decided to have an early night, but had suddenly changed his mind at the last moment.

'I'm having such a lovely evening,' he said. 'I think I'll stay up for a while.'

I had just been to the bar when one of the girls in our party came up to me. She looked anxious. 'I don't think your manager is very well,' she said.

Jack looked pale. I went over to see what was wrong, and asked if I could do anything for him.

'I've got a terrible headache, love,' he said, and fell on my shoulder and passed out.

We rushed him to hospital where I was told he had had a massive brain haemorrhage. For the next two days, he fought for his life. I fought every step with him. I was numb, but I was fighting. I couldn't leave him. I felt so helpless and vulnerable. There was nothing I could do, and yet I had to do something to stop my mind from fearing the worst. Every time I heard footsteps, I anticipated it was the doctors coming to tell me the news I expected to hear at any moment, but fought hard to black out of my brain.

After forty-one hours, the doctors told me there was nothing they could do for him. Jack was clinically dead. The haemorrhage had done too much damage. He was being kept alive only by machine. The hospital needed permission to switch off the life-support unit. There was no hope.

I was hysterical; heartbroken. It was a decision I could not make. I didn't want to make it, either. I rang his sisters in Yorkshire and told them the tragic news and explained exactly what had happened. Then I asked for their consent. They refused. They told me how much they admired our friendship and our relationship and said Jack would have wanted me to take the decision. It was only right.

It was the worst decision I have ever had to make in my life. I hope I am never faced with anything like it again. I prayed for guidance; I sought advice and help from the doctors. Only when they assured me there was absolutely nothing that could be done to save Jack, and he couldn't recover from such an attack, did I tell them to go ahead. It was a tremendous burden to have to bear, but I was told he didn't suffer.

Jack Hanson was dead. He was sixty-four. It was the lowest point of my entire life. I had to be put under sedation myself, I was so distraught. I was emotionally drained. I had lost the best friend I ever had. The tour was cancelled immediately.

Shortly after the news of Jack's death reached England, I received a telephone call from Mike Yarwood. In his latest television special, which had been recorded some months before and was due to be screened within a matter of days, there was a sketch featuring an impression of me in which I referred to Jack in my usual style. 'Isn't that right, Jack?' had become a loved and legendary saying in show-business circles, I said it all the time, although never on stage. Mike had the courtesy to phone and say he would cut the sketch from the show if I felt offended. I told him to keep it in, and added Jack would have loved it.

Jack had always stressed that he wanted to be buried, and his sisters weren't at all distressed that he wanted to be buried by my family. He had cut himself off from his own family after the war, and it was only in recent years he had re-discovered them and they'd become wonderful friends. His sisters and I have remained very close ever since.

The body was flown home to Britain where Jack was buried in West London. He had never been deeply religious. He was straightforward and honest: a good man. I am sometimes boringly religious myself, yet there are some marvellous people who never practise religion at all, but behave like good Christians. Jack was a good Christian.

At his funeral, I was so proud. I never realized how much the man was loved and respected by the profession. I cried. There were so many people at the cemetery to pay their last respects and say a sad and fond farewell. The biggest names in show business were there, and *all* the hierarchy from television and theatre, including Lord Delfont, Bill Cotton and Michael Grade. It was a remarkable turn-out.

I took a whole year to reassess my life after Jack died. It was only his undying belief in me that *made* me survive. When anything went wrong, he had always been there to help me; to share the good times and comfort me if things got rough. He was the most important person in my life. I miss him dreadfully. When I go home and make a cup of tea and he's not there to talk to, that hurts. Now I miss him in a different kind of way because I know he is still here with me all the time. Time can never heal completely, but it helps. My regard for him and his contribution to my life will never diminish. I am a very gregarious person by nature, but I miss talking to him most of all. We could communicate together; I always found him very easy to talk to whenever I needed him.

Since his death, I have become a better performer because I feel he is watching me closely. I make a joke now. Instead of saying, 'Isn't that right, Jack?' it has become, 'I'm doing it for Jack.'

He was always there with good advice. He told me once that I would be wrong to accept the leading part in *La Cage Aux Folles*, when it was offered to me first. He categorically and adamantly begged me not even to think about it. He said I had made myself into a unique personality and added: 'You don't need to do this. Let actors do it instead.' He also advised me against a part in the play, *The Staircase*, when I was approached and, although I desperately wanted to appear in *Privates on Parade*, he said 'No.' He told me to look instead towards restoration comedy. He said I would be wonderful. Jack knew me so well.

It is nice to hold on to memories. Once during *Hello, Dolly!*, he became very philosophical. 'Dan,' he said, 'I am so sorry. I have one deep regret now.' God, I thought, what have I done wrong now? 'You will never see what I see,' he continued. 'How you are always there. How you never let up, that makes me so proud.'

Nowadays, when I have a decision to make that will affect my life or my career, I have to keep asking – 'What would Jack have done?'

When Jack Hanson died, somebody cut away part of my body. I died a little, too.

A short time after he passed away, I was going through some of the many items he had given to me as presents for birthdays or anniversaries during our time together, wallowing in the memories each one brought back. I was particularly fond of a beautifully crafted and ornate box that had been a gift for my fiftieth birthday in 1977. I had always marvelled at Jack's exquisite taste. He had a rare ability to find the ideal present for each special occasion and obviously spent a great deal of time choosing each gift.

I opened the box carefully and found it still contained the tissue paper I had wrongly assumed had been put there to protect such a delicate object. Yet, on a much closer inspection, I came across a cassette tape nestling underneath the paper, which had remained undiscovered for over seven years. I simply couldn't understand how I had missed finding it all those years before.

With trembling fingers, I placed the cassette on the tape recorder and switched on, not really knowing what to expect. There was a short pause before a warm and familiar voice came over the speakers. It was Jack. I shivered; it came as a tremendous and emotional shock to hear him again. My body went cold. In his deep, velvet voice he recited a poem he had composed specially for me on my fiftieth birthday:

FROM DRAGS TO RICHES

Half-way: My Gift for Danny on a Very Special Birthday

There are beginnings,
There are endings,
There are long, long in-betweens,
There are good times,
There are bad times
But life is what life means,
And life I have had, my friend, from you
For almost half my years,
In every good or bad disguise,
With all the hopes and fears
That crowd our onward journey
Towards our final goal,
And life for me has been a thing of beauty,
Rounded whole.
For this I give you all my thanks
And all my deepest love,
To last through times,
Through every change,
Until the final move,
And after that in memory,
When you, I hope, survive,
You know that thanks to you, my friend,
I knew *I* was alive.
Thanks, Dan.

11
'The best-dressed woman in the world'

It always astounds me that for a man who dresses up in a wig and a frock to earn a living, I have as many woman fans as Tom Jones and Engelbert Humperdinck. All of my fan mail is from women, from all over the world, and I have had more proposals of marriage from ladies than I care to remember.

Women like me. I don't degrade them. Sleazy impersonators usually get their laughs by having people laugh at them. I do the reverse. I love laughter, glitter and glamour. I love women too much to denigrate them; mine has been a more subtle, warm approach. I will send up their allure; the joke may be about women, but it is fundamentally on their side. Up until a few years ago, my audience was predominantly female. Now, I think it's an equal split. The whole attitude to life has changed. But the men don't see the frock. They see simply a comedian who makes them laugh. What amazes me, though, is that I don't have a gay following.

I have always looked upon myself as a character actor, or as Laurence Olivier calls me, 'an illusionist'. I create glamorous illusions and shatter them. I am a puppeteer. I manipulate my ladies, but I am never destructive, or negative and I never mean to offend. I am tremendously flattered whenever Mike Yarwood or Stanley Baxter does an impression of *me*. I look upon it as a great tribute to my talent and standing in the profession. You can say you have arrived once you have been mimicked. I love it, it appeals to my sense of fun. In the same way, none of the special 'ladies' I have caricatured on stage has ever been offended. I think they secretly admire my interpretations. I know many who do, and they all love my outfits. When Ginger Rogers saw me do a 'Fred and Ginger' routine at the Prince of Wales, she was amazed at the detail we included and adored my portrayal of her immensely. But unless you copy their look totally, you lose the whole idea of the character.

One of the reasons why none of my 'ladies' has ever objected to me is that I have always been as fair as I can be and I try to make my 'ladies' as attractive as I possibly can. I try to pick the best period of their lives to represent and re-create. Mae West's was in the thirties. She was the greatest comedienne of the time. She wrote all her own material and her gags were so near to the knuckle that she was arrested several times and spent the odd night in gaol in New York. I only ever met her once, in 1948, when she was appearing at the Prince of Wales in a wild-west melodrama she had written herself, called *Diamond Lil*. I went backstage and was introduced to this petite lady with tremendous presence. I was very surprised at how tiny she was. If ever someone decided to stage a musical about Mae's life, then Barbara Windsor would be marvellous in the role.

For Marlene, I have always chosen to depict her in her forties when she was sultry and sensational. I wouldn't ever dream of portraying her in her eighties, that would be too cruel. It is always far better to remember a star as they were in their heyday, in their prime, because sometimes in later life the illusion can be shattered completely. And yet, in Australia, I saw one artiste do an outrageously seedy imperson-ation of Dietrich as she is today. A decrepit old lady was wheeled on stage with a drip feed and wires going into her arms while singing 'Falling in Love Again'. It was completely and utterly tasteless, and an affront to the word entertainment.

I have featured Elizabeth Taylor in my repertoire of Hollywood legends since my days at Winston's. She was one of the very first of my ladies and has kept me in good material for a long time. We performed a very funny sketch when the film *Cleopatra* was being made, at the start of the sixties, amid all the controversy and surrounding publicity. I played Elizabeth Taylor as Cleopatra, Barry Cryer was Caesar. She saw the sketch many times and loved it. When I appeared at the Prince of Wales theatre, we did a parody on Elizabeth Taylor, but I had to change the lyrics to the song three or four times during that run because she was divorced, married and divorced again to Richard Burton in such a short space of time.

In February 1982, I was one of the honoured guests to be invited to help her celebrate her fiftieth birthday in a smart London disco off Burlington Street. I was terribly flattered to have been asked to such a shimmering occasion, even Richard Burton was *not* on the guest list. He had to gate-crash the party after it had started, and we spent most of the evening together chatting. It was a happy memory. I have still kept a little bunch of violets, the menu and one of her candles from the event.

When she appeared on stage for the first time in London in *The Little Foxes* at the Victoria Palace, I took Wayne King along with me to see her. We went backstage after the show, and he was totally taken by the lady. He was in awe, like a little schoolboy, not quite sure of himself in her company. But she does tend to have that effect on most people. It's called charisma. Here was a grown man, who had toured the world, and met some of the biggest names in show business, and he was mesmerized by this fascinating lady. She was so nice . . . and is still an incredibly good-looking woman.

The 'ladies' in my life have been flamboyant, elegant and so utterly glorious. All have the most exquisite style. When people come to see Danny La Rue, they come to see glamour. I once did an interpretation of Hilda Ogden from *Coronation Street* in one of my television specials and it was quite a good portrayal of a rich and colourful character. I had rollers in my hair, large wrinkled stockings and a cigarette permanently dangling from my mouth. The next morning, I was flooded with letters from my fans saying how dare I spoil my wonderful image by acting this way. I never did anything like it again. Image is so important.

I have always been a firm believer in spectacular extravagance. With my shows, everything is of the highest quality and the outfits with which I create my illusions have always been the very best. When I first started out in the business, I always bought the best clothes I could possibly afford, even when I was earning very little. My idea was to let women live out their own dreams through my shows. I'd dress up to the nines with feathers, sequins and gorgeous gowns, and be outrageous and cheeky, yet fantastic to look at. The clothes and the spectacle are the essential ingredients – to make the characters I create look glamorous and alluring. Yet, I don't think of the clothes I wear as gowns. To me, they are all props, the tools of my trade. I believe the reason I am successful in a frock is because I never see the frock. I make sure they are all wonderful and then it's forgotten. There is a certain style in the interpretation of my work that makes the audience very comfortable, but they know I don't care about the frocks, whether they cost £1 or £10,000. It's like a huge joke at a party. The costume is the moment, the entrance, like flicking through a magazine. But it is an illusion, you see what you want to see. I am completely cool about my costumes, too. If I liked wearing them too much, I wouldn't be good at what I do, I would flaunt it too much. Bob Hope once called me: 'The best-dressed woman in the world.'

I like the best. I don't like imitations. I am a complete perfectionist when it comes to my work. It is so important that the fabrics of my outfits move perfectly. I use clothes well. I don't say that with pride, it is simply the truth. I believe I look like every woman wants to look, but wouldn't dare. Because of *Dallas* and *Dynasty*, fashion in that sense has gone totally over the top. What I try to do when I am designing a new outfit, is to exaggerate the clothes, which exaggerates the characters, which is just the effect I am looking for. Most of the time, the characters are so unique the clothes design themselves.

Not long ago, many of my costumes would have been considered fancy dress, fantasy creations and certainly unwearable offstage. But now I think that women could actually wear some of them, like Mae West's outfit or Zsa Zsa Gabor's, or Marlene Dietrich's for that matter, not for everyday use, but perhaps for special occasions.

I try not to wear high fashion because things date so quickly, and yet I set my own trends. Evelyn Laye was always worried about her clothes, and she loved me because she thought I was a fashion plate and could help her. I wore catsuits long before they became fashionable and I am sure I encouraged the wearing of wigs. People simply didn't wear wigs before I started wearing them in my act. I'm lucky though, I don't have to wear one when I am being *me*, because I don't know how some people in the public dare to be seen in *their* wigs. But they are so wonderfully practical for women. I could name hundreds of women who wear them. No one would ever know. They just have their hair copied. It's marvellous when you're travelling.

I have a superb collection of wigs today, numbering well over a hundred, of which some cost over £600. Wig Creations of London started it all off for me, but I have since used all my own people. Richard Mawbey looked after my wigs for over eight years before going freelance, though he still helps me out whenever I need it. He is a very talented man. I discovered him working as a hairdresser in Blackpool, and persuaded him to join me. Since going out on his own though, he has worked on such West End shows as *La Cage Aux Folles* and *The Mystery of Edwin Drood*.

These days, good wigs are made from real hair so that they can be created into any shape by a competent hairdresser, although yak hair is used to give more body to styles like my interpretation of Tina Turner. At one time nuns used to sell their hair, while a lot was imported from the Far East. A good wig will last for about a year before it has to be refurbished. I have kept a lot of mine from way back although the hair texture has changed over the years.

Of course, it is vitally important that each wig is styled and then matched against the costumes to create perfect harmony. In the early days, Berman's were responsible for making my outfits, for the shows at Winston's and later at Danny La Rue's. Cynthia Tingey, who later designed for several major West End shows, created them all. She had an acute eye for detail and devised some very clever outfits.

Shortly after the club opened, however, I met a brilliant young designer called Mark Canter with whom I had great empathy. We worked together for nearly twenty years, and he certainly helped to revolutionize costume design. Mark had a mind that could turn the merest hint of an idea into a stunning creation. He was like a magician, waving a magic wand. He made some outstanding costumes. From our initial discussions, he would interpret my own suggestions into sketches and from these into finished garments.

Before he joined me, Mark Canter was in publicity and used to design advertisements. As a hobby, he set his mind on designing for the fashion world, and later collaborated with Disley Jones on a spectacular cabaret for Cecil Landeau, before concentrating on late-night cabaret and revue. He created costumes for all my West End shows, except *Hello, Dolly!*, for my tours and especially for my pantomimes, for which he was responsible for some of the most outrageous, over-the-top yet highly glamorous fashions I have ever seen. He also looked after the costumes in my film, *Our Miss Fred*, although Berman's executed the outfits for the rest of the cast. The last show Mark designed and created the costumes for was *Aladdin*, my pantomime at the London Palladium, for which he came up with a spectacular wardrobe of garments.

Mark believed firmly in making his outfits comfortable above all else. He used to say that as soon as I stepped out on stage, I had to be able to forget what I was wearing, to concentrate on entertaining. It was his job to see there were no hitches. To see a woman fiddling with a slipping shoulder strap was bad enough, but it was much worse to see a man dressed as a woman doing it. He was acutely aware he was designing clothes for a man to dress as a woman, but he prided himself in being able to make me look as good as any woman. The clothes were made to create impact, to produce 'ooohs' and 'aaahs' from the audience whenever I appeared on stage in a different design . . . and applause if we were lucky. We were, on most occasions.

Mark was also very shrewd because he made my clothes in such a way as to eliminate all my instantly noticeable manly points.

'We always have to cover the collar bone,' he said. 'It's massive, and the upper arms as well. But you would never realize it is being done.' He knew what he was talking about. He put his thoughts into practice so subtly that no one ever noticed. He softened my shoulders with the introduction of frills and sparkle, and made the sleeves wide and flowing. He would often use ornate embroidery and beading on the hem, cuffs and neck, all acting as a form of distraction, which in turn actually helped to make my waist look slimmer. I never wore sleeveless dresses. To balance my typically masculine frame – broad shoulders and narrow hips – most of my outfits were made in light fabrics that moved well in motion, like chiffon and organza.

Nothing was ever bought ready-made or off the peg, including shoes. I only take a size 6½ or 7, but it would be impossible to match up some of the exotic styles, so they are all hand-made. Even the simplest skirts and blouses were made up specially because they had to be exaggerated and made in proportion for a man to wear as a woman – that was the difference. No expense was spared in getting everything to perfection. We often experimented and imported a lot of material from Switzerland. It proved quite an expensive business buying sixty and seventy metres for just one outfit, since some of the material cost £125 a metre. I had one ballgown made up for me which took 100 yards of tulle and a woman actually wrote to me asking where she could buy a pattern for the frock to make it up herself!

Where Mark was particularly clever in his designs was in the way he made the clothes fall into the correct line, or move in exactly the right direction he wanted them to move, by the use of the finest stiffeners. The effect was unbelievable. Long trains had to float in the air, or follow me delicately downstairs; stoles and capes had to be draped to perfection. This was where his cunning workmanship was used, designing new and exciting ways to overcome all the problems. He was more than a dress designer, he was a draughtsman, mathematician and inventor as well. If an outfit had to sparkle in the theatre lights, he would sew hundreds of jet beads into the hem or bodice in such a way as to be invisible until the lights shone on them in a particular way. It was pure genius.

Mark always insisted I had marvellous legs, and designed a lot of clever outfits to show them off, some with thigh-high splits, or open-fronted. But my legs aren't really as good as they look. I know they look great, because they are intended to, and I don't shave my legs.

Accessories are also very important. It is no good wearing a silly string of beads with a £6,000 gown. It's important for me to wear the right jewellery, so I have an enormous collection of necklaces, bracelets, rings and earrings to chose from. For jewellery, I try to have authentic pieces copied, but it is very difficult these days. It is becoming more and more expensive. Paste used to come from Czechoslovakia, but only a small amount comes from there now. They tried to use the technique in Hong Kong but after a month you were left with just the glass, and that was no good at all. I wear real diamonds as well. My mother told me to invest in jewellery when I was younger so that if everything else got taken, I'd still have something left to sell.

For *Queen Passionella and the Sleeping Beauty* at the Saville Theatre, Mark designed some of the most elegant and witty costumes he had ever created. They were so glamorous and inventive. I was applauded on every single one of my entrances, which was a true mark of how good they were. I had thirty-four changes of costume.

In the course of the show, I did a gentle send-up of Shirley Bassey for which Bryan Blackburn had written a brilliant parody on 'Big Spender'. I wore a typical Bassey costume, which had cost in excess of £2,000. It was pure lace, with exotic feathers, and looked rich and terribly expensive.

The lyric to the song went: 'I came from Tiger Bay, I always walk this way, *this* came from C&A,' referring to the dress. It was a dreadful mistake. For weeks afterwards, I was inundated with letters from people with the same complaint. 'Can you tell me in which department of C&A you bought your dress?' said one. 'I've looked everywhere and I can't find it,' was typical of another. They had really believed me.

I have known Shirley Bassey for ages, she is one of my closest friends in show business and I have seen her through all the good times and the bad. She always goes hysterical when she sees me as Bassey, and she has often come up on stage with me. She is a wonderful example of a shining British star and I have the highest regard for her. She is a glamorous woman and a great, great talent, but very volatile and a very emotional lady.

I have had many letters from the public asking where they can buy similar clothes to mine which, of course, they can't. It's as simple as that. Mine are unique. One tiny woman told me how much she would love to copy one of my outfits. I asked her if she realized one of the sleeves would be enough to do the whole job and still would swamp her. I am over six-feet tall, and bigger people can certainly wear clothes better than smaller people. The tragedy of small people is that their clothes tend to swallow them up.

Another lady wrote to me to say she thought I would be amused at part of a conversation she had heard between two senior citizens when I appeared in a striking lurex dress.

One of the ladies asked: 'Did you watch him when he walked? Just like a racehorse.'

'Yes,' said the other. 'And I wish I had one of those shiny *durex* dresses he is wearing.'

I also get a lot of letters from ladies with breast cancer asking my advice on how they can still look natural after having a breast removed. A lot of them are very sad letters, but there are a large number of amusing ones, too. Many women accept it marvellously and have such courage and positive attitudes. I don't mind sharing a few secrets with them, but I tell them I get my cleavage effect purely by the use of make-up and clever shading, nothing more. I do advise women to have a false bosom built into their dresses. Cushions of bird seed, of all things, are so effective, because they move about in such a natural way.

One of the most essential requirements for any of my outfits, as far as I am concerned, is the practical necessity of ease of access. I probably make the fastest changes in show business for some of my shows, particularly pantomimes, where I might have up to twenty-five different changes of costume to make during the show. So I need to be able to get in and out of garments at speed. For that reason, everything is built into my outfits these days – the bust, made from foam rubber, the shape . . . everything. Because my changes are very quick, I always say the important thing is to get into the *next* costume. If the zip gets stuck, it's far better to rip the dress to get out of it than struggle and waste time. There will always be plenty of time to put it right before the next show.

Every time I change, I do it totally: tights, shoes, jewellery, even down to the nail polish. That is why there is such an element of surprise from the audience. I tend not to put on weight because I use up so much energy in a show that water just runs off me. When the adrenalin starts working, I bubble.

After Mark Canter and I parted company, I used several people for some of the costumes, bits and pieces really, nothing substantial. I have always been a great admirer of Eric Lloyd. I was in shows with him from way back, when I was in the chorus and he was a principal artiste. I have always found his work of the highest standard, and he is so wonderfully reliable. He makes a lot of clothes for Wayne King.

I discovered Anne Galbraith one evening while watching television. There was a show, featuring the American singing duo Captain and Tenille, and I saw Toni Tenille wearing a most fabulous cloak, which was exactly what I wanted for my act. Once the programme had finished, I contacted a friend of mine at the BBC and between us we tracked down the creator of the cloak. It was Anne. She had such an impressive track record in show business, having made clothes for Shirley Bassey, Stanley Baxter, Dick Emery, Susan Hampshire and Barry Humphries. Indeed, she made the famous Australian flag dress which Dame Edna Everage wore on one of her television specials. Anne had also worked in New York with Jackie Gleeson and Jane Taylor. Before branching out on her own, she worked for Berman's for a while on such television series as *The Forsyte Saga*.

It turned out that she had always wanted to work for me, but she wouldn't approach me because she thought I already had someone making my costumes. That was in 1979, and we have worked together ever since. Anne, who has become a very dear friend, is constantly working on new and exciting creations for the future, with which to dazzle the audiences. She has brought a slightly less outrageous, far more sophisticated, style to my clothes in recent years, although her Tina Turner creation was pure pyrotechnics.

Anne was also responsible for making my costumes for *Hello, Dolly!* and although I only had seven changes to make throughout the entire musical, the least number of costumes I have ever had for one of my shows, they were the best clothes any Dolly had ever worn, including Barbra Streisand in the movie version. Each of the outfits cost an average of £5,000, while the Dolly dress itself, for the restaurant scene, cost nearly £6,000, one of my most expensive designs.

The most expensive outfit I have ever had made for me cost a fortune. It had £6,000-worth of orange fox on it and another £2,500-worth of black fox just for starters. I would hate to think what it would cost to make today, although I have stopped using fur for a long time now, and have joined the anti-fur campaigners. I prefer to use exotic feathers, man-made fibres and fake fur to create the same effect. Often the outfits cost more than the stars I am creating wear themselves.

I have collected literally thousands of costumes during my career in show business. Today, they are kept in storage in Tunbridge Wells, in Kent, where my pantomime outfits have one whole room to themselves. At the last estimate, they were valued at well over a million pounds, although to me they are priceless. The cheapest outfit I possess is the one I have worn as Margaret Thatcher, which cost a mere £250 by comparison. I don't know if she has ever seen me on stage or television, but I received a very warm letter from her during the Falklands crisis, thanking me for my help in raising money for the South Atlantic fund.

I am by nature a hoarder, I never throw anything away. I often reuse fabrics from time to time, and I have some outfits which are made of material that is no longer in existence, which can be revamped and re-styled. Styles keep changing all the time, coming in and out of fashion at the merest whim, so there will come a time when even the most dated outfit can be used again. I would never sell any of my costumes, instead I give them away, to theatres, dramatic societies and music halls. I have given quite a lot to the Theatre Royal, Stratford East, and to several other groups who have difficulty finding enough money. I can remember what it was like when I first started out in the business, so if I can help out I do as often as possible.

Make-up has always played a large part in my career. Any good actor should know about it. I could make-up for any part now: experience has taught me how. It takes me half an hour to put on my make-up and it is a process I insist on going through alone. Nobody is allowed to watch me transforming myself into my 'ladies' because I believe it would spoil the mystique. I would certainly never allow the public to see me, that would be totally unfair. I never let myself be photographed during the process, either, though many newspapers have asked if I would. I am a great believer in *not* giving away my secrets.

Naturally, I have to shave before I can make-up, but a little acts as shading. I use cream pan-stick, very fine but dark, and lots of eye make-up. Luckily, I have good eyes for the stage. I use a powder eye-shading, too, because it is easier to change colours for different roles and, of course, false eyelashes add the finishing touches. I never pluck my eyebrows; I just wax over them so they're completely erased and then I can draw in more feminine lines instead.

I must admit, I have a few physical advantages which have helped me enormously to create my ladies over the years. I used to hate my turned-up nose when I was a boy, people thought it girlish. I used to sleep with a clothes peg on it to try and make it longer and change its shape. I was fed up with being called pug nose at school. Now it is my greatest asset. I also have a very good skin and very few lines on my face for my age.

Over the years, I have built a huge reputation for myself in the profession for my expertise at make-up, and several of my colleagues have approached me in the past and asked for my advice and help. My very good friend Donald Sinden, that distinguished and very fine actor, was one.

In 1967, long before we became friends, he was appearing at the Royal Shakespeare Company in *The Relapse*, in which he played the part of a fop – Lord Foppington. In every role Donald creates on stage, he always tries to model his appearance on someone he knows. But for this particular part, he was stumped. During the period in which the play was set, it was commonplace for men to wear extravagant make-up on their faces, fops especially. So Donald needed someone to turn to. He chose me. He got hold of one of my photographs and based his make-up for the play on mine. It was a marvellous gesture, but it didn't end there.

A few years later Donald's son, Marc, found himself in a similar position. He was appearing in *The School for Scandal* in the West End and was having great difficulty with his own stage make-up. Then he remembered me. Fortunately, I was only across the road at the Prince of Wales at the time, so Marc decided to come over and see me and get some first-hand advice.

I was delighted to be able to help him and I was flattered that a legitimate actor of the highest order should turn to me when he needed help – like father, like son. I made him up in my dressing room for his performance that evening and he then had to walk back to his own theatre, the Duke of York's, across Leicester Square in full stage make-up. He told me afterwards, it took him twice as long to get back, and involved a lot of fast talking.

More recently, singer Boy George has gone on record as saying I inspired him greatly with his own make-up, which is a nice gesture. We met once when we were appearing on a television show together, and spent most of the time talking about make-up. I think he is very clever. I like anything that works. Gimmicks are fine if you have the talent to back it up. George has great talent, and he actually holds a unique place in my career. In 1984, he became the first man I had ever caricatured in costume on stage. George had a special place in my line-up of 'ladies' for a pantomime appearance at the Theatre Royal, Plymouth where I was starring in *Mother Goose*.

The greatest gift any artiste can have in show business is respect, from your profession, and from your audience. I am so lucky to have been accorded both. Although I cannot for the life of me understand how a grown man can walk out on stage in a frock and command utter respect, I do feel now that I have become part of the establishment. Marjorie Proops called me 'a beloved national monument'. Respect and admiration has come from some most unexpected quarters, too. Rock singer Alice Cooper actually wrote to me to say how much he had been influenced by me.

A few years ago, I wanted to feature a Bunny Girl character in one of my shows, which was unheard of at that time because no one had ever been given permission to use the mascot of the Playboy Club in this way before on stage. It was a copyrighted figure and as such a valuable commodity. Playboy just wouldn't sanction it. Hugh Hefner, who founded the Playboy empire, gave me the go-ahead personally, and I became the only person who was allowed to use the character.

At Wakefield one evening, the Theatre Club had been taken over for a private function by the local rugby club and I found myself playing to an audience of bruisers, big beefcake figures of men. I hadn't the faintest idea how they would react to me, so I took the initiative, went on stage and attacked. 'Here I am,' I said. 'If any of you don't like me, you can all piss off.' The roof went up. The audience stood up and applauded. From then on I had them in the palm of my hand. We had the same high regard for each other.

When I was appearing in my own show at the Prince of Wales, I got a telephone call one morning from some friends at the Royal Shake-speare Company. There had been a tragic death in the company recently, and they were staging a benefit show to raise money for the young man's widow. Ticket sales weren't very good, so they asked if there was anything I could do to promote the show and generate business.

That morning, I was due to appear on a live radio show with Pete Murray and, during the course of the programme, I mentioned details of the show in question and told about the tragedy. It was a revelation. The show almost sold out within a few hours. As my donation to the benefit fund, I took my entire company from the Prince of Wales to see the production. When I reached my seat in the auditorium, I was presented with a programme, which had been signed by every member of the Royal Shakespeare Company. The message read: 'We the under-signed are privileged to be in your profession.' It was very moving.

I have always had the utmost respect for the 'ladies' in my life. I don't think the characters would ever work without it. And of all my 'ladies' I have featured in my act over the many years there was only one character that didn't work for me – Barbra Streisand. I think I was on to a loser from the start. She has such a sensational voice, whereas mine is merely pleasant. I don't really like her a lot, either. I can remember she once came into my nightclub and wore a very large and very outrageous floppy hat, which she refused to take off all night. I thought she was very rude and showed no consideration for the other people in the room. Maybe she needed such a huge hat to make her huge nose look smaller. Who knows?

However, I loved Marilyn Monroe, although she became the only character I have ever dropped completely from my act. It was a joy to re-create her fabulous illusion. In *Queen Daniella* we performed a tribute, with me as Monroe and two of the boys from the company as Jack Lemmon and Tony Curtis from the movie, *Some Like it Hot*. I was very fond of the portrayal, but she became too sad and had a great effect on the public who became melancholy. I only like laughter.

I based a lot of my pantomime characters on another dazzling Holly-wood blonde, Jayne Mansfield. I met her once and found her bubbling and bright, a complete contrast to the image she had projected to the media. After she had finished filming in England, I was lucky enough to get hold of one of her dresses from Berman's, which was sensational. But after her awful death in a car accident in 1967, I just couldn't bring myself to wear it on stage any more, and gave it away.

Since I started in show business, I have always detested the word 'drag'. There is nothing wrong with the word itself, it is what it conveys that bothers me. The sleaziness of it all. 'Drag' comes from Shakespeare, derived from the phrase 'the dragging of the skirts', referring to the male actors who played female parts, so it has a legitimate meaning. The reason men were cast as women was because in Elizabethan times it was thought immoral for a woman to appear on the stage.

I have rarely been into the 'drag' pubs. So many of the performers who work there are transvestites, anyway, and they make me feel like a lorry driver. Although I find some of the acts very amusing, I have been put off by the way they exaggerate their movements – the mincing walk and limp-wristed gestures – to the point where it is so stupid. If you study people closely, you will find there is very little difference between the way men and women move. There is a subtle dividing line.

I know many clever people who have put on skirts, but who have remained totally unconvincing. Anyone can actually dress up as a woman. Great actors like Laurence Olivier and Alec Guinness have both put on frocks and done very well indeed. It takes a very good actor to play the part of a woman well, and with conviction. I have never looked upon myself as a female impersonator. I am certainly not a mimic either. I have never tried to re-create other people's voices in my life; impressionists do it far better than I can. I am basically an actor playing a woman; I have discovered it is much more humorous to present a delightful characterization. Putting on a frock is nothing, it is being able to be effective. I must be a pretty good actor because I don't think I could have survived so long in the business and achieved so much if I wasn't. I take on the look of the people I am caricaturing. I re-create their image as a mirror. I never watch them on television, or at the cinema, I simply get a picture of them and base the look on that. Once the characters have been decided upon, a suitable script is commissioned from writer Bryan Blackburn. When everything works out at that level then, and only then, is the costume designed to fit the illusion. It is the finished piece in a great jigsaw puzzle. But the characters must always be identifiable from the moment I walk out on stage. That's why I can get away with very cheeky material because underneath they know it is only Dan. A woman couldn't get away with anything like I do. And I wouldn't have sustained my audience for all those years if they thought I simply loved dressing up. They would be uneasy, and feel uncomfortable, and so would I.

I do so much admire the women I characterize, I pay tribute to them in my own way. In our business, a woman has to be at least twice as good as a man to succeed. It is awfully unfair.

When I first started out in the business I found my own inspiration in such artistes as Gracie Fields and Dorothy Squires, no-nonsense performers who just got up on stage and did it without fuss, and they did it well. Although I didn't model myself on anybody, there were some very good comediennes around at the time, like Revnell and

West, and Suzette Tarri, and my performance developed through watching, taking it all in, and learning. Dorothy Squires has been a constant source of delight and inspiration. When I do Dot Squires on stage, I nudge the audience in the ribs. She loves it.

These days the very special 'ladies' in my life have so much in common. They are all major international stars instantly recognizable and loved the world over. They are all larger than life, and personify the very essence of the word *glamour*. And, what is far more important, they have tremendous staying power in a very fickle business. Yet, they are all completely different and have their own idiosyncrasies, like Dolly Parton with her two marvellous assets; Bette Midler and her funny little walk; and Tina Turner who exudes sexual magnetism with every breath, which is very hard for a fella in a wig to emulate.

Joan Collins has established herself as a sensational and sensuous sex symbol to millions and I have great admiration for her. She is the last glamorous star, and unfortunately there's no one else as exciting. We have known each other for longer than either of us would care to remember. Her father, Joe Collins, booked me in pantomimes in the late fifties. Joan is a survivor in the show-business jungle, but nevertheless has emerged with a great personality and talent to match. I am sure she would be outraged by my portrayal of her, but delightedly so. There is no malice on my part, only a gentle send-up, played out in a designer outfit straight from *Dynasty*, shoulder pads and all. It's a very topical re-creation and goes down like a bomb. I am sure that even Joan doesn't realize how popular she is throughout the world. There are very few marvellous characters like Joan around these days. When they do come along, I grab them with both hands.

My 'ladies' are certainly not young. Indeed, several of them are actually older than I am, while the others are nudging middle age. But we have grown together. Unfortunately, I think the days are long gone when I could attempt a younger character like Madonna, although she would have been absolutely perfect for me. She's got the lot; I am a great fan. But then, I wouldn't attempt to caricature anyone I didn't like, it simply wouldn't work and there would be no satisfaction.

I would very much like to characterize Katharine Hepburn, and I think I would be very convincing; I adore everything she does. In a completely different context, I would like to play Lady Bracknell in Oscar Wilde's *The Importance of Being Earnest*, because that is high camp at its best. It would be a tremendous experience to attempt that role.

The lines are so funny and she is such an eccentric lady. I would feel very comfortable in the part.

Throughout my career, I have carried one item of theatrical attire with me at all times, which has given me a tremendous lift and boost to so many of my gorgeous creations. At the very start of my life in show business, I designed and made my own pair of 'falsies' out of Dunlopillo shavings: as Mae West once said, 'Dunlop's finest, 30,000 miles and still going strong.' I am very superstitious about them. I lost one once and there was a terrific panic. I was running around the theatre shouting: 'Lock the doors, one of my tits is missing.'

If I ever do retire, I would like to have them dipped in gold, and auctioned off at Sotheby's.

12
'Danny La Rue will never become a doddery old tart'

There will never be another Danny La Rue.

There are very few one-offs in show business; I am unique because I am the only man in a glamorous frock who has become a major star, not only in Britain, but also in Canada, Australia and New Zealand. Only my own stubbornness has prevented it from happening in America as well.

I am a complete one-off, and this is not conceit or big-headedness in any way, it is simply my professional side talking. There has never been anyone like me before. George Lacey and Douglas Byng were big names in the same field, but no one has made history like me in virtually every medium of the entertainment industry. I am the only star from light entertainment ever to have headlined seven major West End shows, which pleases me no end.

I have retained my position all the way because I am a product of the people and desperately try to live up to them. The audiences dictate what every performer does in his career. They make demands and we follow. What the public have liked about me is that I have never abused my profession or compromised my talent. I have done everything tastefully. I am not sleazy. I am very much aware of my public and I know I have never let them down.

In any business, standards are so important, and mine must live up to the faith the public have in me. I am very aware of my position and status in show business and would think twice if I believed anything I did would prejudice that standing. An artiste's personal behaviour at all times must be scrupulous and above suspicion.

The public know me and everything I stand for and hopefully they are never disappointed. Professionally, if I say my shows will be glamorous, they will be. No expense will be spared to deliver the goods. If you have built up a reputation you *must* try to retain it – the public demand it. But I'm like a village shopkeeper – I always give good service – and when you do that people come back. I think I am a very lucky man because there are not many people who hear laughter and applause every single night of their working life.

I am very disturbed by certain people's behaviour in show business. When a person is in the public eye, he should always act with dignity, and respect himself and his profession. We owe an awful lot to our public. There must always be integrity and love. I loathe unprofessional artistes and I'm afraid there are quite a few of them. They have no love for this great business of ours and behave dreadfully. They have tremendous influence through their standing, and yet they let everyone down. The trouble is, show business seems to have lost a lot of its professional attitude in recent years with so many artistes taking liberties with their audiences, fobbing them off with any old rubbish, in the name of entertainment, instead of working hard at their trade at all times. It is a situation I find utterly abominable. We work in a very hard business, and we must never neglect it for a minute because it can slip away so quickly. Artistes should never take their success or their audiences for granted and should always strive to better themselves. It's a hard life and needs lots of dedication and discipline.

I have always prided myself in knowing my audience and I have always given them the very best at all times. I will also know exactly when to stop doing my glamorous ladies. I have been in the business long enough and my career has always been based on good timing. I have my own built-in radar system and when it says stop, I'll stop. There will be no comebacks, either. I don't intend to do a dozen farewell performances. I will announce a final national tour and then it will be goodbye to the 'ladies' I love. I have learnt there is always a surprise around the corner and you have to be prepared to take advantage, but I will stop doing my 'ladies' long before I need to. My only vanity is to wish to be considered the very best when I finish.

I will never forget my horror when I saw Mistinguett, the fabulous French entertainer, in London once, still refusing to retire graciously when she was well past her best. I saw this wizened old lady, who could barely walk down a staircase, trying desperately to entertain. She was living purely on her name and reputation alone and performing on auto-pilot. It was so embarrassing, I felt so saddened for her. I vowed it would never happen to me. I want to stop while I am still looking wonderful on stage. Danny La Rue will never become a doddery old tart. Nobody will have to tell me to give up graciously.

I once did a caricature of Mistinguett and that whole French feeling with Josephine Baker and Edith Piaf. Piaf was an incredible woman. I met her in Paris, it was an amazing experience. She was a very plain woman, quite ugly really, yet she could have been beautiful because she had such a fantastic personality, and what a voice. Mireille Matthieu was another one of my Parisian parodies. I thought she was a doll that you just wound up.

I was always intended to be a performer. I am really an artiste born to be in show business. So there will be no retirement. I am still as stage-struck today as I was when I was a youngster watching Jimmy O'Dea at the Cork Opera House. I will simply move on to doing other things within the business. I would eventually like to try my hand at restoration comedy, or farce, or even straight acting. I have had so many compliments about my acting ability from the legitimate side of the industry, I would like to put it to the test to see if I really am any good. I have so much experience now from performing, with the success of Dan in his frocks, that it can only help me in any acting career. I am not stupid enough to want to play *Hamlet* or *King Lear*, but light comedy would be good for me. Failing that, I would like to direct. But I won't ever leave the business altogether. I couldn't just walk away, not now that it has become my life for so long. I couldn't see a future *without* appearing in pantomime, either. It is the best time of the year and I'll do pantomime until I drop. I have built up a tremendous reputation for myself over the years. The reasons my pantos have been so successful throughout my career is that parents come to see me knowing they are going to enjoy the show themselves because it is slightly adult, yet they also know their children are not going to be offended. It is a wonderful feeling to open a pantomime and know you are going to 'kill' the audience. That is the excitement of this business and it has happened to me every year since I first started as an Ugly Sister with Alan Haynes. Whether I have played to a full house, or a half-empty theatre, I have never had a bad reaction.

So the only time I will ever retire completely from show business will be when they carry me out of the door in a box. Then there can definitely be no comebacks.

The late Doris Stokes, the world-famous medium and spiritualist, told me, shortly before she died, that I hadn't achieved anything yet. She said I hadn't even touched the fringe of my career, and that it was going to take off in a different way completely. That pleased me because there is far more to Danny La Rue than just a frock. Doris, who was a dear friend, also believed me to be psychic and I think that in a way I am, although I don't understand enough about it to be sure. Perhaps I simply have great intuition.

During the 1986 Christmas season, I was appearing in pantomime at the Theatre Royal, Bath. I was staying in a lovely apartment in a very elegant block close to the famous Royal Crescent. It was very cosy and warm, and yet every night for several weeks I felt extremely cold and agitated when I was in my bedroom. Occasionally, I would wake up in the night shivering, and would hear noises as if there was some kind of party taking place upstairs. One morning, I asked Anne Galbraith, who was staying with me, if she had heard anything, but she shook her head and looked extremely puzzled. When I suggested there might have been a party going on upstairs, she shrugged her shoulders and told me it couldn't possibly have happened because the people there were quite elderly. I was thoughtful, but dismissed her comments and the events of the previous night as one of those things, perhaps my imagination was playing tricks. I thought no more about it . . . until it happened again, and again, and, on each occasion, I could actually hear muffled voices in what appeared to be a great panic, as if there were a number of people rushing to get out of the room. I couldn't understand what was going on at all, and I still felt very cold at night, despite the central-heating and my thick bedclothes. It was only when I discovered an inventory of items in the flat, which had been prepared by the owner, that the story resolved itself and started to make some sense. In a footnote to the inventory, there were a few background details on the apartment itself, which were very revealing.

The building which housed our apartment had been erected on the former site of an old hotel. During the war the building had been bombed and a substantial number of residents killed in the part where our flat now stood. My bedroom had been the reception area.

As soon as I finished reading the story, I went back into my bedroom, and addressed the room. 'I am very, very sorry,' I said. 'I hope you will all rest in peace and I will have a special Mass said for you at church.' I never heard another sound, or felt cold again.

I was once told by a clairvoyant that she saw a magnificent lady hovering over me as I worked. She told me the lady was French, from the nineteenth century, and she had chosen me, and would guide me. I do believe that maybe there are good spirits and evil spirits. The power of evil is very strong, but I prefer to think the power of good is stronger. The simplicity of truth is miraculous. I have had several experiences like the one in Bath and, apparently, I am receptive, the spirits seem to like me.

My own religion has always been the stabilizing influence between my very public show-business life and my private life. My faith has kept me from going under on a number of occasions. The first thing I do when I arrive in a new town is to locate a church for Mass. That is very important to me. However, I have been saddened in recent years because Latin is no longer the universal language of the Church. When I was a child, the service was always in Latin, no matter where you were. A lot of people argue that once Latin stopped being used, they were alienated from the church. Before, you could go into any Catholic church in any country in the world and the service would be exactly the same. It was a very welcoming experience. Nowadays, if I am abroad, I feel like a stranger in my own Church because I cannot understand the language any more.

Although I believe totally, I also have the right to question my religion. God has put me on this earth and given me a brain and a mind to question. I have my religion, but I do not accept everything it stands for. There is a lot of its doctrine with which I disagree. Of course, I suffer when I question my beliefs, but who can go through this ever-changing world of ours, when we see children dying from starvation in one part of the globe, from oppression in another part, and from drug abuse in a third, *without* questioning and trying desperately to come up with an answer.

I am quite amazed, as a world traveller, that, in this day and age, the contraceptive has not been accepted by the Church. It has been very painful for me as a humanitarian that the Church quells it. It is almost like watching someone cut off their legs and doing nothing about it. It saddens me in this modern life to see people in the third world countries with masses of children where poverty is a way of life and starvation commonplace. Women should not be regarded like machines in that way to produce babies and to go on and on producing them. The idea of family love is not just having sex and breeding children, that's not good enough. There has to be more to it.

To me Christianity means holding out your hand to your fellow man. It is a love for your neighbour and a total awareness of him, and complete respect for him. That is the single doctrine by which I try to live my own life. Yet, there are some religions purporting to teach Christianity that scare me. Bible-bashing evangelists frighten the life out of me, preaching hell-fire and damnation. That's not Christianity, it's fanaticism.

One of the sad indictments of our world is that religion, like politics, can be utterly destructive. It is nothing new and certainly not a symptom of our modern times. There have been wars, death and destruction, and persecution carried out in the name of religion throughout history.

The worst problems in the world today seem to be caused by politics and religion. Far too much is done falsely in the name of religion. If things were carried out in the true name of religion, it would be a wonderful world to live in. If people understood the true doctrine of the holy laws instead of twisting their meanings to suit their own ends, we would all live in peace and harmony. Unfortunately, we don't.

My native country saddens me deeply when I see how brother can kill brother. Some people adopt the same philosophy on life as Scarlett O'Hara: 'I'll think about it tomorrow.' That's not good enough. I think of the sadness of destruction, the lack of love, fellowship and kindness. I don't understand why people want to kill. Violence is completely and utterly abhorrent to me, as it is to most people. I don't believe in passports – we should tear all the barriers down. We are all brothers and sisters together; it is only the barriers that have created violence, and people saying, 'This is my country and that is yours. Keep out.' I don't know how the people of Northern Ireland can say: 'This is our country and you belong on the other side of the barrier.' It is one country. It is Ireland, no North, no South.

I would give anything to see Ireland re-united. I would be ecstatic to see peace in our lovely land. I have travelled the whole of the country and the people have been very nice to me wherever I have been, and I have spoken about my feelings to them. I cannot understand the mind of someone who puts a bomb in a pub or a shop. It can only achieve international hatred and condemnation for Ireland. I was in New Zealand when Lord Mountbatten was murdered. I felt so ashamed. I was insulted because I was Irish. Ireland is a wonderful poetic country, with a marvellous literary background, and yet, there is this enormous hatred, and that wipes out anything else.

I find it particularly sad, not only for my country, but also as I travel the world, to see how much changes in so little space of time. Once you felt free to walk through airports in safety, now you are frightened to move too quickly in case of trouble. Whenever I get off a plane anywhere in the world, I walk very slowly through to immigration or duty-free, in case anyone with a gun thinks I'm running, and takes a shot at me.

The state of the world saddens me. That is why I am so thrilled that I only offer laughter, nothing more. It is a great joy to me and I am hearing more and more laughter now than I have ever heard before. I think it acts as a release for people. It takes them away from all the problems.

Some people get far too carried away. I am often asked how I can equate what I do on stage – where I am often bawdy – with my religion, and they question my right to be a Catholic. I simply remind them where Jesus Christ was when he first met Mary Magdalene. She was a whore in a bawdy establishment. I also maintain honest vulgarity is *of* the people and I have always believed that religion should reflect a tremendously broad view of life. Actually I find such attitudes offensive because I am a seasoned performer. These so-called pseudo-intellectual religious people who try to catch me out should respect that I know my business instead of crediting me with no intelligence.

Nobody would ever say I was offensive in pantomime. I love children; I wouldn't do anything to hurt them. But in nightclubs it is a completely different story. Still, there are some performers who will say things on television, I wouldn't utter anywhere. I have never used a four-letter word in my act and never will. I don't think it is funny. People only use language like that because they are not articulate.

Bernard Manning is accepted today as a very risqué performer, far more bawdy and vulgar than I could ever be and, like me, he is a practising Catholic. I have the highest regard for the man and his religion. He is one of the most generous and benevolent men I have ever had the pleasure of knowing.

Just before I go out on stage for any performance, I always cross myself. Once at the Palace Theatre a stagehand took great exception to my ritual. 'I have the highest admiration for you personally,' he said. 'But I think what you are doing with all that make-up on your face is awful.'

'God doesn't see the make-up,' I replied. 'He only sees the person underneath.'

There is no such thing as a good Catholic: you are either Catholic or you are not. But as a Christian, I find I must always review myself and my values because that is where the truth lies. I became involved with St Peter's Hospice in Bristol in 1980, and sometimes it is painful to visit the wards, meeting and talking to such wonderful people. I know every person I speak to is going to die, maybe the next day, or in a few weeks' time. Some will be teenagers, and some in their seventies, and that is crucifying. They are such a happy bunch of people, so warm and friendly; they make me cakes and we sing songs together.

When I was first asked to go along, I didn't think I would have the strength or the resolve to carry it through. I was frightened. But I do it now because it gives me a most wonderful feeling. The people I meet have so much grace and dignity, so much incredible courage, I learn a great deal from them. They give me a new strength and conviction to cope with my meagre problems. I am shattered when I come out, it drains me utterly, and all I know is that I have to hold on to my religious beliefs because it makes me a better person. What else is there?

My religion has also taught me never to be a greedy performer. I have always been aware of the need to put something back into the business and I look upon touring as part of that duty to my profession and my public, but a delightful duty at that. Provincial theatres are the lifeblood of our industry, but they have been sadly neglected by some of the big-name stars in recent years who should know better, and who should tour more. There are some very beautiful theatres to play all over Britain with fabulous audiences who have been starved of glamorous entertainment. But many of my colleagues seem to ignore them and that's very sad. They refuse to tour, preferring instead to build their careers purely on television with the minimum of live work. Many of them are simply lazy and, once successful, they turn their backs on their roots. Unfortunately, those who do tour, often do it on the cheap, taking advantage of the public, thinking they will accept a drop in standards. I have never been like that. I am probably the only person who tours a show that is too expensive. It costs me money to put on. I could make much more money just going out on my own, but I don't think that is giving value for money. I always present the best possible show that I can, and the public are aware of it.

I have always thrived on the intimacy of an audience and I get a tremendous feeling when I go out on the road. I also feel responsible for the people around me in the true sense of the word 'equity'. I am very conscious of the fact that when I am working there are a lot of people working with me. It does make an awful lot of difference to me. I have worked hard to keep my colleagues. I have always believed in surrounding myself with very good people and I have tried to keep this alive by working with a *lot* of people, but this obviously cuts down what I earn. I could earn far more by halving the company, but I don't do it. It's not my style and I also know the public are not idiots. I believe they come to see the best-dressed, best-performed touring show in Britain. It is champagne and caviare at beer and crisps prices. It is important to me to keep West End traditions.

For several years now, I have been presented on my British tours by Brian Shaw, a dynamic young entrepreneur. He has shown great faith in our business by staging numerous tours all over the country with the biggest names in show business, and he has emerged as one of our leading promoters.

Since the early eighties, I have toured with my entire company in a superb luxury coach. It has everything on board – television, videos and a microwave oven. I think it is a very romantic way to tour, it has echoes of the music hall and concert party – a happy band of strolling players.

I am happier on the move these days because I am afraid the traditional summer season by the sea as we know it is over. One of the last bastions of British show business is rapidly disappearing. It has all become a question of economics. At one time, summer shows were big business with seasons at virtually every seaside resort in the country, starting in May and running through to October. They were well-patronized by holidaymakers, too, to such an extent that twice-nightly performances were given at most places. But with the coming, first of television, and then cheap foreign holidays, traditional summer season started to go to the wall. The demand has all but gone these days because there is so much else vying for people's attention and hard-earned cash in the entertainment stakes.

There are still several major resorts presenting summer season shows of the highest quality, at Blackpool, Bournemouth, Great Yarmouth, Torbay and Scarborough, but these are exceptions. The whole market, once so lucrative, has become a dying breed. Expenses are so high these days that it is impossible to stage a glamorous show at the seaside without charging far more than people would expect to pay. So it becomes prohibitive. To give the public exactly what they want would cost a fortune, and I don't really think we ever charge enough money, anyway. Summer season is still the one show that is relatively cheap to see. In Australia and America, people would expect to pay three times as much for a ticket as they do in Britain, to see a comparable show. People over here would faint if they were asked to pay that kind of money, and yet, they willingly part with it to see a West End show. There just aren't the number of people taking their holidays in Britain these days, and those that do haven't got the kind of money they would need to go and see a different show every night, like they used to do in the great halcyon days of summer season.

Among other things, there simply are not enough big names to guarantee big business throughout the season, and profits at the end of the summer. All-round standards have dropped. I firmly believe that summer season has to undergo some drastic changes if it is to survive and make a viable comeback.

And yet . . . only a few years ago, pantomime in Britain was in exactly the same position. Today, it has become one of the only growth areas in the industry. It is thriving and enormously successful, and safe in the hands of people like Duncan Weldon, of Triumph, who created *Mother Goose* especially for me. He has done more than most to re-establish pantomime as a major form of entertainment in Britain today.

One of the ways in which I try to put back something into life in general, and show business in particular, is through my work for charity. I am a great believer that people in the public eye should use their position and standing in society to help out charities in need. Yet charity work should be done and not talked about. It is very private. But I do enjoy getting involved with charities that help children. I also give a lot of my time to causes to help the aged. I love them because elderly people have had a life and they deserve all our support and help in the twilight of their years. They have given so much to us, and we should show our gratitude and support. Every Christmas and summer season, I become part of a different local community, and I do as much as I possibly can to help that community during my visit. I have always done it. I am lucky enough to have my health so it is no chore, and I am only too pleased to help out.

In 1984, I was chosen to become the ambassador for the British Hospital Broadcasting Association and during my tours, whenever I visited a different town or city, I tried my best to go along to the local hospital radio station to show my face and hopefully cheer up a few less fortunate people confined to bed.

In June 1965, I became a member of the distinguished show business charity organization, The Grand Order of Water Rats. The late Cyril Dowler proposed my admission, Johnnie Riscoe was my second. It was a very great honour to be accepted into this select fraternity, a responsible lot of brothers for whom I have the highest regard. The organization does amazing work for charity and gives an awful lot of money to the underprivileged, besides helping our own colleagues in less fortunate circumstances.

The Grand Order of Water Rats takes its emblem from the water rat itself, one of the lowest and most unloved forms of life. We call ourselves the lowest, but we try to live up to, and strive for, the highest achievements. As former King Rat, Wal Pink, said: 'We will elevate the lowest to the highest in the firmament of good fellowship and charity. A Rat is a vole, and vole is an anagram of *love*. That's what we'll be, a brotherhood of love.' Rats spelt backwards becomes star!

The Order was founded in 1889 and in all that time the Lodge has been very select, with only about 700 members privileged to share the title of Water Rat. In 1973, I was voted Rat of the Year for my services to charity. I was so flattered. Yet there was an even greater honour in store for me. In 1986, I was elevated to the rank of King Rat, the highest and most revered accolade that can be bestowed in show business. Every member of the Order votes for their King, so it is a heartfelt election. When my name was read out at the annual ball in November, I have never heard so much applause and so many cheers. It was one of the greatest highlights of my life and such a tremendous compliment coming from my fellow professionals. There have only been sixty-eight different King Rats since the Order was formed, including some of the legendary names in show business – Dan Leno, Little Tich, Will Hay, Bud Flanagan and Ted Ray. It was a supreme privilege to be in such exalted company.

It is very obvious that I love my profession. It is my life and has been since I first started out in show business all those years ago. Through it all, I have been very concerned for my colleagues and I have never knowingly offended any of them. People tell me one of my greatest qualities is that I am, what is laughingly called, a generous performer. I don't hog the scene. But I also think I am a good and generous friend. I am always there if needed. It's unforgivable to be a bore.

No other business could have opened up so many doors for me to meet some remarkable people. I have been extremely lucky through it all. Life has been very fair to me, and it has given me an experience that is worth more than all the money in the world.

Money changes people. Money changes life. I made so much that I didn't realize how important it was supposed to be until I lost it all. I soon learnt it's not important at all. I am in a much better state of mind since I put my house in order than I ever was before. These days I am easily satisfied as long as I have a bed, towels and hot water, and a good meal inside me. I have done it all before: I have made millions – but couldn't enjoy them because I was busy making more – and lost millions. I have had lovely houses, but I never saw them because I never had the time to indulge myself. In five years, I saw my house at Henley just four times.

I think it would all have been different if I had had a family of my own. Then I would have needed to keep my feet firmly on the ground. I would have loved children. If there is one thing I regret more than anything about my life, it is not being married. I would have enjoyed my own family life so much. But then, I am very fortunate to have a brother and sister with wonderful children, and now grandchildren, so I have always had youngsters around me, and I think they have helped to keep me young at heart. Still, I think I would have made a pretty good dad myself. It would have been nice to try.

I am a gypsy by nature, I love travelling. I get uneasy if I am anywhere for too long and want to move on to somewhere else. I wouldn't like to live anywhere permanently at this stage of my life, although I have two lovely homes: one in London, near to my beloved Soho where I was brought up; and one in Sydney, Australia.

The big joke in show business a few years ago in the days of touring variety was that everybody hated going to play in Scotland. It was the graveyard for so many English entertainers and comedians. Des O'Connor once fainted on the stage of the Glasgow Empire through sheer terror at facing such a hostile audience. Fortunately, I have never had such problems. I have a tremendous following in Scotland, in Ireland and in Wales. It's the Celtic blood in me, an empathy that breaks down the barriers. Some performers have certain regions in which they are very successful, but I have been able to travel almost everywhere with equal acclaim.

Although I am gregarious and like to be around people, I also like my own company very much. I can balance myself out now by spending fifty weeks of the year working hard at my profession in the glare of the camera and public eye all the time, and two weeks in my own company, totally alone. And that's enough for me. For relaxation, I like walking – which is very difficult for me living in central London because I am recognized wherever I go – and holding dinner parties for my friends. I adore sitting around a dinner table with some good food and fine company, and just talking. I think all Celts are good talkers because we are all romantics at heart.

My tastes in life are very catholic, with a small 'c'. I adore good theatre and, when I am in London, I go as often as I can. You can't beat the excitement and immediacy of live theatre no matter how good or bad. I also like good music, but nothing noisy. I have never been to a disco in my life.

I am very partial to good wine, although I don't drink spirits and I have never smoked in my life – apart from one brief episode as a youngster. Usually, during Lent, I don't drink at all for six weeks. It's self-discipline, not religious. It is so important to give up something you really like. It makes it harder, but far more rewarding, when you succeed.

Throughout my life, I have been extremely lucky and I thank God for my good fortune. I have never missed a single performance through illness because I have never really been ill. I have had bouts of flu and bad colds, like everyone else, but nothing serious. I stupidly worked once when I had pleurisy during the run of *Queen Daniella* and my doctor was very annoyed with me because I insisted on going on stage every night. He told me I would get a bad chest every year through my stupidity. And, of course, I do.

In 1985, I developed nodules on my throat, which I had removed almost immediately, and I was forbidden to talk for two weeks. I could communicate only by writing everything down on a note pad. At the end of the stipulated period, the doctor asked me if I had learnt anything from my fortnight of sustained silence. 'Yes,' I said. 'I found out I can't spell.'

Like all performers, I have great weaknesses. I suppose I should be a lot stronger than I am. My company accuse me of being hard-headed and soft-hearted, but I don't suffer fools gladly and lose patience with idiots. But they are normal traits, I suppose. I don't know if I will ever need a psychiatrist because I am very good at exorcising myself, my act does that. I still draw a veil over sadness and things I want to shut out of my mind completely.

I am a very practical man. My mother and my background taught me great discipline which has helped me throughout my career, and given me great determination.

I have really had a marvellous life. I started with absolutely nothing and, even with all the losses, I have much more than I ever dreamed was possible. There is very little I would ever change, either. I have loved it all. And I am pleased to say that I did my best; the public seemed to like me.

If I could be remembered for one thing, I would like to think I was good at making people laugh. Laughter is the greatest thing in the world. And if someone had told me when I was twenty-one that I would become an international star by running around the stage in a frock covered in feathers and sequins, *I'd have laughed*.

Index

La Rue, Danny *cont'd*
  202; Scarborough (1978), 185;
  Eastbourne (1980), 202; Paignton
  (1982), 57, 202; Torbay, 241;
  clubs, 165–8, 181, 182, 185; in Aus-
  tralia, 192, 193, 228; Walton Hall,
  172, 194–207; overcoming fear of
  flying, 175, 180–84, 188; Australia
  and New Zealand, 42, 57, 59, 72,
  105, 173, 175, 176, 181, 182, 201,
  202, 212, 213, 218; Canada, 176–
  80, 186
Laye, Evelyn (Boo), 25, 220
Lee, Vanessa, 67
Leigh, Vivien, 126, 159
Lemmon, Jack, 229
Leno, Dan, 243
Liberace, 38, 91, 104, 115, 133, 136,
  149, 170, 198, 211, 212
Lidell, Alvar, 38
Lillie, Beatrice, 159
Little Tich, 243
Littlewood, Joan, 104, 122, 123, 187
Lloyd, Eric, 225
Lockwood, Johnny, 192
Logan, Jenny, 105, 116, 131
Lovis, Mr, 128
Lowes, David, 111, 113, 114, 134
Lucan, Arthur, 38
Lunt, Alfred, 159

MacLaine, Shirley, 126
Madonna, 231
Maharajah of Baroda, 92, 93
Maharajah of Cooch Behar, 93
Manning, Bernard, 239
Mansfield, Jayne, 229
Margaret, HRH The Princess, 106,
  118–20, 155
Marian-Crawford, Howard, 128
Marks, Alfred, 163

Marshall, Ralph, 70, 79
Martin, Mary, 178, 179, 208
Marvin, Lee, 126
Matthews, Jessie, 185
Matthieu, Mireille, 235
Mature, Victor, 101
Mawbey, Richard, 211, 220
McCallum, John, 176
McKenna, Siobhan, 82
McLennan, Rod, 116, 176
Meadows, Bertie, 96
Meadows, Harry, 88, 93, 100
Melvin, Glenn, 110
Merman, Ethel, 208
Merrick, David, 149, 150, 207
Midler, Bette, 231
Miguel, 115
Miller, Max, 35
Mills, Richard, 148, 165
Minnelli, Liza, 123, 124
Miranda, Carmen, 131
Mistinguett, 234
Monkhouse, Bob, 110, 165
Monroe, Marilyn, 106, 229
Mordaunt, Sir Charles, 196, 197
Mordaunt, Harriet, 196
More, Billie, 113, 121
Morecambe, Eric, 176
Moreland, Johnnie, 88
Morrison, Aletta, 88
Mortimer, John, 77
Mountbatten, Lord Louis, 58, 238
Murdoch, Richard, 36
Murray, Pete, 133, 228
Mussolini, Benito, 41

Neagle, Dame Anna, 35, 91, 212
Nesbitt, Robert, 95
New, Derek, 177
Newcombe, Clovissa, 105, 116
Newman, Nanette, 119